PAUL AND THE AGON MOTIF

SUPPLEMENTS
TO
NOVUM TESTAMENTUM

EDITORIAL BOARD

VOLUME XVI

LEIDEN
E. J. BRILL
1967

PAUL
AND THE AGON MOTIF

TRADITIONAL ATHLETIC IMAGERY
IN THE PAULINE LITERATURE

BY

VICTOR C. PFITZNER

LEIDEN
E. J. BRILL
1967

PREFACE

The following work was accepted as a doctoral dissertation by the Evangelical Theological Faculty of Münster, Westphalia, in the Summer Semester of 1964. My sincere thanks are due to the Faculty and especially to Professor Dr. K. H. Rengstorf who suggested the study, watched over its progress, and finally gave constructive criticism in preparing it for publication.

Most of my three and a half years of post-graduate studies were pursued in the Institutum Iudaicum Delitzschianum in Münster. To the director, Professor Rengstorf, and the other members of the staff, especially those involved in the compilation of the Josephus Concordance, I wish to express my appreciation for both helpful hints and congenial working atmosphere.

In addition I wish to acknowledge my indebtedness to the editors of Novum Testamentum who in 1964 kindly accepted this study for their series of Supplements, and to the E. J. Brill Press of Leiden whose cooperation has overcome the problem of the distance between us. Finally I cannot omit to express my thanks to certain members of the Lutheran Church of Australia who have materially supported the printing of this book.

Over two years have passed since it was first completed. The return to Australia, as well as parish and lecturing duties, have made difficult a reworking of some sections and additions from recent literature, as well as a complete check of all references. For all errors and omissions the author alone remains responsible.

Malvern (Adelaide), South Australia   V. C. Pfitzner
Christmas, 1966

ABBREVIATIONS

ARW	=	Archiv für Religionswissenschaft
Ath. Mitt.	=	Mitteilungen des Kaiserlichen Deutschen Archäologischen Instituts, Athenische Abteilung
AuC	=	Antike und Christentum
BAG	=	W. Bauer (ET by W. F. Arndt and F. W. Gingrich), Griechisch-Deutsches Wörterbuch zu den Schriften des NT und der übrigen urchristlichen Literatur
BFChTh	=	Beiträge zur Förderung christlicher Theologie
Blass-D.	=	F. Blass, Grammatik des neutestamentlichen Griechisch, bearbeitet von A. Debrunner
Bonn.-Lip.	=	Acta Apostolorum Apocrypha I-II 2, Ed. R. A. Lipsius and M. Bonnet
BuG	=	Botschaft und Geschichte II, Gesammelte Aufsätze von M. Dibelius, herausgegeben von G. Bornkamm
CAP	=	The Apocrypha and Pseudepigrapha of the OT, Ed. R. H. Charles
cf.	=	confer
ch.	=	chapter
CIG	=	Corpus Inscriptionum Graecarum, Ed. A. Boekh et al.
col(s).	=	column(s)
cp.	=	compare
Cremer-Kögel	=	Cremer H.-Kögel J., Biblisch-theologisches Wörterbuch des neutestamentlichen Griechisch
Danby	=	The Mishnah, ET by H. Danby
Diels	=	Die Fragmenter der Vorsokratiker, Ed. H. Diels-W. Kranz
Ditt.Syll.	=	W. Dittenberger, Sylloge Inscriptionum Graecarum
DSS	=	Dead Sea Scrolls
ed.	=	edited
e.g.	=	exempli gratia
Eidem	=	E. Eidem, Pauli bildvärld, Athletae et Milites Christi
Ep Th Lov	=	Ephemerides Theologicae Lovanienses
esp.	=	especially
ET	=	English Translation
ExT	=	Expository Times
f(f).	=	following
Field	=	F. Field, Notes on the Translation of the NT
FRLANT	=	Forschungen zur Religion und Literatur des A und NT
GuV	=	R. Bultmann, Glauben und Verstehen (I-III)
HAT	=	Handbuch zum Alten Testament
Hatch-Redpath	=	Hatch E.-Redpath H. A., A Concordance to the Septuagint (I-II)
HC	=	Hand-Commentar zum Neuen Testament
HNT	=	Handbuch zum Neuen Testament
ICC	=	International Critical Commentary
KAP	=	Die Apokryphen und Pseudepigraphen des AT, Ed. E. Kautsch
KEK	=	Meyer's Kritisch-exegetischer Kommentar über das NT
KNT	=	Zahn's Kommentar zum NT

LCL	=	Loeb Classical Library
Liddell-Scott	=	H. G. Liddell and R. Scott, A Greek English Lexicon (New edition by H. S. Jones)
LKlT	=	Lietzmann's Kleine Texte für Vorlesungen und Übungen
LXX	=	Septuagint
M-M.	=	J. H. Moulton and G. Milligan, The Vocabulary of the NT illustrated from the Papyri and other Non-literary Sources
MNTC	=	Moffatt NT Commentaries
MPG	=	Migne, Patrologia. Series Graeca
MPL	=	Migne, Patrologia. Series Latina
MT	=	Textus Masoreticus
NTD	=	Das Neue Testament Deutsch
op.cit.	=	opere citato
p(p).	=	page(s)
Pauly-W.	=	A. Pauly and G. Wissowa, Realencyclopädie der Klassischen Altertumswissenschaft
RAC	=	Reallexikon für Antike und Christentum
Rahlfs	=	Septuaginta, id est Vetus Testamentum Graece (I-II), Ed. A. Rahlfs
RB	=	Revue Biblique
RGG	=	Die Religion in Geschichte und Gegenwart
RSV	=	Revised Standard Version
SAB	=	Sitzungsberichte der Preussischen Akademie der Wissenschaften zu Berlin, philos.-hist. Klasse
Schmid	=	L. Schmid, Der Agon bei Paulus
Schürer	=	E. Schürer, Geschichte des Jüdischen Volkes im Zeitalter Jesu Christi (I-III)
SNT	=	Die Schriften des NT
Strack-Bill.	=	H. L. Strack and P. Billerbeck, Kommentar zum NT aus Talmud und Midrasch
s(v).	=	sub (voce)
ThHk	=	Theologischer Handkommentar zum NT
transl.	=	translated
TWNT	=	Kittel's Theologisches Wörterbuch zum NT
v.l.	=	varia lectio
ZNW	=	Zeitschrift für die neutestamentlicher Wissenschaft
ZThK	=	Zeitschrift für Theologie und Kirche

INTRODUCTION

1. The Problem and the Sources

The use of the athletic imagery in the thought of Paul is not only relatively frequent when compared with his use of other pictures and metaphors, but also stands in the service of singularly important motifs in his letters. This is generally recognised. Less clear, and in fact problematical, have been the attempts to ascertain and define these motifs. In the attempt to establish the importance of this imagery —which we may in short refer to as the picture of the Agon — for Paul's thought, one is immediately confronted with a *threefold task*: 1. the search for possible contemporary sources, or at least literary or non-literary parallels for the use of this picture,[1] 2. the establishment of the manner, meaning, and purpose of Paul's use of the image, and 3. the ordering of the theological motif(s) suggested by the image in the thought of the Apostle.

From the beginning it must be observed that the oft–noted frequency with which the picture of the Agon appears in the thought of the popular moral philosophy of Paul's day does not yet provide a complete solution to the first of the three tasks set above. It is true that this is one of the most frequently occurring images in the *Cynic-Stoic diatribe*, one which serves to reflect the very core and essence of its ethic. This fact has long been recognised and worked out by the classical philologists who have at the same time been able to trace certain lines of development leading up to the use of athletic imagery in the diatribe, beginning most clearly already with Xenophanes.[2] In the field of NT studies it is particularly Rudolf Bultmann and Paul Wendland[3] who have long since noted a certain

---

[1] Here the question must also be asked whether the Pauline use of the Agon imagery simply reflects a certain stage in the development of a traditional concept of the Agon used in a transferred sense.

[2] Cf. especially E. Norden, "In Varronis Saturas Menippeas Observationes Selectae", in: Fleckeisen's Jahrbücher für klassische Philologie, Suppl. XVIII, 1891, pp. 298ff.; R. Heinze, "Anacharsis", in: Philologus 50, 1891, pp. 458ff.; cf. also J. Geffcken, Kynika und Verwandtes, Heidelberg 1909, and P. Wendland, Philo und die kynisch-stoische Diatribe, Berlin 1895.

[3] R. Bultmann, Der Stil der paulinischen Predigt und die kynisch-stoische Diatribe, in: FRLANT, Göttingen 1910, and P. Wendland, Die urchrist-

parallelism of literary style and form common to the letters of Paul and the diatribe. If such a general stylistic relationship can be established between the two, it also becomes probable that the frequency of certain concrete pictures and images used in early Christian literature —from Paul to the Apostolic Fathers —for example those of the athletic contest, of military life, of the body, of milk and solid food,[1] can also be traced back to the influence of the diatribe, or at least to that of the terminology of the preachers of the popular moral philosophy of Paul's day. This relationship, in particular the striking linguistic parallels between the Pauline use of Agon terminology and that of the diatribe, is now generally acknowledged by most of the commentators, at least in Germany.[2]

What is the truth of the recognition? The truth lies in the correct observation that with the athletic image one is dealing with a traditional usage which has its own history and development. Consequently the attempt to explain Paul's use of this imagery simply as an example of his literary skill, his acute powers of observation, and his consideration for his readers in offering them illustrative pictures from every-day hellenistic life, overlooks both this tradition and the frequency of the image in Paul, together with the striking correspondence of terms which accompany the picture of the Agon in Paul on the one hand, and that of the diatribe and Hellenistic Judaism on the other. At the same time, and this is equally important, individual striking parallels,[3] though of liguistic importance,

---

lichen Literaturformen (HNT), Tübingen 1912, pp. 356f. E. Norden had also already asserted the influence of the diatribe's style and use of imagery on Paul, both in his "Observationes Selectae" and in: Die antike Kunstprosa, Leipzig [2]1909.

[1] Cf. I Cor 14:8, 3:2, 12:12-27.

[2] Cf. e.g. the remarks on I Cor 9:24-27 in the commentaries of Lietzmann (HNT), and J. Weiss (KEK), and also M. Dibelius, Die Pastoralbriefe (HNT), Tübingen [3]1955, pp. 55 and 81, O. Michel, Hebräerbrief (KEK), Göttingen [11]1960, on Hebr 12:1ff., 11; also J. Weiss, Urchristentum, Göttingen 1917, p. 318 (ET: New York 1959, p. 418). E. Eidem, in: Beiträge zur Religionswissenschaft der religionswiss. Gesellschaft zu Stockholm 1, 1913/14, p. 219, concludes that "die paulinischen Agonbilder durch die kynisch-stoische Redeweise bedingt sind".

[3] E.g. the striking linguistic parallel noted by Wendland (Literaturformen, p. 357) between I Cor 9:24 πάντες μὲν τρέχουσιν εἰς δὲ λαμβάνει τὸ βραβεῖον, and Lucian, Anach. 13 πάντες αὐτὰ (τὰ ἆθλα) λαμβάνουσιν; οὐδαμῶς, ἀλλ' εἰς ἐξ ἁπάντων ὁ κρατήσας αὐτῶν.
H. Vollmer, Die alttestamentlichen Citate bei Paulus, Freiburg 1896, p. 82 note 3, traces back similarities between the two passages to a source used by both!

lose their weight with the recognition that one is here confronted by a popular, traditional metaphor, so common that in Paul's epistles, as in the writings of his contemporaries, a single term suffices to recall to mind the whole athletic image in its metaphorical use.[1]

The above considerations already provide an answer to the literary question which could arise at this point. Is Paul dependent on sources for his use of the Agon picture? Once a parallel use has been established, or more correctly, a parallelism in terminology, it does not follow as a necessary consequence that a literary relationship between the two is indicated. It is not at all a question of dependency nor of literary evaluation with which one is here confronted; important is rather the recognition that Paul is using a popular picture, "the common property of popular philosophers, whose sermons could be heard in the streets and squares of Tarsus, as in other Hellenistic towns."[2] In other words, *Paul on his part simply reflects a traditional use of the athletic image.*

An examination of the Cynic-Stoic material parallel to Paul's use of the Agon metaphor is nevertheless still necessary. Such an examination has a twofold importance. In the first place it can aid to an understanding of Paul's thought especially in the case of individual terms which belong to the traditional Agon picture. In the second instance it will help to bring into relief that which is peculiar to, and entirely new in Paul's use, and to clarify the motive and concern which prompted the Apostle to adopt the image. If these two purposes are clearly kept in mind such an examination is preserved from the outset from the danger of developing into nothing more than a 'religionsgeschichtliche' or 'begriffsgeschichtliche' study.

At the same time a certain but limited right must be granted to the claim that in certain instances —above all in I Cor. 9:24-27 where the image of the athletic contest receives its fullest treatment in Paul—there is possibly a direct reference to the public games familiar to his readers.[3] This view does not necessarily run counter

---

[1] Gal 2:2, 5:7, Phil 2:16 (τρέχειν) and Phil 4:1, I Thess 2:19 (στέφανος).

[2] Cf. M. Dibelius-W. G. Kümmel, Paulus, Berlin ²1956, p. 29 (ET: London 1953, p. 31), and Dibelius, Aufsätze zur Apostelgeschichte, Paulus auf dem Areopag, Göttingen 1951 (ET: Studies in the Acts of the Apostles, London 1956, pp. 26ff.), for a classical example of an exegesis based on his own observation above.

[3] Ph. Bachmann, Erster Korintherbrief (KNT), Leipzig ³1921, p. 327, thinks that the reference in 9:24ff. is to the Isthmian games which would

to the positing of a traditional usage of the image, since even here
the concrete features of the games are also called to mind. Less
convincing, however, is Deissmann's attempt to illustrate II Tim
4:7 by means of an inscription from the second century A.D. found
in the theatre at Ephesus (ἠγωνίσατο ἀγῶνας τρεῖς, ἐστέφθη δύω).[1]
In the light of the many other linguistic parallels at our disposal
from outside of Asia Minor it is more than questionable to assume
that Paul and the inscription drew from a common source which
Deissmann limits to the "Formelschatz" of Asia Minor. This process
of locating verbal parallels naturally has its importance, but only
if it is also recognised that every individual passage must be seen
within the wider context of a vocabulary which was 'in the air',
which had become the jargon and common property of every-day
speech. Once again it must be stressed that this fact precludes the
possibility of seeing in any of the Agon passages in the letters of
Paul conscious references or adaptations of other passages whether
from the diatribe or from inscriptions.

As already stated at the beginning, the observation that Paul is
using a traditional image, one which is frequently found in the
diatribe and which was doubtless a commonplace in the message of
the wandering moral philosophers of his day, provides only half an
answer to the first question posed by this study. This already becomes clear when one notes the equally numerous occurrences of
the picture in the writings of *Hellenistic Judaism*, especially in
Philo and IV Maccabees. This fact has led Adolf Schlatter and
Alfred Juncker to assert that the use of the athletic image was
handed down to Paul per medium of the Greek-speaking synagogue.[2]

---

have been most familiar to the Corinthians; so also Robertson and Plummer,
First Corinthians (ICC), p. 193. Karl Baus, Der Kranz in Antike und Chris-
tentum, Bonn 1940, goes too far in his view; "Wenn man sich an die grosse
Verbreitung und Beliebtheit der antiken Agone erinnert, wird man es für
mehr als wahrscheinlich halten, dass Paulus zu diesem Bilde greifen konnte
auf Grund eigener Kenntnis der Spiele" (p. 170); similarly W. M. Ramsay,
Pauline and other Studies, London 1906, pp. 331f., and A. Deissmann,
Paulus, Tübingen ²1925, p. 58 (ET: New York 1957, p. 71).

[1] A. Deissmann, Licht vom Osten, Tübingen ⁴1923, p. 262f. (ET: Light
from the Ancient East, London, ²1911, p. 312): "Solche Inschriften hat
Paulus wohl auch in seiner Zeit gelesen". For the inscription cf. The Collection of Ancient Greek Inscriptions in the British Museum, Part III, No.
604.

[2] Cf. A. Schlatter, Die Theologie des NT II, Stuttgart 1910, pp. 255f. =
Die Theologie der Apostel, Stuttgart 1922, p. 298, and A. Juncker, Die Ethik
des Apostels Paulus, Halle 1904-1919, II p. 127. E. Stauffer, TWNT I, pp.

A final word on this possibility must be left to the end of the study. It may suffice to observe here that the Hellenistic Jewish sources which come into consideration are themselves influenced by Stoic thought and language. It is therefore improbable that Paul was dependent entirely and solely on the Greek-speaking synagogue for his use of the image. The Hellenistic Jewish parallels may, however, present themselves at first sight as closer analogies to Pauline usage, without necessarily forming a bridge from the Stoa to Paul.

This line of development —from popular moral philosophy to Hellenistic Judaism to Paul —easily suggests itself. But it is more than doubtful whether such a rigid scheme of development in the traditional use of the Agon image can be adhered to, and certainly not in the sense of a chronological sequence. Whether we are to find the direct impetus for Paul's use of the picture in his immediate contact with the popularised language and imagery of his day or in his contact with the hellenistic synagogue, is, as we shall see, relatively unimportant. It is probable that the use of the Agon image, especially as found in the martyr-Acts of IV Maccabees and in the writings of Philo of Alexandria, became familiar in the Greek-speaking diaspora, but the possibility that Paul possessed hellenistic Jewish sources is highly questionable.[1] Here again any talk of direct literary dependency is out of place.

The sources which require examination for an understanding of the background to Paul's use of the athletic metaphor are however not limited to those already mentioned. The Stoa was not an original school of thought but rather a collector and assimilator. The background of the diatribe's use of the Agon motif must also be sought in order to gain a fuller picture of the motive for its use in the diatribe. In the second instance it must be asked whether there was something intrinsic in the Greek conception of the public games themselves which readily fostered the concept of an ethical ideal and typified this ideal, quite apart from the use of the athletic imagery to typify a moral struggle in the form of a metaphor. Conse-

---

134ff. and especially in his Theologie des NT, Tübingen 1941 (ET: London 1955), note 50, protests against the prevailing view since Wendland, and instead emphasises Paul's dependence on late Judaism for his hellenistic thought, including the metaphors from the stadium.

[1] The evaluation of such a possibility is naturally to a large extent dependent on the dating and location of such writings as IV Maccabees, Wisdom and IV Ezra, in which the Agon as a moral struggle and contest of martyrdom appears.

quently the first question to be asked concerns the position and nature of the public games and gymnastics in general in Greek thought, life and culture. An examination of this nature is by no means superfluous, since, as we shall see, it has direct bearing on the question whether Paul could take up the picture of the games (as in I Cor 9:24-27) and presuppose that his readers would immediately understand his argument, or whether it was rather the very traditional character of the image which made it possible for him to employ it.

A further problem in this study is posed by a phenomenon which belongs to the development of every language, the tendency for metaphorical terms to lose their original connotation and reference through continued popular use. A word-study of ἀγών, ἀγωνίζεσθαι and related terms, reveals this same paling process. Consequently, while seeking to discover and preserve the unity of Paul's metaphorical use of athletic terminology, it must also be taken into account that, wherever these terms are to be found isolated and outside of complexes where the occurrence of other terms clearly suggests the athletic image, it is quite possible that the original reference to the games has been lost.[1] Only a study of contemporary koiné can help us determine whether this is so or not, or whether, for example, the word in Paul has taken on a new shade of meaning through its frequent use in a military sense.

A final preliminary observation, one which is of extreme importance in evaluating the motives for Paul's use of the image, must be added. In Paul it is instructive to observe not only the parallel use of traditional athletic termini, but also the lack of many of the concepts which are of basic and fundamental importance whether in the diatribe, in Philo, or in IV Maccabees. In Paul such central hellenistic concepts as ἀρετή, πάθη, ἐγκράτεια, ἀπάθεια, ἀταραξία, λογικόν, and λογισμός play no part at all in his picture of the Christian Agon. Such a comparison purely in the sphere of terminology is already instructive for the attempt to pinpoint the Apostle's concern in adopting and adapting this popular picture. At least it shows how little of the Greek spirit of moral idealism he took over in assimilating the metaphor to his purposes, for it is precisely in the lack of many of the central concepts which belong to the hellenistic

---

[1] Such a possibility applies, for example, to Col 2:1, I Thess 2:2 (ἀγών), Col 1:29, 4:12 (ἀγωνίζεσθαι), and to Rom 15:30 (συναγωνίζεσθαι).

moral Agon that Paul's usage becomes transparent and his ability
nevertheless to use this picture possible. His rejection of the termini
mentioned above provides, to a large extent, the clue to his concern
to fill the traditional picture with a completely new content and
meaning.

A problem nevertheless remains. It is just when the centrality
of the Agon motif in Greek thought is appreciated that the adoption
of the image by Paul in the first place becomes less expected, and
the difficulty of ascertaining the new content of the image all the
more acute. It is the ever recurring problem of the interpretation
of language which has been taken over from popular moral philosophy, from the Mysteries, or from Gnosticism. How much of their
original content and connotation has been preserved or discarded
when borrowed terms have become part of the NT vocabulary? In
the case of the present imagery the problem may be formulated as
follows: Granted that the presuppositions for Paul's use of the image
and its terminology were already given, namely the popularity of
the picture and its familiarity to his readers, how could he fit this
image which typifies the Greek spirit of self assertion, of human
achievement and endeavour, into his own theological system of
thought with its emphasis on human impotence and divine grace?
How could he speak so often in the terms of the Agon when all that
this word implied to the Greek mind fell for Paul under the judgment of the wrath of God, when he could use the image negatively,
and categorically state: "So then it is not of him that willeth, nor
of him that runneth, but of God that sheweth mercy" (Rom 9:16)?[1]

But, and this is the burden of the present writer's argument
against the work done on the subject up till now, this is only a
problem if it is assumed that the concept of the Agon also stands in
the centre of Paul's concept of the Christian's *moral* task. Previous
writers have seen in the Apostle's use of the image the most clear
and yet most problematical presentation of the antithesis between
divine grace and human effort. The present work aims at showing
that this problem has been falsely created by the commentators
themselves by transplanting over to Paul the Greek concept of the
moral Agon. In so doing they have reintroduced the problem of an
ethic of achievement when it is far from the Apostle's own mind.

---

[1] The RSV translation of τρέχειν with 'exertion' reproduces Paul's meaning
but destroys the image which, just at this point, is very important for Paul.

Despite the aim to free Paul from any traces of Greek moral idealism they have created a tension in Paul which is foreign to his thinking.

In concluding these introductory and methodological consider-ations reference must be made also to the frequency of the image in the *early Christian writings outside of the NT*, in Christian redaction-al additions to the OT Pseudepigrapha,[1] in the apocryphal Acts of the Apostles, but above all in the writings of the Apostolic Fathers, including the Martyrdom of Polycarp. Even a study which is inter-ested primarily in the theology of Paul must take these passages into account. The question of literary dependency is here legitimate. In examining the parallels one may proceed from the question whether there are features in the later Christian usage of the ath-letic imagery which help to explain the usage of Paul. Conversely it can be asked whether the roots of the picture of the Christian Agon in early Christian literature apart from Paul[2] lie in the thought of the Apostle himself. But here again, as in the case of the relevant passages in Paul's own epistles, one must also reckon with the possibility of a completely independent use of the metaphor, without any conscious or unconscious indebtedness to Paul.[3]

---

[1] E.g. in the Testaments of the 12 Patriarchs and in the Sibylline Oracles.

[2] Included are such passages as Hebr 10:32-33, 12:1-4 and Jude 3.

[3] The large complex in II Clem 7 obviously shows a knowledge of I Cor 9:24-27 but nevertheless reveals a strong non-Pauline colouring which places it into a close relationship with the diatribal and esp. Philonic use of the image. M. Dibelius, "Rom und die Christen im ersten Jahrhundert", in: BuG II pp. 193ff., claims that the famous passage I Clem 5 which pictures the Apostles Peter and Paul as athletes fighting the Agon of martyrdom, shows a conscious borrowing from the Cynic-Stoic diatribe. "Klemens (geht) auf das Martyrium der Apostel aus politischen Gründen nicht ein, im übrigen von den Aposteln nicht erzählen, sondern sie als philosophische Athleten schildern will" (p. 203). This whole section on the end of the Apostles is thus, according to Dibelius, to be regarded as a "moralphilosophische Betrach-tung" (p. 199). On the other hand J. A. Fischer, Die apostolischen Väter, Darmstadt 1956, considers that Clemens could have taken the picture of the Agon from the language of the day, just as did Paul. Possibly, over against the Corinthians, the thought of the Isthmian games was uppermost (see the comment on I Clem 2:4). R. H. Lightfoot also sees the stress on the games in II Clem as inspired by the Isthmian contests (cf. K. Lake, The Apostolic Fathers [LCL], London 1959, p. 126). —That a later use of the image in the Church Fathers which is clearly independent of the thought of Paul cannot be drawn into the discussion, is obvious; cf. however O. A. Sawhill, The Use of Athletic Metaphors in the Biblical Homilies of St. Chrysostom, Disser-tation Princeton 1928, and J. Geffcken, Kynika und Verwandtes, Heidelberg 1909, pp. 18f. (for Gregory of Nazianzus), and p. 37 (for Chrysostom).

2. An Evaluation of Previous Literature

A survey of the previous works on the athletic imagery in Paul
shows that very little specialised attention has been paid to this
phenomenon in his letters, apart from the usual footnotes in the
commentaries pointing out the Apostle's indebtedness to the diatribe. The only monograph which deals directly with the subject is
that by *Lydia Schmid*, Der Agon bei Paulus,[1] a work already fourty
years old and in need of correction and supplementation. In suc-
cessive chapters the authoress deals with the various chief motifs
which she finds suggested by Paul's use of the Agon image, namely
Anstrengung, Ziel, Entwicklung der Kraft, Übung, Kampfregel,
Wetteifer, Lohn, and Darstellungsstreben. She likewise does not
proceed from the assumption of a literary relationship between Paul
and the diatribe. Nevertheless her method is very much open to
criticism. At the beginning she states that the proper procedure is
that of adducing the parallel Greek material only when this promises
to be of value for the understanding of Paul's theology.[2] Such a
statement presupposes a thorough knowledge of the Greek and
Hellenistic background. Only a thorough examination of the pre-
Pauline concept of the Agon can show where and if it promises to
be fruitful for a closer understanding of Paul. An examination of
this nature is missing in her work and contributes to the faultiness
of her presuppositions and findings. Only the parallel material from
the diatribe and from Aristotle's "Ethics" is adduced; the wealth
of material in the sources of Hellenistic Judaism is virtually ignored.
By further ignoring the development and use of the athletic language
and imagery apart from the diatribe, the full range of possibilities
of meaning for ἀγών in the koiné are left out of consideration. The
striking mingling of the athletic and military metaphor both in the
NT and in the Agon tradition must raise the question whether the
Agon complexes in Paul and the isolated occurrences of 'athletic'
terminology can be completely isolated, or whether there is a relationship between the two. It is thus feasible to ask whether the
Agon —as a concept which expresses an aspect of Paul's own
labours and struggles in the ministry of the Gospel—does not also
bear a 'military' character. In actual fact the moral struggle which

---

[1] Unprinted Dissertation, Tübingen 1921.
[2] Op. cit., p. 19 note 1.

Schmid sees as the prime thought behind Paul's use of the image of
the Agon, does not appear in terms of an athletic contest, as in the
diatribe, but rather in terms of the military metaphor (e.g. Rom
6:12ff.).

This brings us to the central criticism which must be levelled
against L. Schmid's work. Despite the fact that she attempts to
avoid systematising Paul's use of the image this is what in actual
fact results from her thesis. Her concern is carefully to differentiate
Paul's ethic from the eudaimonism of the hellenistic ethic. This has
led her to overlook the fact that Paul does *not* only use the image
to illustrate his ethics, but that it in the first place refers to himself
and his own concrete situation as a servant of the Gospel, and in
the second place is used to illustrate certain motifs of the Christian
life of faith. The temptation to seek in Paul the Christian counterpart to popular moral philosophy leads to a distorted picture of the
Agon in Paul. The features which have no parallels in non-NT
sources receive little notice. The way in which Paul, for example,
places the Christian Agon in the eschatological 'already but not yet'
tension in Phil 3:12ff. is not appreciated in its uniqueness; nor is the
application to Paul's own person as a wrestler for the Gospel.

As a general criticism against L. Schmid it must be noted that
she places too much emphasis on the motif of exertion, on the
problem of the responsibility of the human will over against the
divine gift of faith and justification. The contention of the present
work is that this problem does not provide the motive for Paul's
adoption of the athletic imagery. That such a problem is immediately suggested, also in the letters of Paul, is clear. The very terms
ἀγών and ἀγωνίζεσθαι suggest the thought of exertion and maximum
endeavour. But the resultant difficulty only arises as a consequence
of the Apostle's use of the Agon motif in the service of other leading
motifs which he wishes to impress on his readers: the thought of the
Christian's calling in all its earnestness, but above all his own Agon
in the service of the Gospel. It is the eschatological dimension which
gives the Agon in both cases this element of decisiveness, for behind
the use of the image stands the consciousness of having to stand
before the judge 'on that day' to give account as one who has proved
victorious in the "good fight", or not. The emphasis on human
endeavour and exertion, with the consequent problem it raises, only
appears within the greater framework of the Apostle's prime purpose
in using the athletic image, namely, to picture the life of the
Christian as one which is always 'in via', which always lies this side

of the ultimate goal, which gains its determinative earnestness from the necessity to persevere in the faith (cf. Gal 5:7, "You were running well; who hindered you from obeying the truth?").

The only other specialised treatment in German is that offered by E. *Stauffer* in Kittel's Wörterbuch zum NT.[1] Here, in contrast to L. Schmid, only the Hellenistic Jewish material is sketchily outlined and the vital origins of the athletic metaphor in the diatribe are dismissed —obviously as insignificant —with several words. In his Theology of the NT the author specifically rejects the view that the genuine hellenistic elements in Paul's thought, including the metaphors of the stadium, reached him through anything but the medium of late Judaism.

Stauffer finds five 'Denkmotive' in the Christian Agon to which the faithful are called (TWNT, p. 136), ideas which are elaborated under the catchwords Ziel, Verzicht, Widerstände, Leidenskampf, and Heil der Vielen. The work of Stauffer contains the same basic mistake and is in need of the same supplementation as that of Schmid. To discover leading motifs or emphases in Paul's use of this imagery is not yet to discover his central concern. Consequently Stauffer also overlooks the self-apologetical character which underlies the most important Agon passages in the Pauline literature. Most of his references to the image in his NT Theology have no bearing on Paul's writings, but are only of interest in so far as they serve his "Theology of Martyrdom" (Appendix I F). At one point Stauffer approaches the central Pauline emphasis when he speaks of the struggles and suffering of the Christian life as being viewed by Paul in perspective with the victory of the cause of Christ.[2] But this thought, the wrestling for Christ and his Gospel, is not followed up.

The most thorough and reliable treatment of the subject is still to be found in the Swedish thesis of *Erling Eidem*, Pauli bildvärld I, Athletae et Milites Christi.[3] Most probably due to language diffi-

---

[1] TWNT, ἀγών and derivatives, I pp. 134ff.; ἀθλεῖν, I pp. 166f.; βραβεῖον, I pp. 636f. (cf. also Stauffer's NT Theology, note 50 and Appendix I F). In TWNT note also A. Oepke, γυμνάζειν and γυμνασία, I p. 775, E. Fuchs, σκοπός, VII pp. 415f., and H. Greeven, πάλη, V pp. 717f; most recently O. Bauernfeind, τρέχω and δρόμος VIII pp. 87ff.

[2] "Er (Paulus) denkt an die Kämpfe und Leiden des Christenlebens selbst, eines Lebens, das in seiner Ganzheit unter dem Zeichen des Kreuzes steht und in diesem Zeichen die Sache des Christus zum Siege bringt" (op.cit., p. 139).

[3] Lund, 1913. L. Schmid was unfortunately unacquainted with the book

culties and the age of the work (1913) it is hardly known in the
German and English speaking world, even though the author himself has given a short summary of his findings in "Beiträge zur
Religionswissenschaft der religionswiss. Gesellschaft zu Stockholm."[1]
After an extensive introduction to the problem of tracing the origins
of Paul's pictorial language and of ascertaining its meaning, Eidem
devotes detailed attention to the language of the stadium, theatre
and amphitheatre to be found in Paul, examining each individual
passage by itself (pp. 90-186). The author correctly observes that
many of the terms which originally referred to the picture of the
Agon may have lost their metaphorical significance in Paul's time,
especially in their isolated occurrence.[2] Most of his work is a formal
analysis of the 'Bildwert' of the various terms, and little attention
is paid to the question of the theological purpose of their use, or the
theological problems which arise. It is nevertheless necessary to
note that Eidem observes a tendency in the later letters, also in the
Pastorals, to reserve the use of this image for the teacher in the
Church.[3]

On the question of the origin of these images the author considers
that the Apostle's personal experiences and observations here played
a minor role. "Der relative Mangel an Anschaulichkeit spricht am
ehesten für einen Ursprung aus der Tradition."[4] Eidem correctly
notes this tradition in the Cynic-Stoic diatribe, in Philo, and in the
other writings of Hellenistic Judaism. The Agon images in Paul
have most probably been conditioned by Cynic-Stoic diction.

In addition to these specialised studies several more recent works
must be mentioned. *W. A. Beardslee*[5] observes the close connection
between the athletic and military metaphors, but while recognising
the eschatological character of the latter fails to see that this also
applies to Paul's picture of the Agon in its various uses. It is already
indicative of Beardslee's interpretation that he deals with the ath-

---

which also gives a valuable list of older works on the subject in question (cf.
esp. p. 17 note 4).

[1] No. 1 (1913/14), pp. 212ff.
[2] Op.cit., pp. 214 and 18.
[3] Ibid. p. 218.
[4] Ibid. p. 219.
[5] Human Achievement and Divine Vocation in the Message of Paul,
Studies in Biblical Theology No. 31, London 1961, p. 68f. —For a further
discussion of commonly held false views on Paul's use of the Agon imagery,
see the beginning of the second part of this work.

letic imagery under the heading "Progress, Growth, and Perfection", and here in connection with the motif of progress in Paul. Unfortunately this emphasis on progress is carried through almost exclusively with a 'Stoic' conception of the Agon, that is, as a moral struggle.[1] His work thus reveals the same basic mistake as L. Schmid's.

The same failure to recognise the wider context within which the gymnastic imagery of I Tim 4:7ff. is found can be noted in the essay of *C. Spicq* on this passage.[2] According to this writer all the sporting metaphors of St. Paul cast the human factor in the spiritual life of the faithful into full relief. The Apostle of grace uses them to define precisely the cooperation of man with the work of God. Timothy is here exhorted to develop the latent possibilities and abilities of the inner man (p. 235), whereby the possibility must exist that, if he is encouraged to strive after religious perfection, this goal can be realised. The command to exercise gives us to understand, says Spicq, that Timothy is to perfect and increase his "ressources natives", his "bonnes dispositions initiales" (p. 236f.). It is clear that Spicq's interpretation cannot deny its Roman Catholic colouring. But one must ask whether the Christian γυμνασία is here described in terms almost parallel to those of the diatribe. Timothy's training in godliness is still largely seen in the realm κατὰ φύσιν, instead of being placed within the sphere of the καινὴ κτίσις. Again, according to Spicq, the entire energy of the man who trains is stimulated by the results he expects. To excel in his acts—this is the motive for his effort (p. 238). If we remember the position of the addressee of the Pastorals it becomes clear that such a statement reveals a distorted view of the selfunderstanding of the minister of the Gospel. It is not the personal goal and glory of Timothy which is central, but rather the glory of God and his goal in the preaching of the Gospel.

Reference may finally be made to the interesting article of *A. Ehrhardt*.[3] In a scholion to Demosthenes he finds a reference to an Orphic writing with the title 'Steliteutica'. The reference provides

---

[1] "The athletic metaphors usually emphasise the strenuous moral exertion which is necessary for victory" (p. 68).

[2] "Gymnastique et Morale, d'apres I Tim 4:7-8", in: RB 54, 1947, pp. 229ff.; cf. also his related essay "L'Image sportive de II Cor 4:7-9", in: Eph Th Lov, 1937, pp. 209ff.

[3] "An Unknown Orphic Writing in the Demosthenes Scholia and St. Paul", ZNW 56, 1957, pp. 101f.

us with one "fragment out of the first book—or hymn as the case
may be—of this Orphic work, κατὰ γὰρ τῶν ἀγωνιζομένων οἱ στέφανοι,
'for the competitors, namely, are the crowns'" (p. 106). Ehrhardt
considers this passage from the Steliteutica, which must have only
been composed at the beginning of the second century A.D. or even
later, to be important for an understanding of the problematical
phrase in I Cor 9:25. After noting the stylistic similarity of the
preceding verse with a Neo-Pythagorean sentence, and acknowledg-
ing the parallels in the Stoic diatribe, he concludes that these "similarities go a long way to show that Paul was here referring to a
popular conception of man's religious task on earth as a struggle
before the face of the God-head, who Himself had arranged the
contest for him" (p. 109). He further believes that the fragment
helps to explain Paul's seeming selfcontradiction in vv.24f., since it
shows that more than one victor's crown was to be won in the
contests. As we shall see, this argument is completely unnecessary,
even if the final point be granted as valid. The valuable contribution
of Ehrhardt's essay remains in his corrective emphasis on the importance of the role of the "presiding authority, a god, an emperor
or a civil magistrate, in whose presence the contest was held and in
whose name the prizes were given" (p. 110). Thus one must agree
with his criticism of the modern lexicographers "including not only
E. Stauffer, but also W. Bauer, and the editors of Liddell and Scott,
who have been misled by the spirit of competition" (ibid). He also
rightly notes that this concept of the Agon as a contest to be fought
out in the presence of God is also to be found in the sources on the
Jewish and Christian martyrdoms.[1] But he is driving his point too
far in asserting that "the essential figure in the ancient ἀγών was
not the victorious athlete, but the presiding authority" (ibid). Both
features remain essential in the picture of the Greek games.

A purely formal and less profitable treatment of Paul's athletic
imagery is given by *W. Straub*.[2] Here the distinction is drawn between the various literary forms or genre which occur in his use of
the Agon terminology (Bildwörter, Metaphern, Bildsprüche, and
Gleichnisse), but the Agon tradition which lay before Paul is over-

---

[1] E.g. IV Maccabees and the Martyrdom of Polycarp. A closer study of
I Cor 9:24-27 soon shows, however, that neither the thought of the heavenly
crown nor that of God as the presiding judge is uppermost in Paul's mind.
The point of the image lies elsewhere —see infra.
[2] Die Bildersprache des Apostels Paulus, Tübingen 1937.

looked, and any attempt to determine Paul's concern or motive in using the imagery is entirely missing.

Adolf von Harnack also has some important observations for our study in his book "Militia Christi".[1] The value of his work lies above all in the correct recognition of the close relationship between the athletic and military images in Paul in their application to the work of the minister of the Gospel.

---

[1] A. von Harnack, Militia Christi, Die christliche Religion und der Soldatenstand in den ersten drei Jahrhunderten, Tübingen 1905, esp. pp. 12-17.

A

THE HELLENISTIC AGON TRADITION AND ITS ORIGINS

CHAPTER ONE

THE SPIRIT AND IDEALS OF GREEK ATHLETICS

1. The Spirit of Rivalry and Self-assertion

It is by no means insignificant that the public games assumed a central position in the life of the Greek peoples, for there was something intrinsic in the Greek "Lebensideal" itself which readily found expression in these games and in the whole sphere of athletics.[1] The idea of developed competitive contests in sports is typically Greek. Physical training in the sense of culture of the body played no important independent role in the other ancient cultures, for wherever such training was practised it was primarily for military purposes. Herodotus, for example, reports that the Persians taught their youth only riding and archery (I 136). The competitive spirit of the games was as far removed from Jewish thinking as it could have been, quite apart from the offence in the sight of God caused by the nakedness of the athlete, whether training or competing.

For the Greek, on the other hand, the spirit of contention and competition was one of the major sources of impetus urging him on to activity and self-assertion. It is thus understandable why the word 'agon', apart from being used to designate the ἀγῶνες γυμναστικοί, ἱππικοί and μουσικοί, found such a wide use in the thought and language of the Greeks. It was used not only for the united struggle of the people in war,[2] but also for every kind of contest in civil life.

---

[1] On the spirit and cultural significance of the games cf. Pauly-W. I cols. 841ff. (s. Agones); J. Jüthner, "Herkunft und Grundlagen der griechischen Nationalspiele", in: Die Antike 15 (1939), pp. 231ff.; H. J. Marrou, Geschichte der Erziehung im klassischen Altertum, München 1957, passim; also the older works of E. Curtius, "Der Wettkampf", in: Göttinger Festreden, Berlin 1864, pp. 1-22; J. Burckhardt, Griechische Kulturgeschichte IV, Berlin/Stuttgart 1889ff.

[2] Cf. e.g. Herodotus IX 60: ἀγῶνος μεγίστου προκειμένου ἐλευθέρην εἶναι ἢ δεδουλωμένην Ἑλλάδα; also VIII 102.

Not only in the field of athletics was the victor celebrated. Feats in every field of endeavour were acclaimed, so that the entire civic life of a Greek became, as it were, an Agon, a sphere in which to exert himself and excel over others.[1]

This desire for supremacy in achievement, as a characteristic of the Greek mind, can also be observed by comparing the Greek and Roman public games. The Greek Agones provided the citizens with the opportunity to pit their strength and skill against each other. The Roman "Ludi" or "Venationes" on the other hand contained no vestige of this ideal. Here the citizens were passive spectators, observing the bloody contests of the gladiators merely for the sake of entertainment.[2]

The spirit of φιλονεικία and the quest for fame are consequently fundamental for the picture of the Agon, whether in the games, in public life, or in the arts. At the athletic contests—at least at the ἀγῶνες στεφανῖται—fame and victory itself are the true goal, because they grant the victor that which is in essence the goal of every Greek, that he might become the object of awe and admiration, and that his name might be remembered even in death.

These thoughts may be traced back to the Homeric writings. Here already the love of fame has a central position in the ethic of the heroes. Achievement, success, honour, power, prowess and skill, these all constitute the ἀρετή of the Homeric hero. The superior exercise of physical or mental strength and skill, to excel, to establish oneself as the best in contest and competition, to complete the heroic feat, this is the ἀριστεία which places him above all others. This ideal is best summed up in the maxim (Iliad 6,208 = 11,784): αἰὲν ἀριστεύειν καὶ ὑπείροχον ἔμμεναι ἄλλων. The hero embodies in his life and feats this ideal of ἀρετή, and his life becomes an example for those who follow. He is not afraid to boast of his prowess or superi-

---

[1] Cf. J. Jüthner, RAC I, p. 187: "Dem ehrgeizigen, durchaus agonal eingestellten Griechen, der bei jeder Betätigung von dem Gedanken beseelt war, es den anderen zuvorzutun, wandelte sich jegliche Bemühung in einen Agon, dessen erfolgreiche Durchführung ihm Anerkennung und Ruhm bringen sollte, während ihm eine Niederlage unerträglich schien". This spirit could even be extended to drinking contests; cf. Aelian Var. Hist. 2,41: ἐκ δὲ Διονυσίου τῇ τῶν Χοῶν ἑορτῇ προύκειτο ἄθλον τῷ πιόντι πλεῖστον στέφανος χρυσοῦς.

[2] The Greek ἀγῶνες μουσικοί as literary and rhetorical contests did however still live on in the Capitoline contests, founded by Domitian in 86 A.D.; cf. Müller, Handbuch der klass. Altertumswissenschaft VII, p. 176.

ority. This is rather his very aim, to be able to say, εὔχομαι εἶναι ἄριστος (Il. 23,669), or ἀλλ' ἐν πρώτοισιν οἴω ἔμμεναι (Od. 8,180).

In Homer this ideal is already closely connected with the athletic contests.[1] Laomedon invites his guest Odysseus to participate in the games and adds: οὐ μὲν γὰρ μεῖζον κλέος ἀνέρος ὄφρα κεν ᾖσιν ἤ ὅ τι ποσσίν τε ῥέξῃ καὶ χερσὶν ἐῇσιν (Od. 8,145ff.). It is the desire for, and the pursuit of, this nobel fame which is the "innerste Triebfeder dieser ritterlichen Sittlichkeit". And although the concept of ἀρετή changed in the history of Greek thought, this "agonistische Lebensideal" remained as one of the "bezeichnendsten Aspekte der griechischen Seele."[2]

Even though—as we shall see in the next chapter —the Greek games showed signs of decline long before the beginning of our era, they and the spirit which they both reflected and fostered did not die out, even under Roman influence. Lucian, writing in the second century A.D., makes Solon say to the Persian Anacharsis, with reference to the honour and glory which the athletic seeks: "If anyone were to take away from life the love of fame, what good would still be left to us?"[3]

2. The Nature of the Games as Holy

Contests between the gods belong to the oldest myths of Greek literature. Rivalry between the deities forms an essential part of the background in the Homeric epics, especially in the Iliad. Hesiod pictures the contest for power between Zeus and Prometheus, the representative and champion of mortals, in the form of an Agon.[4] Furthermore, both Homer and Hesiod know of many heroes in whose honour games were held, and the origins of the four great national games are popularly to be found in the myths of the gods and heroes.[5] Even their spirit is traced back to a divine origin.[6]

---

[1] The word ἀγών appears 29 times in Homer, but continually in the sense of assembly or place of assembly. Cf. e.g. Il. 24,1: λῦτο δ' ἀγών, and Od. 8,260: καλὸν δ' εὔρυναν ἀγῶνα. Ἄεθλος is used for the games, and for the toils of Hercules (Il. 8,363) and of Odysseus (Od. 1,18).

[2] Marrou, op.cit., p. 26. Cf. also Pindar Isthmia VI 10ff.

[3] Lucian Gymnas. 36.

[4] Hesiod Theog. 535ff.

[5] Cf. Pindar Olymp. X, and Ath. Mitt. IX 31: ἐν τοῖς κατ' ἐνιαυτὸν τιθεμένοις εὐχαριστηρίοις ἀγῶσιν Ἡρώοις.

[6] J. Jüthner, Herkunft und Grundlagen etc., p. 231: "Nicht nur die fest-

In this respect the account of the funeral games in honour of Patroclus in Book 23 of the Iliad is instructive.[1] The situation, including the proceedings themselves, clearly indicates that the contests here have a cultic character: they appear within the framework of the herocult.[2] Thus we can observe a second characteristic feature of the early Greek ἀγῶνες; they are frequently designated as ἱεροί.

The connection of the games with the cult of the gods in historical times follows not only from the aetiological legends attached to them, but also from the manner in which they were conducted. All the local festivals with their athletic contests stood under the patronage and protection of a deity to whose honour and service the whole assembly was dedicated.[3] That the dramatic contests in Athens arose out of the cult of Dionysius is clear from the fact that until very late the dramas were only performed on the festival of this deity.[4] The following additional features also serve to reflect the religious character of the games.[5] A breach of the peace during the conduct of the games was a serious and punishable offence against the patron deity. Before the image of the deity the contestants vowed to comply with the rules of the games, and to him they brought their offerings and prayers for victory and later, if successful, their statuettes and crowns.[6] Wherever possible the

---

lichen Kampfspiele, auch der Wettkampfgedanke an sich muss nach der Meinung des Volkes höheren Ursprungs sein".

[1] The reliability of this account in tracing the historical origins of the Greek games is of no interest to us here; cf. Jüthner, op.cit., pp. 237ff., and Meier, in: Pauly-W. I col. 841.

[2] The heroes who are helped to victory by the gods (e.g. Il. 23,768ff. and Od. 8,193ff.) are themselves superhuman beings. But elsewhere it is clear that only he who is helped by the gods and enjoys their favour has any hope of success; cf. Pindar Isthmia VI. Cf. also note 6 infra.

[3] Cf. Dionys. Hal., Art. rhet. I 1,2: θεός γε που πάντως πάσης πανηγύρεως ἡγεμὼν καὶ ἐπώνυμος, οἷον Ὀλυμπίων μέν Ὀλύμπιος Ζεύς, τοῦ δὲ ἐν Πυθοῖ Ἀπόλλων.

[4] Cf. Müller, op.cit., p. 199. In the theatres stood images of the gods.

[5] For the following see above all Meier, op.cit., cols. 841ff., and Jüthner, op.cit., pp. 240ff.

[6] On the religious symbolism of the crown cf. Deubner, "Die Bedeutung des Kranzes im klassischen Altertum", in: ARW 30 (1933), p. 78ff., and K. Baus, Der Kranz in Antike und Christentum, Bonn 1940, pp. 153f.: "Nach der Vorstellung der antiken Menschen ... wird in der Person des Siegers derjenige bekränzt, zu dessen Ehren die Spiele abgehalten werden ... Entsprechend der religiösen Bewertung der Spiele selbst, wurde auch der Kranz religiös bewertet" (ibid., p. 155). Connected with the presentation of

games were held in the vicinity of the sanctuary, and it became a firm practice to cut the victor's crown, wreath or palm branch from a tree in the sacred grove. When sometimes objects of value were also given as prizes, these were regarded as gifts of the festival's patron god. The contests were sometimes called ἀγῶνες ἐισελαστικοί from the triumphal processions which accompanied the victor into his home town and to the altar of the deity on which he placed his crown.[1] The games consequently appear as a form of λειτουργία in which the deity is served and honoured by artistic and physical achievements.[2]

Passages such as Pausanias V 24,9 and VI 23,1ff., as well as non-literary evidence (cf. Ditt.Syll. 795B and 1073,40) can be multiplied to show that the religious significance[3] of the games was not even lost in the first centuries of our era, even at a time when the games were supported by benefactors and held in honour of the Roman Emperor (Josephus Ant. 15.267ff. and Bell 1.426ff.). Much of the later Christian polemic against the games is also understandable only on the background of their character as "sacred contests".[4]

---

the victory crown to the deity there may also be the thought that victory has been gained not only by personal effort, but also by divine aid.

[1] This practice is still well known in the Christian era, as can be seen from Or Sib II, 39: μέγας γὰρ ἀγὼν εἰσελαστικὸς/ἔσται εἰς πόλιν οὐράνιον.

[2] Cf. E. Curtius, op.cit., p. 13: "Um ihre Götter zu ehren, glaubten sie ... vor allem die Blüthe der Jugend in ihrer Gesundheit und Kraft den Göttern darstellen zu müssen, ... auch in freudigen Wettkampfe sollten ihre Jünglinge zeigen, dass sie sich reichlich empfangenen Gottesgaben zu voller Entwickelung zu fördern nicht träge gewesen seien. So sind die Wettkämpfe ein Opfer des Danks, dessen die Götter sich freuen." Cf. also Meier, op.cit., col. 841: "Nicht nur die musischen Agonisten, die unmittelbar in Kulthandlungen eingreifen, sondern auch die gymnischen (werden) während der Feste den im Kulte beschäftigten Personen gleich erachtet."

[3] H. Eheloff, "Wettlauf und szenisches Spiel im hethitischen Ritual", in: SAB Philos.-hist. Kl. 1925 No. XXI, p. 270, cites an Egyptian inscription dating from 1200 B.C. which tells of a cultic race at the spring festival in which the winner received the position of royal reinsman. It is likewise interesting that other non-Greek athletic contests in antiquity, such as the 'lismu' (race) at the Babylonian spring festival and the races at the corresponding. Germanic festivals also had a cultic significance. In addition F. Dölger ("Köpfe von Isispriestern mit der Kreuznarbe", AuC II, Münster i.W. 1930, pp. 294ff.) has drawn attention to a cultic battle within the Isis Mysteries —although the athletic image is missing.

[4] Cf. esp. Tertullian, De Spectac. 11: ... et apparatus agonum idolatria conspurcat de coronis profanis, de sacerdotalibus praesidibus ...; De Coron. 13: Numquid et agonisticae causae disputabuntur, quas statim tituli sui (i.e. as holy) damnant, et sacras et funebres scilicet? Hoc enim superest, ut

3. THE GREEK GYMNASIUM AND ITS IDEALS

The Greek gymnasium is of interest not only in so far as it formed a centre where the agonistic ideals of Greek life were inculcated and fostered, but also because the education which it offered largely contributed to the popularization and extension of athletic imagery. From its beginnings the gymnasium was a centre of the sports in which the youths—at first the sons of the nobility—were trained and exercised from an early age onward in the various contests, taught to comply with the rules of the games and to undergo painful exertion.[1] The entire curriculum of the gymnasium, including the studies in grammar and the musical arts, became saturated with the spirit of competition, so that examinations in all spheres were regarded as contests offering the possibility of showing personal superiority over the next person.[2] Victory lists of the successful competitors were issued.[3] Life in the gymnasium was a continual winning or being defeated, a continual measuring of one's own powers over against those of the other, whereby superiority was an aim in itself without necessarily being directed towards any practical use of the strength and skill developed.

Education in the gymnasium was based on the principal that everything was to be reached through training and exercise, through the maximum development of the individual with his innate latent powers. The ideal of this training may best be summed up in the term καλοκἀγαθία understood as embodying the ideal of a completely developed mind in a body which has reached its maximum degree of perfection. The sports, music and all the arts are placed in the service of this end. Originally the man who was καλὸς καὶ ἀγαθός was no doubt the accomplished athlete, and if in the Greek system of education there was an ethical element, this was actualised largely in and through the sports. Physical beauty—especially the beauty

Olympius Jupiter et Nemaeus Hercules et misellus Archemorus et Antinous infelix in Christiano coronentur, ut ipse spectaculum fiat, quod spectare taedet.

[1] For the following cf. J. Öhler, s. Gymnasium, in: Pauly-W. VII, cols. 2004ff.; J. Jüthner, op.cit., p. 863; above all Marrou, op.cit., pp. 66ff., and C. Spicq, "Gymnastique et Morale, d'apres I Tim 4:7-8", in: RB 1947 (54), pp. 230ff.

[2] Examinations were also called ἀγωνάρια or διαδρομαί; Öhler, col. 2014.

[3] Those who excelled in the 'animi palaestra' were often called πένταθλοι; cf. E. Norden, Fleckeisen's Jahrbücher für klass. Phil. Suppl. XVIII, Leipzig 1891, p. 299 note 1.

of the naked body—and its cultivation had true meaning for life since for the Greek it was the medium for the actualisation of his personality.[1]

At the present point we are not interested in finding out how Paul may have taken up the three main features of the games as they have been outlined: the spirit of rivalry and self-assertion which they embodied, their holy character, and the ideal of perfection through training. It is first necessary to see how these features were taken up in a metaphorical use of the pictures provided by the games. We turn, then, to an examination of the growth, terminology and content of what we may call the Agon tradition.

---

[1] Marrou, p. 74.

CHAPTER TWO

THE AGON MOTIF IN GREEK AND HELLENISTIC PHILOSOPHY

1. From Xenophanes to Aristotle

It is significant that the more important gymnasia, for example the Lyceum and the Academy, also became centres of intellectual training and philosophy, in which such leading philosophers as Plato and Aristotle taught. It is the philosophers who not only reflect the decay of the original spirit of the games as a result of the growth of professionalism, but also seek to discover the true meaning and purpose of the games and athletics or, as in the case of the Cynics and Stoics, coin a new picture of the entire life of the sage as an Agon, retaining the terminology of the public games.

In tracing the evolution of what may be termed a philosophical concept of the Agon, a picture which reached the peak of its popularity and fullest form in the diatribe and the representatives of late Stoic moral philosophy, it is necessary to bear in mind the decay of the spirit of the games. It is only against this background that the polemic and the *criticism* of the tragedians and philosophers against the games and athletics in general on the one hand, and on the other hand their *defence* against the philosophers on the part of those seeking to retain the original glory of the games, is understandable.[1] The very exaggeration of the importance of the sports in early Greek education later became fateful for their evaluation. At the same time the fame attached to the panhellenic games and the exaggerated desire to have a share in this fame led to a professionalism which, by means of its specialization and minute regulations for training and diet, destroyed the noble ideals of the games and converted athletics into a trade, in the vulgar sense of the word.[2]

---

[1] The defence of gymnastics by Flavius Philostratus is no doubt prompted by the attacks of the Cynics and Stoics. Similar motives may well lie behind Lucian's 'Anacharsis'.

[2] Cf. Marrou, op.cit., pp. 93f. and 192ff. For the polemic of the tragedians and philosophers against this trend see esp. E. Norden, op.cit., pp. 298ff, and R. Heinze, "Anacharsis", in: Philologus 50, 1891, pp. 458ff.

In the sphere of education the Sophists provided the reaction by demanding from their pupils exertion on the intellectual plane.[1] Sports were still played and remained an essential part of the curriculum of the gymnasium but ceased to be the first object of the ambition of the youth.

While the tragedians of the fifth century occasionally lash out in vitriolic attacks against the athletes,[2] we find other voices pointing to something higher and more important than the glory to be won at the games. The famous elegy of *Tyrtaios* already reveals a rejection of the old ideal of the nobility which was largely determined by the games, and stresses over against the achievements which an athlete might perform in the contests the true ἀρετή of the warrior. The relevant lines run:

> Οὔτ' ἂν μνησαίμην οὔτ' ἐν λόγῳ ἄνδρα τιθείμην
> ὄυτε ποδῶν ἀρετῆς οὔτε παλαισμοσύνης,
> οὐδ' εἰ Κυκλώπων μὲν ἔχοι μέγεθός τε βίην τε,
> νικῴη δὲ θέων Θρηίκιον βορέην,
>
> .   .   .   .
>
> οὐδ' εἰ πᾶσαν ἔχοι δόξαν πλὴν θούριδος ἀλκῆς
> οὐ γὰρ ἀνὴρ ἀγαθὸς γίγνεται ἐν πολέμῳ,
>
> .   .   .   .
>
> ἥδ' ἀρετή, τόδ' ἄεθλον ἐν ἀνθρώποισιν ἄριστον
> κάλλιστόν τε φέρειν γίγνεται ἀνδρὶ νέῳ.[3]

This is however not merely a return to the hero-ἀρετή of the Homeric epic, for here manly virtue is newly orientated in the citizen's obligation to the Polis. A similar Polis-consciousness can be detected in the elegy of *Xenophanes* which marks the beginning of a development towards a philosophical picture of the Agon.[4] In this passage the poet claims in the name of 'philosophy' that his σοφίη is better than all the glorious victories in the games:

---

[1] Aristophanes in his attacks on the Sophists in Clouds 1002ff., ascribes the decay of gymnastics to the rise of Sophistry with its verbal Agones.

[2] Cf. Euripides Frg. 282N: κακῶν γὰρ ὄντων μυρίων καθ' Ἑλλάδα οὐδὲν κάκιόν ἐστιν ἀθλητῶν γένους; also Sophocles Aias 1250.

[3] Tyrtaios 12, 1ff., in Poetae Lyrici Graeci II (ed. T. Bergk), pp. 17f.; cf. G. Bornkamm. "Der köstlichere Weg —I Cor 13", in: Das Ende des Gesetzes, München 1961, pp. 93ff.

[4] Xenoph. Frg. 2B (Diels I p. 128, line 7ff.).

..... ῥώμης γὰρ ἀμείνων
ἀνδρῶν ἠδ' ἵππων ἡμετέρη σοφίη.
ἀλλ' εἰκῇ μάλα τοῦτο νομίζεται, οὐδὲ δίκαιον
προκρίνειν ῥώμην τῆς ἀγαθῆς σοφίης.

The wealth and good order of the Polis is in no way profited by all the athletic feats of strength. It is wisdom alone which is of value to the state.[1]

Together with this claim for the superiority of σοφία we also find in the writings of the *Presocratics* the emphasis on the exercise of the soul over against the exercise of the body. Here the Cynic-Stoic picture of the Agon of the sage in his struggle to live κατὰ φύσιν, subjecting his impulses to the law of reason, is already suggested.[2] This is clear from Democritus (Diels II, p. 192, lines 17ff.): ἀνθρώποις ἁρμόδιον ψυχῆς μᾶλλον ἢ σώματος λόγος ποιεῖσθαι. ψυχῆς μὲν γὰρ τελεότης σκήνεος μοχθηρίην ὀρθοῖ, σκήνεος δὲ ἰσχὺς ἄνευ λογισμοῦ ψυχὴν οὐδέν τι ἀμείνω τίθησιν ... ἀνδρεῖος οὐχ ὁ τῶν πολεμίων μόνον, ἀλλὰ καὶ ὁ τῶν ἡδονῶν κρέσσων ... θυμῷ μάχεσθυ μὲν χαλεπόν.[3]

Democritus defines the struggle against the passions as a matter of exercise and discipline, and in adopting the terms πόνος and ὑπυμονή points the way to the terminology of the diatribe: πόνος συνεχὴς ἐλαφρότερος ἑαυτοῦ συνηθείῃ γίνεται —οἱ ἑκούσιοι πόνοι τὴν τῶν ἀκουσίων ὑπομονὴν ἐλαφροτέρην παρασκευάζουσιν.[4]

The secondary reports of the teaching of *Socrates* present him as stressing the true and profitable exercise of the mind and soul over against the exercise of the body.[5] Καλοκἀγαθία is conceived of in a strictly ethical sense.[6] More important in tracing the Agon motif, however, is the word attributed to Socrates in Plato's Gorgias (526

---

[1] Cf. also Diodorus Sic. IX 5: ὁ Σόλων ἡγεῖτο τοὺς μὲν πύκτας καὶ σταδιεῖς καὶ τοὺς ἄλλους ἀθλητὰς μηδὲν ἀξιόλογον συμβάλλεσθαι ταῖς πόλεσι πρὸς σωτηρίαν, τοὺς δὲ φρονήσει καὶ ἀρετῇ διαφέροντας μόνους δύνασθαι τὰς πατρίδας ἐν τοῖϛ κινδύνοις διαφυλάττειν.

[2] Cf. Heraclitus (Diels I, p. 176, line 1): σωφρονεῖν ἀρετὴ μεγίστη, καὶ σοφίη ἀληθέα λέγειν καὶ ποιεῖν κατὰ φύσιν ἐπαΐοντες.

[3] Cf. also Heraclitus (Diels I, p. 170, line 3): H. Quiring, Heraklit, Worte tönen durch Jahrtausende, Berlin 1959, prefers to understand θυμός as 'Mut' (p. 117 note 16). However the passage from Democritus would seem to suggest that B. Snell is correct in translating 'Begierde' (Snell, Die Fragmente des Heraklits, Tübingen 1949, p. 29).

[4] Diels II, p. 193 lines 12f.

[5] Cf. Xenophon Mem. I 2,4.

[6] Xenophon Conv. 2,4.

Df.). He here pictures his work as τὴν ἀλήθειαν ἀσκῶν, trying to live and die as a virtuous man, and concludes: παρακαλῶ δὲ καὶ τοὺς ἄλλους πάντας ἀνθρώπους ... καὶ δὴ καὶ σὲ ἀντιπαρακαλῶ ἐπὶ τοῦτον τὸν βίον καὶ τὸν ἀγῶνα τοῦτον, ὅν ἐγώ φημι ἀντὶ πάντων τῶν ἐνθάδε ἀγώνων εἶναι.[1] Striking here is that the whole life of the philosopher and his attempt to live and die as βέλτιστος is considered as an 'agon'. Although the use of the word in this context approaches that which is to be found especially in Philo and the Diatribe, the phrase τὴν ἀλήθειαν ἀσκῶν distinguishes it from the purely moral application of the concept in Stoic and Cynic thought.

Plato himself reacts strongly against the spirit of competition which has reached such an exaggerated importance in his time,[2] and seeks to lead the sports back to their original purpose, namely as a preparation for war.[3] On the other hand he assigns to athletic exercise its own educational value and moral worth in the development of the intellect and the formation of the character and personality.[4] According to him the rational and temperamental parts of the soul are to be harmonized through a mixture of the arts and gymnastics, and thus trained to manage and direct the third part of the soul, the seat of the innate insatiable desires.

The passage in Plato which demands most attention is that in Phaedrus 247 B in which he describes the ascent of the soul to the vision of the ultimate realities. The soul in its ascent is likened to a pair of horses with a reinsman. Plato here presupposes the teaching of the tripartite soul as expounded in the 'Republic'. The reinsman is the λογιστικόν part of the soul, and the willing and troublesome horses the θυμοειδές and ἐπιθυμητικόν respectively. The last must be held in check by the reinsman since it continually seeks to drag the trio back to earth. The struggle which ensues is described with the words ἔνθα δὴ πόνος τε καὶ ἀγὼν ἔσχατος ψυχῇ πρόκειται.[5] The simi-

---

[1] Epictetus (IV 8,26) pictures Socrates as summoning into the σκάμμα all who desired to learn to differentiate between reality and appearance.

[2] Leges VII 796 A&D, VIII 830 A.

[3] Rep. III 403ff. and 410 Bff.; the guards of the state are to undergo πόνους and ἀγῶνας (413 D) to extinguish the innate human vices and strengthen the virtues of courage and endurance, for the guards are ἀθληταὶ .... τοῦ μεγίστου ἀγῶνος (403 Ef.).

[4] Rep. III 410 C-412 A; cf. also IV 441 E-F.

[5] Cf. the ἄμιλλα καὶ ἱδρὼς ἔσχατος in 478 B. In this connection note also Rep. X 608: "For great is the Agon ... whether one is to become good or evil, so that one is not lead astray either by honour or money or any power

larity of this struggle, as a feud between the λογιστικόν and ἐπιθυμητικόν of the soul, with the Agon of the diatribe is apparent. The aim
of the struggle is however quite different. In Plato the soul struggles
to gain a vision of the eternal ideas of righteousness or justice,
temperance and knowledge; in Stoic thought the Agon has as its end
ἀπάθεια and ἀταραξία. Nor could one as yet see the Agon here as a
designation for the whole life of the philosopher. More important in
this respect is a passage in the Laws where we read of the battle
against the desires and passions, of γυμνασία and ἀγῶνες in the
pursuit of ἀρετή (here courage).[1] Here the Agon clearly has the
connotation of a test or trial.

In his Nichomachean Ethics *Aristotle* frequently makes use of
athletic imagery. The goal of ethical behaviour is εὐδαιμονία, and
this is to be achieved through the guidance of reason over the
impulses and passions.[2] This happiness is to be found at the mid-
point between the two extremes of ὑπερβολή and ἔλλειψις.[3] Just as
the expert in running or wrestling avoids immoderate or too little
training, so the pursuit of virtue always has τὸ μέσον as its goal,[4]
a goal which is accessible to all through μάθησις, ἐπιμέλεια and
ἄσκησις.[5] Virtue may be one's own as an innate possession but it has
no value until it is transformed into activity, for ὥσπερ δ' 'Ολυμπίασιν
οὐχ οἱ κάλλιστοι καὶ ἰσχυρότατοι στεφανοῦνται ἀλλ' οἱ ἀγωνιζόμενοι
(τούτων γάρ τινες νικῶσιν), οὕτω καὶ τῶν ἐν τῷ βίῳ καλῶν κἀγαθῶν οἱ
πράττοντες ὀρθῶς ἐπήβολοι γίνονται.[6] To illustrate the virtue of
courage Aristotle uses the example of the gymnastic games, showing
the necessity of keeping the goal in sight and of persevering. Just
as the boxer must not be distracted or discouraged by the pain of
his πόνοι, so also the brave man must not be deterred by wounds or
even the thought of death.[7] The whole range of athletic terms is to
be found here —ἀγών, πόνος, τέλος, ὑπομονή and στέφανος—but is
only used to form an illustrative parallel.

---

whatsoever, or by the art of poetry, to neglect righteousness and the other
virtues."

[1] Leges 647 C&D: ... ἄπειρος δὲ δήπου καὶ ἀγύμναστος ὢν τῶν τοιούτων
ἀγώνων ὁστισοῦν οὐδ'ἂν ἥμισυς ἑαυτοῦ γένοιτο πρὸς ἀρετήν, σώφρων δὲ ἄρα τελέως
ἔσται μὴ πολλαῖς ἡδοναῖς καὶ ἐπιθυμίαις ... διαμεμαχημένος καὶ νενικηκώς

[2] III 12, 1119b, 13.
[3] VI 1, 1138b, 21.
[4] II 2, 1104a, 15 and 5, 1106b, 3.
[5] I 9, 1099b, 17.
[6] I 8, 1099a, 3.
[7] III, 12, 1117b, 2.

2. The Agon Motif in Cynic and Stoic Moral Philosophy

It is the Cynics, followed by the Stoics, who first developed a complete and unified picture of the Agon of the sage. The old noble ideal of καλοκἀγαθία as exemplified in athletic achievement here receives a decidedly ethical interpretation. The methodical Cynic polemic against the folly of the games and of athletics is best seen in the reports of the sayings of Diogenes found in the writings of Dio Chrysostom and Diogenes Laertius.[1] This polemic became one of the recurring themes of the diatribe. The Cynic argues for the priority of ἄσκησις ψυχική over ἄσκησις σωματική. Purely physical exercise must first be transferred to the spiritual plane, or mental plane, before it has any moral value.[2] With scorn for pride in pure physical achievement as folly, the Cynics now claim that they are the true athletes in their struggle for virtue.[3] The prize in this struggle is not the corruptible crown of the public games, nor are men the antagonists of the sage, but rather poverty and exile, dishonour and one's own impulses and desire.[4] It is by waging a continual battle with himself that the philosopher becomes κρείττων, becomes the victor in the true Agon of life with its task of gaining ἀρετή, καλοκἀγαθία[5] and thus εὐδαιμονία.[6]

In picturing the task of the philosopher as an Agon against pleasure and pain (Dio Chrys. Or. VIII 284), the Cynics and Stoics claim to be following the great example set by their patron Hercules.[7] They strove to remove the popular opinions held concerning Hercules and his great feats by asserting that those men erred who thought that he had fought against beasts, for the beasts were allegorized as the vices of men which the hero sought to extirpate in his

---

[1] Especially Dio Chrys. Or. VIII & IX. Cf. also the play on words with ἀθλητής and ἄθλιος in Or. XXVIII 534, also found in Epictetus Diss. III 22, 57 and Clem. Alexandrinus, Paedagogus II 1,2. For Diogenes' polemic see further E. Norden, op.cit., p. 300, and F. Heinze, op.cit., p. 460.

[2] Diog. Laert. VI 70; cf. Dio Chrys. Or. XXVIII 535 and Lucian Anachars. 21 where τὰ περὶ τῆς ψυχῆς are placed above the διαπονήσεις τῶν σωμάτων.

[3] Demetrius de eloc. 260: τὸ Διογένους τὸ ἐν Ὀλυμπίᾳ, ὅτε τοῦ ὁπλίτου δράμοντος ἐπιτρέχων αὐτὸς ἐκήρυττεν ἑαυτὸν νικᾶν ... πάντας ἀνθρώπους καλοκἀγαθίᾳ.

[4] Dio Chrys. Or. IX 11f.

[5] Cf. Stobaeus Flor. IV 12, Diog. Laert. VI 27.

[6] Dio Chrys. Or. VIII 280: ὁ δὲ ἀνὴρ γενναῖος ἡγεῖται τοὺς πόνους ἀνταγωνιστὰς μεγίστους καὶ τούτοις ἀεὶ φιλεῖ μάχεσθαι ... οὐχ ὑπὲρ σελίνου, ὥσπερ αἱ αἶγες, οὐδὲ κοτίνου καὶ πίτυος, ἀλλ'ὑπὲρ εὐδαιμονίας καὶ ἀρετῆς ...

[7] Cf. Dio Chrys. VIII 27 and 30.

global wanderings. Not Hercules' toils as feats of strength, but rather his πόνοι as moral struggles, are the inspiration and example of the sage in his own toils against the ἡδοναί.[1]

It is, however, the representatives of the late Stoic school which here demand our chief attention, indicating the popularity of the athletic metaphor in Paul's own day. The true Agon of the sage is one of the most frequently recurring pictures in the moral discourses of Epictetus, Seneca, Marcus Aurelius, and Plutarch.[2] Hercules again appears as the great example of the moral athlete toiling for virtue.[3] Particularly strong, again, is the traditional contrast between the vain and futile efforts of the athletes in the games and the noble and courageous struggles of the moral athlete in his pursuit of virtue.[4] However over and above this traditional critique we now find in the diatribe a more highly developed and wider appropriation of the athletic imagery and terminology in the service of its own philosophy. The contest into which man enters, if he wishes to follow the Stoic way of life with its struggle against the desires and passions, and the whims of fortune which threaten to disrupt his peace of mind, is the Olympic contest of life itself.[5]

What has been said above concerning the agonal conciousness of the Greek applies to an even higher degree to the Stoic. His entire life in every department of activity, especially his moral endeavours, are pictured as an Agon.[6] The goal of his moral striving is to be found

---

[1] Cf. Ragnar Höistad, Cynic Hero and Cynic King, Uppsala 1948, p. 71. Note also the ἄθλοι/ἀγῶνες of Isis in Plutarch, De Iside 27.

[2] For summaries of the Stoic ethic see M. Pohlenz, Die Stoa, Geschichte einer geistigen Bewegung, Göttingen 1948; A. Bonhöffer, Die Ethik des Stoikers Epiktet, Stuttgart 1894; C. Schneider, Einführung in die neutestamentliche Zeitgeschichte, Leipzig 1934, esp. pp. 77ff.; R. H. Pfeiffer, History of New Testament Times, London 1949; R. Bultmann, Das Urchristentum im Rahmen der antiken Religionen, Zürich 1949; C. K. Barrett, The New Testament Background: Selected documents, 1957.

[3] Eg. Epict. Diss. III 22,57 & 26,31; IV 10,10. Seneca adds the example of Cato, unconquered by toils and contemptive of pleasure, De Const. Sap. 2,2.

[4] In II 18,22f. Epict. contrasts the noble Socrates with the σαπρούς ... πύκτας καὶ παγκρατιαστάς; cf. also III 22,58 and Seneca Ep. 80,2f.

[5] Epict. III 22,51: Ὀλύμπια μέλλεις ἀπογράφεσθαι, ἄνθρωπε, οὐχί τινά ποτε ἀγῶνα ψυχρὸν καὶ ταλαίπωρον; cf. Encheiridion 51: νῦν ὁ ἀγὼν καὶ ἤδη πάρεστι τὰ Ὀλύμπια.

[6] This corresponds to the stress on πρᾶξις or 'actus' over against a merely metaphysical or theorizing philosophy. Epictetus, in a polemic against the mere study of books, contrasts the γυμνασία and ἀγών against sense impressions in the sphere of action with the reading of a treatise on the subject (IV

in ἀναισθησία or ἀπάθεια which is not so much non-sensation or insensibility as impassibility and imperturbability, the state in which "one is no longer at the mercy of pleasure and pain".[1] This aim may also be expressed with the words αὐτάρκεια and ἀταραξία which indicate the self-sufficiency of the sage and his 'stoic' impassibility.

All the ideas of the above catch-words are subsumed in the sage's endeavour to live according to nature (κατὰ φύσιν or συμφώνως τῇ φύσει[2]). The 'logos' which is the cosmic law ruling the universe is at the same time present in the human mind and intellect. The end for rational man is thus to submit to the direction of the λογικόν or ἡγεμονικόν within him, thereby living in accord with the universal Logos, and in harmony with Nature.[3]

All that threatens to disturb the equanimity and imperturbability of the sage, his sense impressions, passions and emotions, and the whims of fortune, must be overcome under the direction of his 'ruling reason'.[4] Thus the *scope of the Stoic Agon* is delineated. It is a struggle against the domination of φαντασία and the πάθη, and against besetting τύχη.[5]

In describing this contest the full range of athletic imagery is employed. As noted above the term ἀγών (Latin 'certamen') is now fully appropriated and used absolutely of the Stoic struggle itself.[6] The sage appears as the ἀθλητὴς ἄθλου τοῦ μεγίστου, τοῦ ὑπὸ μηδενὸς πάθους καταβληθῆναι.[7]

This contest is the Olympic contest of life itself, the ἀγὼν ὁ μέγιστος, not in wrestling or the pancratium, but ὑπὲρ αὐτῆς εὐτυχίας

4,11-13). Seneca writes: 'sic imperfectum ac languidum bonum est in otium sine actu proiecta virtus, numquam id quod didicit ostendans' (De Otio 6,2); cf. also 1,4 and Esp. 94,45.

[1] M. Aurel. 3,3. This state is true 'freedom', cf. Epict. Fragment 35 (Florilegium Cod. Paris 1168, 501E): Οὐδεὶς ἐλεύθερος ἑαυτοῦ μὴ κρατῶν.

[2] M. Aurel. 5,21; 4,51; 7,74; Epict. Diss. I 2,5ff.

[3] M. Aurel. 2,16; 3,9; 5,1&26; Seneca Epist. 76,10.

[4] M. Aurel. 9.7; Plutarch De Gen. Socr. 584E.

[5] An examination of the Stoic moral Agon reveals the basic influence of Greek dualistic anthropology in which the higher principal in man, his soul and reason, is contrasted to his corruptible body, the seat of the ἐπιθυμίαι. The one is νοῦς καὶ δαίμων, the other γῆ καὶ λύθρος (M. Aurel. 3,3). Epictetus says of man: ψυχάριον εἶ βαστάζον νεκρόν (M. Aurel. 4,41), while Seneca despisingly calls the body the 'corpusculum' (eg. Ep. 41,4 & 65,22).

[6] Epict. II 18,27: μέγας ὁ ἀγών ἐστιν; cf. also Encheir. 51 (above p. 29).

[7] M. Aurel. 3,4. The man who successfully strives against difficulties is an Ὀλυμπιονίκης —Epict. I 24,1f.

καὶ εὐδαιμονίας.¹ God summons man into the struggle with the words: ἔλθε ἤδη ἐπὶ τὸν ἀγῶνα, δεῖξον ἡμῖν, τί ἔμαθες, πῶς ἤθλησας.²

At the same time the diatribe makes large use of athletic imagery as illustrative material. The goal-motif and the picture of life as a forward struggle are both stressed with the example of the runner. It is not for man to peer into the blackness of another's heart but to run straight to the goal with never a glance aside.³ Seneca speaks of the 'cursus' which the soul must run, and at whose end lies the 'summum bonum' when the soul 'nec quicquam amplius desiderat'.⁴ In a manner reminiscent of Paul's words to the Corinthians he urges and spurs on Lucilius who is already 'currentem' his course.⁵ The man whose purpose is in harmony with nature is like the runner who adheres to the principles of running. He it is who is προκόπτων ταῖς ἀληθείαις καὶ ὁ μὴ εἰκῆ ἀποδεδημηκώς.⁶

More widely employed, however, is the picture of the boxer, wrestler and pancratiast.⁷ This figure is suited for expressing the necessity of persistent and unflinching struggle in the face of opposition. The business of life is like wrestling for it requires of man "to stand ready and unshakeable against every assault however unforseen."⁸ The sage should use his hardship and difficulties as the wrestler uses his sparring partners to steel himself for greater battles.⁹ Every object and person is to be used in the exercise of self discipline, even he who reviles, for "he exercises (γυμνάζει) my dispassionateness, my gentleness".¹⁰ The picture of the wrestler is thus

---

¹ Epict. III 25,2f. Elsewhere it is an ἀγών ... ὑπὲρ βασιλείας, ὑπὲρ ἐροίας, ὑπὲρ ἀταραξίας (II 18,27ff.), or with fortune —Plutarch De Amic. Mult. 94: ἀγὼν πάσης τύχης & De Gen. Socr.: ἀγῶνες ἀρετῇ πρὸς τὰ συντυγχάνοντα. In Plutarch it is also the ψυχή which ἀγωνίζεται ... ὥσπερ ἀθλητής, κατὰ τὸν βίον, ὅταν δὲ διαγωνίσηται, τότε τυγχάνει τῶν προσηκόντων (Ser. Num. Pun. 18,561A).

² Epict. IV 4,29f.

³ M. Aurel. 4,18; cf. also 4,51: ἐπὶ τὴν σύντομον ἀεὶ τρέχε. σύντομος δὲ ἡ κατὰ φύσιν, and the phrase ἐπὶ τὸν σκοπὸν διώκειν in Epict. IV 12,15.

⁴ De Vita Beata 9,3; cf. Ep. 17,1: ad bonum mentem magno cursu ac totis viribus tende.

⁵ Ep. 34,2; compare the 'Meum opus es' with the 'are you not my work in the Lord' of Paul in I Cor 9:1. Cf. also Ep. 109,6.

⁶ Epict. I 4,18f.

⁷ Just as the pancratiast always has a ready weapon in his fist, so also the moral athlete has only to call on his ἡγεμονικόν for assistance, M. Aurel. 12,9.

⁸ M. Aurel. 7,61; cf. Teles ed. O. Hense ²1909 = Stob. Flor. iii 1,98: δεῖ, ὥσπερ τὸν ἀγαθὸν ὑποκριτὴν ὅ τι ἂν ὁ ποιητὴς περιθῇ προσώπων τοῦτο ἀγωνίζεσθαι καλῶς, οὕτω καὶ τὸν ἀγαθὸν ἄνδρα ὅ τι ἂν περιθῇ ἡ τύχη.

⁹ Epict. I 24,1f.; IV 9,15f.; Encheirid. 29; Seneca De Provid. 2,2ff.

¹⁰ Epict. III 20,9.

used to illustrate two major themes of the Stoic Agon. Every contest in life is a test of one's strength, and victory in each one gives new strength and confidence for the next. That man is the "invincible athlete" who goes on from one victorious round to the other, persisting despite all temptations of wealth, ease, pleasure and glory.[1] The moral athlete may from time to time suffer a defeat at the hands of his desires but can easily pick himself up and contest again without having to wait another four years for the next Olympic festival.[2] Consequently life becomes one long period of ἄσκησις and γυμνασία in which προκοπή means the advancement from one victory to the next towards the goal of ἀταραξία.[3] In this training the moral athlete must strictly follow his standards, just as the athlete must keep to his diet and prescribed exercises.[4]

This Agon is nevertheless not every man's lot. This is clear from the many passages in the diatribe which insist on the necessity of carefully considering beforehand one's strength and aptitude, and the difficulties which lie ahead. In a large Agon complex in his Encheiridion Epictetus shows how the athlete must first weigh his strength with the rigours and hardship of training and the contest itself before entering the games. He continues: ἄνθρωπε, πρῶτον ἐπίσκεψαι, ὁποῖόν ἐστι τὸ πρᾶγμα · εἶτα καὶ τὴν σεαυτοῦ φύσιν κατάμαθε, εἰ δύνασαι βαστάσαι · πένταθλος εἶναι βούλει ἢ παλαιστής; ἴδε σεαυτοῦ τοὺς βραχίονας, τοὺς μηρούς, τὴν ὀσφὺν κατάμαθε. ἄλλος γὰρ πρὸς ἄλλο πέφυκε.[5] But once the Agon has been taken up any slackening of exertion means defeat; all progress depends on the earnestness with which one contests: μέμνησο, ὅτι νῦν ὁ ἀγὼν καὶ ἤδη πάρεστι τὰ Ὀλύμπια καὶ οὐκ ἔστιν ἀναβάλλεσθαι οὐκέτι καὶ ὅτι παρὰ μίαν ἡμέραν καὶ ἐν πρᾶγμα καὶ ἀπόλλυται προκοπὴ καὶ σῴζεται.[6]

---

[1] Epict. I 18,20-23.
[2] Epict. III 25,2-5.
[3] See Epictetus' picture of the inactive athlete who longs for the games to be proclaimed (I 29,36), and the mock victory of the athlete who lacks an opponent (Seneca De Provid. 4,1), and Plutarch De Amic. Mult. 96A: Just as rivalry and competition goad on those ἀγωνιζομένους ἐν τοῖς θεάτροις, so also adversity (πόνοι) spurs on the man who wishes to live as the λογισμός dictates. For πόνοι and ἀσκήσεις as trials and exercises in virtue see also B. J. Hijmans, ΑΣΚΗΣΙΣ —Notes on Epictetus' educational system, Assen 1959.
[4] Epict. III 23,2; Encheirid. 29.
[5] Encheirid. 29; also III 22,53.
[6] Epict. Encheirid. 51. The optional character of the Stoic Agon does not diminish the fact of its earnestness for the sage. Although Epictetus speaks

The insistence on the right of the sage to take his own life[1] seems to introduce a note of inconsistency into the picture of the Agon until death. But the Stoic himself sees no inconsistency here. Death itself is to be welcomed for "it is better to be rid of the passion which tears us in this life".[2] Suicide may be cowardice and an easy way out of the struggle, but it can also be the brave act of a man whose external conditions render a life of virtue impossible, and whose gorge has risen at falsehood and luxury.[3] This is Stoic self-assertion taken to its final extreme.

However the element of competition seems to be entirely lacking from the moral Agon. The term ἀγών itself loses its connotation of competitive contest, changing from a 'vying for honours with' to a 'contending against'. Peace of mind, satisfaction with one's lot and virtue, not glory, are the goal of the moral athlete.[4] Man is summoned into a noble and glorious contest with many spectators,[5] but the sage is nevertheless not the object of adulation like the athlete. Virtue and its possession are glory enough for him.[6]

The sage is his own judge. Each day is to be lived as though it were one's last,[7] but man need give account to none else except to the 'divine reason' within him.[8] The Stoic often speaks of God. But

---

of progress towards perfection (Encheirid. 51,1-2: ἤδη οὖν ἀξίωσον σεαυτὸν βιοῦν ὡς τέλειον καὶ προκόπτοντα), such perfection is not a passive or static state. The sage must therefore struggle until death releases him from the contest, "dum nodum illum exsolvit et omne vinculum mortale" (Seneca De Vita Beata 16).

[1] Esp. frequent in M. Aurel. eg. 3,1; 5,29; 8,47; 9,2ff.

[2] M. Aurel. 10,8. Cf. 6,28: θάνατος ἀνάπαυλα αἰσθητικῆς ἀντιτυπίας καὶ ὁρμητικῆς νευροσπαστίας καὶ διανοητικῆς διεξόδου καὶ τῆς πρὸς τὴν σάρκα λειτουργίας; death is to be welcomed "for Nature wills it like all else" (9,2).

[3] M. Aurel. 9,2; cf. Seneca Ep. 58,36: exibo, non propter (sc. dolorem) ipsum, sed quia impedimento mihi futurus est ad omne, propter quod vivitur.

[4] Seneca Ep. 78,16: praemium non corona nec palma est nec tubicen praedicationi nominis nostri silentium faciens, sed virtus et firmitas animi et pax in ceterum parta, si semel in aliquo certamine debellata fortuna est.

[5] De Provid. 2,8: Ecce spectaculum dignum ad quod respiciat intentus operi suo deus, ecce par deo dignum: vir fortis cum fortuna mala compositus ...

[6] Seneca Ep. 79,13, and Plato Defin 415 A: ἆθλον ἀρετῆς γέρας τὸ ἑαυτοῦ ἕνεκα αἱρετόν. M. Aurelius rejects the pursuit of glory (4,19) and calls for humility in virtue (5,6). E. Stauffer (TWNT I p. 135, line 7f.) is hardly correct in citing Plutarch Gen. Socr. II 593 E (on the passage see below p. 34 note 8) to prove that, for the diatribe "der Preis, der dem Sieger gesetzt ist .. letztlich jenseits des Lebens [liegt]".

[7] M. Aurel. 7,69; 6,30.

[8] Seneca is his own judge, Ep. 26,4: Non timide itaque componor ad illam diem, quo de me ... iudicaturus sum.

3

these passages must be critically examined within the framework of the whole Stoic system. It is God who summons man into the Agon,[1] it is Zeus who exercise the sage by imposing hardship on him.[2] The Agon is itself θεῖος, God himself being the physical trainer who matches man against difficulties.[3] The moral athlete is to call on the deity for help and strength in the contest.[4]

Such language cannot completely hide the pantheistic 'theology' of Stoicism. What Sevenster has recently written on Seneca's concept of God also applies to the writings of Epictetus and Marcus Aurelius.[5] To obey God means little more than obeying the laws of Nature, and to appeal to the deity is the same as calling on the aid of 'divine reason'. That man walks with the gods who carries out the will of the δαίμων, ὃν ἑκάστῳ προστάτην καὶ ἡγεμόνα ὁ Ζεὺς ἔδωκεν —he is the ἱερεὺς ... καὶ ὑπουργὸς θεῶν, the champion in the highest of championships, who puts to use that which is enthroned within, namely his reason.[6] Such frequent admonitions as 'remember God' are thus not appeals to outside aid, but rather exhortations to man to look to himself and his reason for guidance.[7] The identity of the human soul and the deity means that to offend against the deity is to offend against one's own higher self.[8]

---

[1] Epict. IV 4,29ff.

[2] Epict. III 22,56; cf. 57: The Cynic is οὗτος δ'ὑπὸ τοῦ Διὸς ἀθλούμενος καὶ γυμναζόμενος.

[3] II 18,27f. and I 24,1f.

[4] Epict. II 18,27: τοῦ θεοῦ μέμνησο, ἐκεῖνον ἐπικαλοῦ βοηθὸν καὶ παραστάτην, and III 22,53: ἀνάκρινον τὸ δαιμόνιον, δίχα θεοῦ μὴ ἐπιχειρήσῃς.

[5] J. N. Sevenster, Paul and Seneca, Leiden 1961, esp. pp. 35ff.; cf. also R. Bultmann, "Das religiöse Moment in der ethischen Unterweisung Epiktets", ZNW 13 (1912), p. 178: "Es ist also leicht zu sehen, dass der Gottesbegriff Epiktets nichts weiter ist als eine Personifizierung der höchsten Gedankeninhalte, die der Mensch fähig ist zu erzeugen, der sittlichen Gedanken".

[6] M. Aurel. 5,27 and 3,4; cf. Epict. I 14,12. E. Hatch (The Influence of Greek Ideas on Christianity, with a foreword by F. C. Grant, New York 1957, p. 155) is thus hardly right when he writes: "Epictetus expresses moral philosophy in terms of theology. Human life begins and ends in God." Rather it is the reverse —theology is anthropology.

[7] M. Aurel. 7,59: Ἔνδον σκέπε · ἔνδον ἡ πηγὴ τοῦ ἀγαθοῦ ...., Epict. IV 9,15f.: ἔσωθεν γάρ ἐστι καὶ ἀπώλεια καὶ βοήθεια, Seneca Ep. 80,3: Quicquid facere te potest bonum, tecum est.

[8] Epict. II 8,12-14: ἐν σαυτῷ φέρεις αὐτὸν (sc. θεόν) καὶ μολύνων οὐκ αἰσθάνῃ ἀκαθάρτοις μὲν διανοήμασι ῥυπαρεῖς δὲ πράξεσι.
The situation in Plutarch is somewhat different; here such an identification is missing. Those πεπαυμένοι τῶν περὶ τὸν βίον ἀγώνων δι'ἀρετὴν ψυχῆς γενόμενοι δαίμονες look compassionately on those who are still ἐπὶ ταὐτὸ γυμναζομένους

In view of this one could speak of a profanation or secularization of the Greek games in the thought of hellenistic popular moral philosophy. The Cynic-Stoic Agon is removed from its cultic framework and placed in the sphere of everyday life.

3. THE AGON MOTIF IN THE MYSTERY RELIGIONS AND GNOSTICISM

The picture of the Agon of virtue as found in the diatribe plays no great role in the literature to which we owe our knowledge of the hellenistic mystery religions. In view of the structure of thought in the mysteries this phenomenon is not at all surprising. All the life of the devotee is directed towards the mystic rite in which he is granted the vision of the deity and union with him, thus himself becoming divine. Nevertheless the Hermetic writings speak of an ἀγὼν τῆς εὐσεβείας and even provide a definition of this Agon. The relevant passage runs as follows: ψυχὴ δὲ ἀνθρωπίνη, οὐ πᾶσα μέν, ὁ δὲ εὐσεβής, δαιμονία τίς ἐστι καὶ θεία καὶ ἡ τοιαύτη καὶ μετὰ τὸ ἀπαλλαγῆναι τοῦ σώματος τὸν τῆς εὐσεβείας ἀγῶνα ἠγωνισμένη (ἀγὼν δὲ εὐσεβείας, τὸ γνῶναι τὸ θεῖον καὶ μηδένα ἀνθρώπων ἀδικῆσαι), ὅλη νοῦς γίνεται.[1]

The aim of human striving in the mysteries is to become 'spiritual', freed from somatic bonds. The soul is viewed as having left its heavenly origin, and having become enslaved to matter here on earth. It now longs to be freed of these bonds and the dominion of εἱμαρμένη to which it is here subjected, and to return to its original home. The Hermetic writings show that in this struggle man has been gifted above all other forms of life and matter with λόγος and νοῦς, which themselves stem from God's being.[2] It is the Nous which wars against the evils of human nature which cling to the body which the soul must bear on earth. It is only over the ἀσώματος οὐσία that 'heimarmene' has no power.[3] The Nous can however only take up dwelling in the soul which is εὐσεβής. The ἀγὼν τῆς εὐσεβείας

τέλος and aid them in this same struggle for virtue (De Gen. Socr. 593 D&E). In the same section (593F-594A) the soul ἤδη διὰ μυρίων γενέσεων ἠγωνισμένη μακροὺς ἀγῶνας is granted the help of its daemon by God.

[1] Corpus Hermeticum, Vol. I, X 19, ed. by Nock-Festugière with French translation, Paris 1945. On the passage see R. Reitzenstein, Die hellenistischen Mysterienreligionen, Stuttgart ³1927, p. 295, and J. Kroll, Die Lehren des Hermes Trismegistos, Münster i. W. 1914, pp. 258. 353 and 311.

[2] Corp. herm. XII 12.

[3] Cf. Kroll, op.cit., p. 215.

has its final goal in the complete release from the body when the soul has become completely Nous. This process results in the deification of the soul, that is, its return to its divine origin when it was free of matter, to perfection itself.[1]

The phrase τὸ γνῶναι τὸ θεῖον however clearly suggests the boundaries of the Agon here. It is not limited to the Stoic Agon of man to lift himself above the shackles of the material and the sensual. For the γνῶσις τοῦ θεοῦ is given in the mysteries by means of the sacred rites of initiation in which the soul dies to the material body and its passions and reaches the vision of the deity and union with him. Thus the initiant is himself acclaimed as God.[2]

It is thus evident why the concept of the whole of life as an athletic Agon is here out of place.[3] The struggle of the Nous against the passions is certainly related to that found in the diatribe. This idea and the dualism of soul and body are traditional elements of hellenistic philosophy. But whereas the sage is never released from his Agon, the devotee of the mysteries is released from the struggle by his initiation with its various stages which result in his deification, his perfection and the release from all that is earthly.

The very phrase ἀγὼν τῆς εὐσεβείας with its qualifying genitive draws attention to the difference between the concept of the Agon in the mysteries and that found in the diatribe. Here the term again receives a religious orientation as opposed to the 'profane' philosophical usage, and thus approaches the 'Agon of godliness' in Hellenistic Jewish Literature.

Probably in accordance with their oriental origin, the mysteries show a preference for the military metaphor. The cults of Isis and

---

[1] K. Kerényi, Die griechisch-orientalische Romanliteratur in religionsgeschichtlicher Beleuchtung, Tübingen 1927, pp. 125ff., also points to the recurring theme of martyrdom or "voluntaria mors", in the late-Greek novel. This death, often crucifixion, is also called an Agon (cf. Achilleus Tatios VI 21: ἀγῶνα θεάσασθε καινόν πρὸς πάσας τὰς βασάνους ἀγωνίζεται μία γυνὴ καὶ πάντα νικᾷ). Kerényi sees here a symbolic presentation of the ritual death of the initiated in the mystery-rites of Isis (p. 144) and also draws attention to the Agon as initiation into the mystery in Apuleius XI 24.
[2] For the cultic-ritual background of the term γνῶσις in the mysteries see Reitzenstein, op.cit., pp. 294ff.
[3] There are no indications that the frequently recurring picture of the στέφανος in the mystery initiation rites has any connection with the ἀγὼν τῆς εὐσεβείας. K. Baus, Der Kranz in Antike und Christentum, Bonn 1940, has pointed out the widespread religious significance of garlands and crowns in antiquity.

Mithras, for example, stress the concept of the sacred military service which the devotee enters through the oath of allegiance (sacramentum).[1]

---

[1] Cf. Reitzenstein, op.cit., pp. 20ff. and p. 185 where the prayer to Seth or Typhon is cited: ἐγὼ (εἰμὶ) ὁ σὺν σοὶ συμμαχήσας τοῖς θεοῖς, and esp. Chapter III, Mysten, Gotteskrieger und Gottesgefangene, where references to the 'sancta militia' in Apuleius are discussed. Cf. also F. Cumont, Die Mysterien des Mithra, Leipzig/Berlin 1923, p. 143: The mystic seeks the title "miles" through initiation. Mithraicism placed great emphasis on life as a testing of moral courage. Cumont, p. 148, shows that the ideal was the same as the Stoic goal of ἀπάθεια, the freeing from every sensual impulse.

CHAPTER THREE

HELLENISTIC JUDAISM AND THE AGON TRADITION

The purely hellenistic material at our disposal has shown that at least the linguistic presuppositions were present in the milieu of Paul to enable him to make use of the athletic metaphor. However the fact that the outer form was present cannot detract from the realization that the philosophy represented by the traditional athletic image was diametrically opposed to Paul's own theological thought.

Consequently we are set the task of searching for parallel or illustrative material closer to the intellectual and religious home of Paul, namely in Hellenistic Judaism.[1] In actual fact one here meets a wealth of evidence testifying to the continuance of the Agon tradition, above all in the writings of Philo of Alexandria, and in the Apocrypha and Pseudepigrapha of the Old Testament. That we are here still dealing with the same tradition is further indicated by the striking manner in which the sources reflect decided influences from the thought of the diatribe.

1. Philo

The works of Philo of Alexandria teem with the terminology of the games and with the picture of the Agon of virtue. Here again, however, one should not be satisfied with simply adducing interesting parallels—even when it is realized that they offer further convincing proof of an Agon tradition.[2] These passages should be seen in the light and within the framework of the writer's entire scheme of thought, in order to make the examination completely fruitful. This is all the more important in the case of Philo since a purely linguistic or formal comparison could lead to the false conclusion that Philo is simply carrying on uncritically the image of the diatribe before him.[3]

---

[1] This further stage of the study is also necessitated by the need to examine closer the suggestion of some scholars that Paul received the athletic metaphor from the hellenistic synagogue; cf. the Introduction p. 4 note 2.

[2] See e.g. the list of references in Eidem, Pauli bildvärld, pp. 175f.

[3] P. Wendland, Philo und die kynisch-stoische Diatribe, in: Beiträge zur Geschichte der griechischen Philosophie und Religion, Berlin 1895, has

The recurrence of the traditional features and themes of the Cynic-Stoic picture of the Agon of virtue are not difficult to find in Philo. The polemic against the supposedly holy character of the national games again occurs frequently. The moral athlete is to leave to others the prizes of those unholy contests which the states hold every three years and to apply himself rather to winning the crowns in those contests which are truly holy: ὁ τοίνυν Ὀλυμπιακὸς ἀγὼν μόνος ἂν λέγοιτο ἐνδίκως ἱερός, οὐχ ὃν τιθέασιν οἱ τὴν Ἦλιν οἰκοῦντες, ἀλλ' ὁ περὶ κτήσεως τῶν θείων καὶ ὀλυμπίων ὡς ἀληθῶς ἀρετῶν εἰς τοῦτον τοῦ ἀγῶνα οἱ ἀσθενέστατοι τὰ σώματα ἐρρωμενέστατοι δὲ τὰς ψυχὰς ἐγγράφονται πάντες.[1]

Philo ridicules the efforts of the athletes[2] by pointing out the superior physical strength and prowess of the animals, and by drawing attention to the anomaly that, normally, physical injury to others is punishable, but is rewarded in the arena with crowns and honour.[3] In traditional fashion he contrasts the athletes who take thought only for the improvement of the body with the philosophers οἷς ἔθος ἐγγυμνάζεσθαι διὰ ξηρῶν ἱδρώτων πρὸς τὴν τῶν περὶ τὸν βίον ἀναγκαίων καὶ χρησίμων κτῆσιν.[4]

The true Agon of life which alone deserves to be designated as holy again appears as the contest for virtue in the struggle against the passions and vices.[5] As in the diatribe this contest is called the

---

observed the recurrence of many of the traditional themes of the diatribe in Philo, expecially the emphasis on ἐγκράτεια as the basic moral demand. However, as H. A. Wolfson has admirably shown (Philo I and II, Cambridge/ Mass. 1948), Philo's thought not only contains a revision of Platonism and Neopythagoreanism, but also offers a criticism of Stoicism. "In fact the whole philosophy of Philo may be reconstructed as a criticism of Stoicism" (op. cit., I p. 112). But Wolfson's stress on the unity and originality of Philo's thought seems to be questionable over against E. Schürer's view on the composite and eclectic character of his system (Schürer, III p. 598), a view shared by C. K. Barrett, The New Testament Background: Selected Documents, London 1958, p. 175. L. Treitel, Die Theologie Philo's, Berlin 1923, also warns against seeing in Philo a rehash of Stoicism.

[1] Agric 113 and 119; compare also Mut Nom 106: ἀγωνισταῖς κατὰ τοὺς ἱεροὺς ἀγῶνας λεγομένους with Abr 48: ἀνδρῶν ἀθλητικῶν ... ἐπὶ τοὺς ἱεροὺς ὄντως ἀλειφομένων ἀγῶνας.

[2] Note also the familiar play on words with ἀθλητής and ἄθλιος in the cutting polemic in Vit Cont 41, and also in Plant 39 and Som II 24.

[3] Wendland, op.cit., p. 43.

[4] Spec Leg II 91; cf. also Leg All III 72.

[5] For the Agon of virtue as 'holy' see, in addition to note 2 above, Migr Ab 200, Mut Nom 81f. and Praem Poen 52: λέγω δὲ ἱεροὺς (sc. ἀγῶνας) οὐ τοὺς παρὰ πολλοῖς νομιζομένους ... ἀλλ' οὓς ἡ ψυχὴ πέφυκε διαθλεῖν.

'Ολυμπιακὸς ἀγών itself.¹ It is the κάλλιστος ἀγών² against 'pleasure' for the καλὸς στέφανος which no festival gathering can offer.³

Philo appropriates to himself the whole range of athletic imagery and terminology. Words such as ἄσκησις, γυμνασία, πόνος and ἄθλησις and their related forms, originally at home in the sphere of athletics (clear, for example from the phrase οἱ ἔναθλοι καὶ ἐναγώνιοι πόνοι in Som I 168) now become part of Philo's stock vocabulary in picturing the self-control and renunciation, practice, toil and struggle in the Agon for virtue. The pursuant of virtue is simply called the athlete or agonist. In Philo these terms still carry a ring of their original connotation so that any one of them when standing alone suffices to recall the familiar athletic metaphor.⁵

Philo loves to dwell on the various features of the athletic contests as illustrative material for his moral philosophy. As in the diatribe the comparison with the wrestler, boxer or pancratiast is most frequent, for here the greatest scope is offered in illustrating the need for toil and endurance against the opponent, the passions.⁵ But there are many instances where the athletic picture is metaphorically used without any explicit comparison with the games.⁶

---

¹ Agric 119; Deus Imm 147.

² Leg All II 108; also III 48: καλὸν δρόμον καὶ πάντων ἄριστον ἀγώνισμα; cf. the καλὸς ἀγών in I Tim 6:12 and II Tim 4:7!

³ Cf. also Mut Nom 82: καλόν γε ἀσκητικῇ ψυχῇ πρόκειται τὸ ἆθλον, and Vit Mos II 136: ἀγώνισμα καλὸν ἄρασθαι. For the contrast between the paltry prizes of the games and those won by the moral athlete cf. Omn Prob Lib 113.

⁴ E.g. Spec Leg IV 99: ἄσκησις τῆς ἐγκρατείας, ibid 101: ἄσκησις ἀρετῆς, Congr 108: οἱ περὶ τῶν καλῶν πόνοι, Sac AC 85: ψυχὴν γυμνάζειν.

⁵ E.g. Omn Prob Lib 110ff. For comparisons with the athlete see Jos 223, Leg All III 14 and IV 202. Less frequent is the picture of the runner, but see Som I 171, Leg All III 48, and Agric 91 for the picture of the ἀγῶνες ἱππικοί. In Det Pot Ins 32 the field of Gen 4:8 is taken as a symbol for the ἄμιλλα καὶ διαμαχή which Abel, the φιλόθεον δόγμα fights against Cain, the φίλαυτον δόγμα. This struggle is pictured in terms of a pancration, especially popular in Stoic literature in comparing the struggle of the wise against the foolish (cf. the note ad loc. in the Cohn-Wendland edition of Philo). The picture of the σκιαμαχία is only used negatively, Det Pot Ins 41 and Plant 175. For ὑπομονή still with its agonal connotation see Deus Imm 13: τοὺς διὰ ... ὑπομονῆς ἐπὶ κτήσει τοῦ ἀρίστου διαθλεῖν ἄθλους.

⁶ An excellent example in Migr Ab 27 (God's words to Abraham based on Gen 31:3): ἀθλητὴς τέλειος καὶ βραβείων καὶ στεφάνων ἠξιώθης ἀγωνοθετούσης ἀρετῆς καὶ προτεινούσης ἆθλά σοι τὰ νικητήρια· κατάλυσον δὲ ἤδη τὸ φιλόνεικον, ἵνα μὴ πάντοτε πονῇς ...
See also the full metaphor of the Agon in evil in Agric 111ff.

The position of Hercules as the paradigm of the moral athlete in the Cynic-Stoic diatribe is occupied in Philo in the first place by the patriarchs of the Old Testament. By means of allegorization he converts the various figures who appear in the history of Genesis into the different conditions of the soul.[1] The personalities of the Old Testament, but above all the patriarchs, become embodiments of particular virtues and psychological dispositions. Thus Abraham is the representative of διδασκαλικὴ ἀρετή (virtue which must be learnt in the gradual growth from knowledge to faith), Isaac represents φυσικὴ ἀρετή (virtue as a natural inborn gift or predisposition), while Jacob is the symbol of ἀσκητικὴ ἀρετή (virtue which must be won through exercise and struggle for self-control against the passions).[2] It is especially on the basis of Gen 32:24ff. that Jacob is viewed as *the* type of the moral athlete. He is τοῦ πάλην ἠσκηκότος ... —πάλην δ' οὐ τὴν σώματος ἀλλ' ἣν παλάιει ψυχὴ πρὸς τοὺς ἀνταγωνιστὰς τρόπους αὐτῆς πάθεσι καὶ κακίαις μαχομένη,[3] and again τοῦ ἀθλοῦντος καὶ τὸν ὑπέρ κτήσεως ἀρετῆς ἱερὸν ὄντως ἀγῶνα μὴ διαφθείροντος.[4] However Abraham and Isaac are, with Jacob, "athletes who equip themselves for the truly holy contests, who value lightly physical exercises and take thought for the good condition of the soul through earnest striving for victory over the opposing passions".[5] Moses also is pictured as a wrestler for virtue;[6] Joseph wrestles with adversity and passion in the person of Potiphar's wife;[7] Enoch's life is an Agon of repentance;[8] Noah too is designated as a victorious agonist.[9] The metaphor is even applied to the Children of Israel who, with the giving of the Law, entered "as into a holy contest", a contest in which some proved themselves athletes

---

[1] Cf. Schürer, III p. 649. For the lack of historical perspective, i.e. any sense for God's saving acts with Israel in history, in Philo, see also E. E. Ellis, Paul's Use of the Old Testament, Edinburgh 1957, pp. 52ff.

[2] Cf. esp. Praem Poen 27; Abr 11,52-59; Jos 1; Som I 167-72 (Schürer, III p. 665; L. Treitel, Theologie Philos, pp. 50f; R. Bultmann, Urchristentum, p. 105).

[3] Leg All III 190.

[4] Migr Abr 200; cf. also Som I 126-129, 171; Jos 223; Fug 43; Ebr 82; Sobr. 65.

[5] Abr 48; for Abraham alone as an athlete of virtue see in addition Migr Abr 27 (cf. note 7 supra); Abr 256; Som I 479.

[6] Vit Mos I 48: τοὺς ἀρετῆς ἄθλους Μωυσῆς διήθλει; also Poster C 13 and Leg All III 14.

[7] Leg All III 242.

[8] Praem Poen 15.

[9] Abr 34f.

of true virtue.¹ The entire wandering in the desert becomes an Agon in which some of the Israelites "let their hands sink like athletes who give up opposition" (the picture is probably that of the boxer), "and decide to run back to Egypt to the enjoyment of the passions", while the others τὸν ἀγῶνα τοῦ βίου διήθλησαν with strength and endurance.²

Another phenomenon which deserves close attention in Philo is the frequent use of military imagery, in many instances combined with the athletic metaphor.³ Here once again Philo no doubt reflects the influence of the diatribe where life is also pictured as one long warfare.⁴ The verb μάχεσθαι is used for the struggle for virtue against the onslaughts of the pleasures and passions,⁵ but the military metaphor, in as far as it is related to that of the Agon, is most often represented by the nouns στρατεία and πόλεμος (plus their derivatives). Several times Philo uses πόλεμος of the civil war in the soul of man kindled by the desires and passions.⁶ The close affinity between the uses of πόλεμος and ἀγών is shown by the fact that Philo elsewhere pictures the unending struggle between evil and virtue in man's soul in the terms of an Agon.⁷ Also, in other instances where πόλεμος appears it is clear that Philo could just as well have used the word ἀγών.⁸ The only instances where he seems to prefer

---

¹ Praem Poen 4ff.

² Congr Erud 164f. In Omn Prob Lib 88 it is the Essenes who merit the title "athletes of virtue' because their philosophy is free from the pedantry of Greek wordiness, rather setting them exercices in laudable actions. Four hundred years later the Christian ascetic Nilus of Ancyra writes the following of the Essenes (Text in: Antike Berichte über die Essener, ausgewählt von A. Adam = LKIT No. 182, p. 58): ἀλλὰ τί τῶν ἀγώνων ὄφελος αὐτοῖς καὶ τῆς ἐπιπόνου ἀθλήσεως τὸν ἀγωνοθέτην Χριστὸν ἀνῃρηκόσιν; (!)

³ This observation is of significance in view of the same phenomenon in Eph 6:10-20 (πανοπλία and πάλη), and in II Tim 2:3-5 (στρατεύεσθαι and ἀθλεῖν). Cf. a further mixture of metaphors, though showing dependence on II Tim 2:4, in Ign Pol 6:1f. Cf. also IV Macc 3:4f., also 13:15f., 16:14ff., esp. 9:23f.(!), 11:20-22.

⁴ Cf. Epict III 24,31: οὐκ οἶσθ' ὅτι στρατεία τὸ χρῆμά ἐστιν; and 34: στρατεία τις ἐστιν ὁ βίος ἑκάστου καὶ αὕτη μακρὰ καὶ ποικίλη —the στρατηγός whose commands are to be obeyed is the ἡγεμονικόν; Seneca Ep. 107,9: malus miles est, qui imperatorem gemens sequitur, and Ep. 96: Vivere ... militare est; Marc. Aurel. II 17: ὁ δὲ βίος πόλεμος καὶ ξένου ἐπιδημία...

⁵ E.g. Leg All I 86, II 106, III 190 and 116, Poster C 32.

⁶ Somn I 147: τὸν ὑπὸ τῶν παθῶν ἀναρριπιζόμενον ἐμφύλιον πόλεμον, also Ebr 75: τὸν ἐν ψυχῇ τῶν ἐπιθυμιῶν ἐμφύλιον πόλεμον.

⁷ Cf. Abr 105f.

⁸ The interchangeability is clear from Sacr AC 35 where the Agon is the πρὸς ἡδονὴν πόλεμος; cf. also Leg All III 134.

the military image are those in which he allegorizes accounts of the
Pentateuch which report armed battles.¹

The close relationship between the athletic and military imagery
in Philo is seen at its clearest in the passages in which he mixes
the two metaphors. He himself obviously found the combination
in no way disturbing since they complemented each other. In allegorizing Moses' flight from Egypt Philo writes: στρατευσάμενος
γὰρ στρατείαν τὴν ὑπὲρ ἀρετῆς οὐ παύεται πολεμῶν, πρὶν ἐπιδεῖν πρηνεῖς
καὶ ἀπράκτους τὰς ἡδονάς ... ἀναχωρεῖ, τουτέστιν ἀνακωχὴν ποιεῖται
τοῦ πολέμου ἀθλητοῦ τρόπον διαπνέοντος ...² An even more surprising
mixture is that in Sacr AC 17: καὶ τὰ βραβεῖα καὶ τὸν στέφανον
παραχωρῆσαι τῷ πόλεμον ... πρὸς τὰ πάθη πεποιημένῳ—soldiers could
also receive crowns, but βραβεῖον belongs to the terminology of the
games!

Before turning to the original features of Philo's concept of the
moral Agon attention may be drawn to the interesting passage in
which Moses appears, as it were, in the role of a Stoic sage: τοὺς
ἀρετῆς ἄθλους Μωυσῆς διήθλει τὸν ἀλείπτην ἔχων ἐν ἑαυτῷ λογισμὸν
ἀστεῖον ..., διὰ τὸ προκεῖσθαι σκοπὸν ἕνα τὸν ὀρθὸν τῆς φύσεως λόγον,
ὃς μόνος ἐστὶν ἀρετῶν ἀρχή τε καὶ πηγή.³

The definition of the struggles by means of the genitive ἀρετῆς,
but above all the words λογισμός, φύσις, and ὀρθὸς λόγος⁴ point back
to a Stoic origin. Nevertheless a closer look at Philo's concept of the
moral Agon, and already his terminology, quickly reveals the *wide
gap which lies between him and the diatribe*. Philo is a hellenistic
philosopher, but he also wishes to remain a faithful Jew.⁵

The definition of the Agon is already instructive. Philo is still

---

¹ Cf. the allegorical interpretation of Ex 32:26-28 in Sacr AC 130 where
Moses, avenging the sin with the golden calf, appears as the στρατηγός of the
ἱεροὶ λόγοι (ideas based on reason) who πόλεμον ἀκήρυκτον ὑπὲρ εὐσεβείας
ἐπολέμουν. The battles of the Children of Israel are also interpreted as moral
πόλεμοι —e.g. Mut Nom 265, and Conf Ling 57.

² Leg All III 14 —a similar mixture in III 90.

³ Vit Mos I 48.

⁴ Cf. Diog. Laert. VII 88. This is the objective law of nature by following
which man, the microcosm, lives in harmony with the universe, the macro-
cosm.

⁵ Schürer III, p. 700. The dominant role of Jewish piety in Philo's ethic is
strongly stressed by W. Völker, Fortschritt und Vollendung bei Philo von
Alexandrien, Texte und Untersuchungen 49, 1 (1938) —a correct emphasis
over against the onesided presentations of Wendland and of Treitel (op.cit.)
who overlook this side in drawing the lines of connection with hellenistic
philosophy.

genuinely Stoic in presenting the moral struggle of man as an Agon of virtue.[1] The phrase ἀγὼν τοῦ βίου and the idea it expresses is also at home in the diatribe.[2] But that which is characteristic of Philo, and which reveals the basic influence of his piety, is his understanding of the struggle as an ἀγὼν τῆς εὐσεβείας. True, he usually uses the phrase[3] when interpreting actual struggles and battles in the Old Testament, but these in turn are allegories of the Agon of piety, godliness, and holiness, which the moral athlete must wage. *For Philo the agonist is finally a fighter for God, a 'Gotteskämpfer'*[4] in so far as all of man's speech and actions have a direct bearing on his relationship to God,[5] and in so far as God himself is directly concerned in the contest of his athletes. God is the ἀθλοθέτης, Who has prepared the world as an arena,[6] the βραβευτής Who awards the prizes,[7] and Who crowns all toil.[8] Virtue can only be achieved by toil, but toil cannot in turn achieve virtue without the help of God. The 'Gotteskämpfer' is never self-sufficient in the same sense as the Stoic sage. "It is necessary that the soul should not ascribe to itself its toil for virtue, but that it should take it away from itself and refer it to God, confessing that not its own strength or power acquire nobility but he who freely bestowed also the love of it... Only then does the soul begin to be saved when the seat of anger has received reason as its charioteer, and toil has come to create in it not self-satisfaction, but a *readiness to yield the honour to God*, the bestower of the boon."[9] God is the everpresent helper of the athlete on the

---

[1] E.g. Agric 119: ἀγὼν ... περὶ κτήσεως τῶν ... ἀρετῶν; Mut Nom 14 Migr Abr 200 and Congr 180.

[2] Somn II 145 and Congr 164f.

[3] E.g. Spec Leg II 183, Sacr AC 130, Vit Mos I 307 and II 136, Virt 45 (ὑπὲρ εὐσεβείας καὶ ὁσιότητος) Spec Leg I 57 (ὑπὲρ θεοῦ τιμῆς ἀγῶνας) In all Israel's battles God is the προαγωνιστής; Virt 45, Abr 232.

[4] This feature, and the concept εὐσέβεια brings us closer to the Agon in the Hermetic writings.

[5] Cf. Josephus Contra Ap. 2,171: ἅπασαι αἱ πράξεις καὶ διατριβαὶ καὶ λόγοι πάντες ἐπὶ τὴν πρὸς τὸν θεὸν ἡμῖν εὐσέβειαν ἔχουσι τὴν ἀναφοράν.

[6] Op Mund 78, though the context is strictly not that of the moral Agon. Man, as last created, is the spectator enjoying God's world.

[7] Somn I 153 130. In Ebr III (based on Ex 15:1) Moses sings the praises of God as τὸν δίκαιον καὶ ἀληθῆ βραβευτήν; cf. also Rer Div Her 271. In both instances the word βραβευτής means little more than judge, and can also be applied to Moses in this capacity —Spec Leg IV 64 and 66.

[8] Leg All I 80; οὐκ ἀτελὴς ὁ πόνος ἀλλὰ στεφανούμενος ὑπὸ θεοῦ καὶ μισθοδοτούμενος.

[9] Leg All III 46,137 —quoted by H. A. Wolfson, Philo, Cambridge/Mass,

road to virtue.[1] While the Stoic's prayer for assistance in the Agon is finally only a plea to the God within himself, his 'ruling reason', the prayer of Philo to God as a power outside of himself (Ebr 32) is genuine prayer.

It is Philo's piety which preserves him from the negativism of the Stoic ethic. It is an Agon which is given to man by God, it is a struggle which is to be fought to the honour of God, and one which is rewarded by God. It is this theocentricity[2] in Philo's ethic which precludes the possibility of his expressing its final goal in the negative terms of Stoicism.[3] For Philo the goal of all ethical endeavour is finally "to live to God alone",[4] virtue being a concept which is directly related to God and to his commands.[5] This point becomes further clear when we observe Philo's attitude to the Law of God given through Moses.

Philo follows Stoic thought in picturing the life of virtue as that which is lived according to the law of nature—this being identical with the law of reason.[6] But it is imperative to remember that he shares the concern of the writer of IV Maccabees to prove that the Law of Moses is identical with this rational law of nature.[7] Still within the athletic image he speaks of the laws of the Fathers as the trainers which God has given man for the Agon of piety.[8]

1948, I p. 447. The picture of the charioteer obviously refers to Plato's image in Phaedrus 246f.; cf. above, ch. II 1.

[1] Somn I 179.

[2] Cf. Völker, op.cit., p. 205: "Die Ethik unseres Alexandriners ist gottbezogen ... sie unterscheidet sich daher prinzipiell von der stoischen Sittenlehre." That Philo's piety stands at the centre of his ethic is also clear from the lack of emphasis on the anthropocentric ideals of εὐτυχία and εὐδαιμονία which are to be the final result of the Stoic sage's Agon. The Stoic could never speak of an ἀγὼν μετανοίας or ἀγὼν δικαιοσύνης as does Philo (Praem Poen 15 and 22).

[3] The struggle against the passions has μετριοπαθεῖν rather than ἀπάθεια as its aim (Abr 257; cf. Völker, op.cit., p. 135).

[4] Mut Nom 213, Leg All III 193,13. The highest virtue is thus εὐσέβεια. This is, of course, not to deny that the highest goal which the truly wise and virtuous reaches, is the mystic vision of God. This goal is, however, still closely connected with Philo's piety and ethics.

[5] The opposite of the Agon of piety is the ἀγὼν περὶ τῶν ἐν τῷ διαμαρτάνειν πρωτείων —applied to the contemporaries of Noah in Abr 40.

[6] Cf. the standard phrase ὀρθὸς φύσεως λόγος in Virt 127 and in Vit Mos I 48.

[7] Cf. Treitel, op.cit., p. 49, and Völker, op.cit., p. 66. Cf. also G. Bornkamm, "Die Offenbarung des Zornes Gottes, Röm. 1-3", in: Das Ende des Gesetzes, München 1952, p. 16, and Gutbrod, TWNT, IV p. 1045, lines 36ff.

[8] Cf. Praem Poen 4-6, Spec Leg IV 179, Omn Prob Lib 80.

Despite the philosophical dress of his thought Philo obviously gards the revealed will of God—often allegorically interpreted where the literal sense lacks ethical content—as the basis of his ethic.[1]

Even the familiar scheme, Reason versus Passions, which re-occurs in Philo[2] should not be accepted uncritically as a pure repro-duction of Stoic thought. In the first place he carefully avoids the pantheistic conception of the Logos as the immanent 'world-soul' or ruling principal which pervades all of nature. He does this by distinguishing between the Logos, in the sense of νοῦς, as the mind of God which is identical with His being, and the created mind which is distinct from His essense. The former is and remains es-sentially transcendant, so that the immanent Logos is never identi-cal with God Himself, even though Philo speaks of the 'heavenly' or 'divine' in man.[3] In the second place it is not a matter of a simple antithesis between mind/reason and the body as the seat of the impulses and desires.

Rather, the immanent Logos not only encounters errant matter on entering the body; it meets another soul created by God, one which is however γεώδης (Leg All I 12,31). The Agon in Philo is thus best defined as "the struggle of the rational soul with the body under the dominance of the irrational soul".[4] Furthermore there appears a third factor which differentiates this struggle from that found in the Stoic diatribe, namely the factor of the will. Philo understands it as a manifestation of divine grace that man was given that freedom of action by which God, in a miraculous manner, comes to the aid of his chosen ones in their struggle against the odds of nature.[5] Through his emphasis on the necessity of divine aid he thereby overcomes the mechanical conception of the Stoic Agon where the victory of reason over the passions, or vice versa, depends

---

[1] Völker, p. 199: Philo's ethic is "von dem verpflichtenden Ernst der alt-testamentlichen Forderung getragen". It is true that Philo does speak of εὐδαιμονία, but this is not to be reached by man himself by means of greater effort and application; it is rather a gift of God's grace, a result of the ful-filment of God's commands in the effort to please Him (cf. Migr Abr 128 and 35).

[2] Cf. Logos in Leg All 116 and 155, Abr 243, Rer Div Her 125; λογισμός in Abr 256, Vit Mos 148; νοῦς in Somn II 145, Migr Abr 67.

[3] E.g. Gig 60; Det Pot Ins 29.

[4] Wolfson, op.cit., p. 424.

[5] Wolfson, p. 431. On the freedom of the will in Philo see also Völker, op. cit., p. 59.

ultimately on the relative strength or weakness of the two contestants.

One final feature must also be noted, one which again distinguishes Philo's picture of the Agon from that of Stoicism. The athletic metaphor in the diatribe is virtually incomplete due to the rareness of the image of the victor's prize or crown.[1] The diatribe is on the one hand true to the limits set by its 'theology', and on the other hand carries on the tradition of Greek philosophy with its maxim: "Justice and virtue for their own sakes".[2] Thus the sage considers that "virtue is worthy of choice for its own sake".[3] Philo seems to be following in this tradition when he writes that "prudence is itself the reward (ἆθλον) of prudence, and justice and each of the other virtues is its own recompense (γέρας)".[4] At the same time, however, he frequently refers to the prizes and crowns which are awarded to the athletes of virtue and piety according to their particular feats.[5] "He (i.e. Abraham) reaches perfection with virtue as his instructor and receives as a prize (ἆθλον) trust in God. To him (i.e. Isaac) who through his fortunate natural disposition and through independent hearing and learning has gained virtue falls the prize (βραβεῖον) of joy. To the fighter (i.e. Jacob) who through unabating and restless toils has made the good his own, his crown (στέφανος) is the vision of God".[6] Philo here uses the three main terms for the prizes at the

---

[1] Cf. supra, ch.II 2.

[2] Cf. Plato Rep. X 612B and Aristotle Ethic. Nic. X 6, 1176b, 8-9.

[3] Cf. Diog. VII 89,127 and further references supra, ch.II 2.

[4] Spec Leg II 47,259. Wolfson, who cites this passage (op.cit., II, p. 286), also points to similar statements in Rabbinical literature, above all, in Aboth 1,3. But it should not be overlooked that here the stress lies elsewhere —quite apart from the impossibility of using the category of 'virtue' in the parallels which here come into question. Wolfson himself points out that, according to Jewish belief in individual providence and divine judgement, no righteous deed can go unrewarded, even though this may not be apparent to the eye. (for the idea of reward in Aboth see further 2.16, 3.2, 5.1,2 and 14, 3.17, 6.2) The stress in the Rabbinical literature is therefore rather on righteous action and the study of the Law without reward forming the *motive* for such action —despite the certainty of reward, and without *claiming* this reward (cf. Aboth 1.3, 2.8, and 6.6). The distinction is quite clear in Aboth 6.1: "He that occupies himself in the study of the Law for its own sake merits many things, and, still more, he is deserving of the whole world". (H. Danby, The Mishnah, Oxford 1933, p. 459)

[5] E.g. Sac AC 17, Agr 120, Praem Poen 4-6.

[6] Praem Poen 27. In Mut Nom 82 the vision of God is the καλὸν ἆθλον and the εὐανθέστερος καὶ ἐπιτηδειότερος στέφανος. In Abr 254 Isaac is the prize granted to Abraham by God for his virtuous life.

athletic games.[1] But the decisive point is that the prize or crown is *not claimed* by the athlete, *but granted* by God, for it is God who rewards and crowns all toil.[2] The prizes themselves, though varying, complete the picture of the Agon of piety in that they are all God-related. This emphasis also comes to light in De Abrahamo 34f. where Noah, the τέλειος, is crowned as the victorious agonist and receives the most illustrious proclamation of prize (κήρυγμα λαμπρό-τατον) when it is said of him that "he pleased God".[3] In Philo the ultimate goal and prize are the same—God Himself and His blessings.

2. THE GREEK BIBLE

The Greek public games and the ideals which they represented were completely foreign to Israelitic thought and life. The spirit of competition, the cult of the beautiful —including the beauty of the naked form —and the structure of hellenistic education in which the exercise of the body played a dominant role, are all without parallel in the life and language of the Old Testament people. Naked-ness, an essential feature of Greek athletics, is rather a source and sign of shame, and to be hidden from the sight of man and of God.[4] However—and herein lies the necessity of examining the language of the Septuagint—it is still possible that a hellenistic Jew could have been reminded of the popular picture of the Agon while reading his Greek Bible at certain passages.

In the verses describing Jacob's *wrestling* with the angel of the Lord in Gen 32:24f. the niphal of אבק (only here in the MT) is twice rendered by means of παλαίειν. The same verb, but again obviously without any athletic connotations, occurs in Jud 20:33[5] and in the

---

[1] Cf. also Somn II 90 (ἀγώνισμα ἀρετῆς), Vit Mos II 136 (ἀγώνισμα καλόν).
[2] Leg All I 80; cf. supra p. 44 note 8.
[3] LXX Gen 6:9. An even more surprising allegorization appears in Somn II 129ff. where the laming of Jacob in Gen 32:26 is interpreted as a picture of the soul which, perfected in the contests for virtue, does not boast of its achievements but lames itself, voluntarily remaining behind the incorporial beings, thereby carrying off the victory though seemingly beaten.
[4] Gen 3:7ff., 9:20ff; cf. however the account of David dancing before the Lord in II Sam 6:16, 20ff. For the lack in OT thought of the elements which contributed to the Greek agonistic conception of life, cf. R. Bultmann, Das Urchristentum im Rahmen der antiken Religionen, Zürich 1949, p. 49 (ET: London 1956, p. 47).
[5] Καὶ τὸ ἔνεδρον Ισραηλ ἐπάλαιεν (מֵעִם) ἐκ τοῦ τόπου, i.e. the ambush sallied forth in attack. Codex Vat. simply has ἐπήρχετο.

Greek apocryphal additions to Esther in 1:1e.[1] Nor is it probable that the function of the Greek prize-giver at the games was suggested to the Greek reader[2] by the συνεβράβευσαν αὐτοῖς in I Esdr 9:14. In the context the phrase can mean little more than "they assisted them as leaders/judges".[3]

The verb τρέχειν in the LXX reproduces the רוץ of the MT, in most cases simply as a description of the physical action of *running* or hastening. If this action is ascribed to any particular persons, it is above all the warrior in battle, and the messenger who are meant,[4] certainly not the athlete. The second of these two applications is present in two passages which are of significance for Paul's use of τρέχειν. In the first place Ps 147:4[15]: ὁ ἀποστέλλων τὸ λόγιον αὐτοῦ τῇ γῇ, ἕως τάχους δραμεῖται ὁ λόγος αὐτοῦ, bears strong affinities to II Thess 3:1. The picture of the word as the authorized messenger of the Lord is then further applied to the prophets as his 'runners' — if commissioned by him —in Jer 23:21: οὐκ ἀπέστελλον τοὺς προφήτας καὶ αὐτοὶ ἔτρεχον.[5] This passage is again strongly reminiscent of the picture of Paul as a runner in the service of the Word in I Cor 9:26, Gal 2:2, and Phil 2:16. In considering the imagery of these verses the passages just cited must obviously also be taken into account, despite the lack of reference to the games.

In addition another transferred use of τρέχειν may be noted in LXX Job 41:14: ἔμπροσθεν αὐτοῦ (sc. Leviathan) τρέχει ἀπώλεια (the MT has the verb רוץ in 41:21).[6] But more significant for us are those passages which point to a religious or ethical colouring in the

---

[1] Cf. Rahlfs I, p. 951. Mordecai sees in his vision two dragons rise up ἕτοιμοι ... παλαίειν with each other.

[2] It is now generally accepted that at least the greater part of I Esdras is based on a Hebrew-Aramaic original or prototype; cf. Schürer III, pp. 445f., H. Guthe in KAP I, pp. 1f., R. H. Pfeiffer, History of New Testament Times with an Introduction to the Apocrypha, London 1949, pp. 237ff.

[3] Cf. Liddell-Scott s.v. Possibly the root שׁפט lies behind the Greek word. Cook (CAP I, p. 54) translates "were assessors". In Josephus Ant. 5,232 βραβεύειν is used of the rule of Gideon the Judge βραβεύων αὐτοῖς τὰ δίκαια, and of Samuel in 6,31; cf. also 7,194 and 9,3, used for the giving of legal decisions.

[4] Applied to the warrior Josh 7:21, I Bas 17:48 and 51, II Bas 22:30, Joel 2:7 and 9, Jer 12:5, Amos 2:14; applied to the courier I Bas 4:12, II Bas 18:19-26 (δρόμος = מְרוּצָה the manner of the running of the messenger in 18:27), IV Bas 4:26 and 5:20f., II Chron 30:6 and 10 (οἱ τρέχοντες = רָצִים), Zech 2:4.

[5] Cf. also Jer 14:14, 27:15 and 29:9.

[6] Cf. also Prov 7:23 with its typically Greek phrase περὶ ψυχῆς τρέχειν.

use of τρέχειν. On the one hand the verb is used of those who hasten to do evil, Prov 1:16: οἱ γὰρ πόδες αὐτῶν εἰς κακίαν τρέχουσιν καὶ ταχινοὶ τοῦ ἐκχέαι αἷμα (Is 59:7: ἐπὶ πονηρίαν),[1] Prov 61:5: ἔδραμον ἐν ψεύδει (cf. also συντρέχειν in Ps 49[50]:18). On the other hand he who keeps Jahweh's law sings in Ps 118(119):32: ὁδὸν ἐντολῶν σου ἔδραμον, and in 58(59):5: ἄνευ ἀνομίας ἔδραμον καὶ κατεύθυναν.[2] Traces of this use of the image of running are also found in rabbinical literature, for example Gen. Rabba 1: "He (sc. Moses) ran and relied on the merits of the Fathers", b. Ber. 28b: "I run to the life of the age to come", and Aboth 4:2: "Run (רוּץ) to fulfil the lightest duty even as the weightiest, and flee from transgression".[3]

Similar figurative use is also made of the word δρόμος (and δρομεύς)—for the course or movement of natural objects, I Esdr 4:34 of the sun,[4] Job 38:34 of water, and Sap 17:19 of living creatures. In Job the figure expresses the transience of life, LXX 17:11 Aℵ[2]: αἱ ἡμέραι μου παρῆλθον ἐν δρόμῳ (B βρόμῳ), 7:6 and 9:25: ὁ δὲ βίος μού ἐστιν ἐλαφρότερος δρομέως,[5] while the LXX uses the figure of the runner as a picture for want and poverty in Prov 6:11: ἐμπαραγίνεταί σοι ... ἡ ἔνδεια ὥσπερ ἀγαθὸς δρομεύς ... ἡ δὲ ἔνδεια ὥσπερ κακὸς δρομεὺς ἀπαυτομολήσει.[6]

More significant for our purposes, however, are two verses from Jeremiah which seem to reveal the same religious colouring as that found in several passages with τρέχειν —Jer 23:10: ἐγένετο ὁ δρόμος αὐτῶν πονηρός, and 8:6: διέλιπεν ὁ τρέχων ἀπὸ τοῦ δρόμου αὐτοῦ ὡς ἵππος κάθιδρος ἐν χρεμετισμῷ.[7]

It would be pressing the text, as well as being guilty of a trans-

---

[1] Cf. Rom 3:15 and Prov 6:18: πόδες ἐπισπεύδοντες κακοποιεῖν. (Th. Sm. and Aqu. use the verb τρέχειν here too).

[2] A similar accent also in Is 40:31: οἱ δὲ ὑπομένοντες τὸν θεὸν ... δραμοῦνται καὶ οὐ κοπιάσουσιν, and Prov 4:12: ἐὰν δὲ τρέχῃ, οὐ κοπιάσεις.

[3] Cf. W. D. Davies, Paul and Rabbinic Judaism, London 1955, p. 271, and H. Danby, p. 453. In b. Ber. 28b (shorter version in j. Ber. 4.7d) the simile is taken directly from the games, the statement contrasting the vain running of the athletes.

[4] Cf. Ps 18(19):6: ἀγαλλιάσεται (i.c. the sun) ὡς γίγας δραμεῖν ὁδὸν αὐτοῦ.

[5] Δρομεύς/רוּץ probably here in the sense of courier. In 7:6 λαλιᾶς (accepted by Rahlfs) may represent the original reading.

[6] The verb ἀπαυτομαλεῖν could suggest the picture of the warrior, but the Hebrew כְּאִישׁ מָגֵן probably means insolent man and not armed man. The expansion of the MT in the LXX may well have been caused by this double understanding of מָגֵן, but it is simpler and more in accordance with the context of the LXX version to see here a reference to the courier.

[7] The sense of the Hebrew is: Each persists in running the false course, like a horse rushing into battle.

ference of Greek ideas into Hebrew thought, to view the δρόμος/ מְרוּצָה as a comprehensive metaphor for life as such. Nevertheless the complaint of Jahweh in both cases reveals a figure of speech with almost the same accent as that found in the complaint of Paul in Gal 5:7. Nor is the race in Eccl 9:11 (οὐ τοῖς κούφοις ὁ δρόμος (מֵרוֹץ) καὶ οὐ τοῖς δυνατοῖς ὁ πόλεμος) a complete metaphor for life; together with the reference to warfare—perhaps the δρόμος itself refers to the running of the warrior in battle—it serves to illustrate the thesis that the many facets of life are not determined by strength, skill or wisdom, but by time and chance. Nevertheless the formulation of these two lines is still strongly reminiscent of Paul's words in Rom 9:16.

Of the other terms in the LXX which could serve as athletic termini[1] only στέφανος deserves special attention, expecially in view of the occurrence of the word in Phil 4:1 and I Thess 2:19. Here there is no direct indication what *crown* is meant, whereas in I Cor 9:25 and II Tim 4:8 it is quite clear that the crown belongs to the picture of the Agon. These two passages only find parallels in the hellenistic-influenced writings of the LXX (see Sap 4:2 and IV Macc 17:15 below[2]).

Eidem has shown that the translators of the LXX did not carry through a consequent distinction between στέφανος and διάδημα when translating the Hebrew עֲטָרָה. And he is no doubt right in viewing this phenomenon as an example of the hellenisation of the OT which the LXX often represents.[3] In most instances στέφανος stands for the royal diadem[4], but also represents the corona of the priest (Zech 6:11 and 14; cf. I Macc 10:20), or that worn by the bridegroom (Cant 3:11; cf. II Macc 4:8), as well as the crowns and garlands worn at special festivals (Is 28:1 and 3, Ezek 23:42).

---

[1] Σκοπός is used for lookout or groundmarker, but also as mark or goal in the image from archery in Lam 3:12, and in Sap 5:12 and 21. Στάδιον only appears as a measure of length in Dan LXX Su. 37, 4:9, II Macc 11:5 and 12:9-29.

[2] Apart from these two metaphorical passages, an increasing use of garlands, wreath or crowns by the Jews in hellenistic times is reflected by Sap 2:8, Sir 35(32):2 (at mealtimes), Jud 3:7 and 15:13, I Macc 10:29, 11: 35, 13:37 and 39, II Macc 14:4 (as tribute or tokens of honour), III Macc 7:16; cf. also Schürer III, pp. 91f., 14, 42, 80 note 20, and 132 note 39.

[3] Eidem, p. 125f. LXX Is 28:5 and 62:3 clearly show this lack of distinction.

[4] II Bas 12:20, I Chron 20:2, Is 22:17 and 21, Esth 8:15, Job 19:9, Ps 20[21]:3, Sir 40:4 etc.

However the picture of the diadem is also used figuratively: of Jahweh who will be the "crown of hope" of the holy Remnant (Is 28:5), and of Israel itself who will be a "crown of beauty" in the hand of Jahweh (62:3).

More significant are the numerous passages in which the crown becomes a symbol of blessing and honour. In the Psalms God crowns the year with His goodness (64[65]:11), the righteous with His favour as with a shield (LXX 5:12), man, His creation, with honour and glory (8:5), with loving kindness and mercy (102[103]:4). In Proverbs the instructions and commands of parents are a crown of grace (LXX 1:9), wisdom crowns those who embrace her with a crown of glory (4:9), a virtuous woman is a crown to her husband (12:4), riches the crown of the wise (14:24), and a hoary head and children the crown of the righteous and the aged (16:31 and 17:6). Sirach repeats the last-mentioned image, the "crown of sons", in 50:12. Otherwise it is the fear of the Lord (1:11 and 18, 25:6) and wisdom (6:31, 15:6) which are pictured as a στέφανος.

The Late-Jewish writings further point to a wide use of the image of the crown, especially the crown of righteousness as a reward granted to the righteous.[1]

The *Agon termini* understandably appear seldom in the LXX where the Greek represents a translation from an original Semitic. Is 7:13 reads: μὴ μικρὸν ὑμῖν ἀγῶνα παρέχειν ἀνθρώποις; καὶ πῶς κυρίῳ παρέχετε ἀγῶνα; (the MT has לאה niph. = to weary). The idiomatic use in this passage is nevertheless interesting in so far as it offers a parallel to the κόπους παρέχειν in the NT.[2] The verb ἀγωνί-

---

[1] Epist Arist 280 and Test Levi 8:2 and 9 (R. H. Charles, The Testaments of the Twelve Patriarchs, Oxford 1908, p. 42f.); cf. Test Ben 4:1: στέφανοι δόξης. The rabbinic literature also speaks of the crowns of glory which the righteous will receive in the future world; b.Berak. 17a, 34: "In the future world there is no eating or drinking, no begetting or generating, neither commerce nor change, neither enmity nor envy, nor strife; but the righteous sit there with their crowns upon their heads and bask in the glory of the Shekinah" (cf. Strack-Bill. I, p. 210 and IV, p. 1132f. and 1143). —In Test Abr 16f. death meets Abraham and informs him that his righteous deeds have become a crown for his (i.e. death's) head (cf. Bousset-Gressmann, Die Religion des Judentums, Tübingen ³1926 [HNT] p. 297). —More frequent is the saying of the Rabbis about the three crowns, e.g. Aboth 4:13 "There are three crowns (כתרים), the crown of the Law, the crown of the priesthood, and the crown of kingship; but the crown of a good name excels them all" (Danby, p. 454). Cf. Strack-Bill III, p. 116f. for the other numerous references to this saying.

[2] Gal 6:17, Matt 26:10 = Mk 14:6, Lk 11:7, 18:5 (κόπον παρέχειν).

ζεσθαι[1] is used twice by Theodotion in Dan 6:15 (= MT 6:14): ἠγωνίσατο (sc. Darius) τοῦ ἐξελέσθαι αὐτοῦ (sc. Daniel) καὶ ἕως ἑσπέρας ἦν ἀγωνιζόμενος τοῦ ἐξελέσθαι αὐτόν. The Aramaic text has שָׂם בָּל לְ (set his mind on) and מִשְׁתַּדַּר (strove, exerted himself) respectively. A similar pale use of the verb is found in I Macc 7:21: ἠγωνίσατο Ἄλκιμος περὶ τῆς ἀρχιερωσύνης. In both instances the word implies the total application of strength, utmost endeavour and exertion. This also applies to the lines in Sir 4:28: ἕως θανάτου ἀγώνισαι περὶ τῆς ἀληθείας, καὶ κύριος ὁ θεὸς πολεμήσει ὑπὲρ σοῦ. The fact that the verse is based on a Hebrew original form, as well as the parallelism with πολεμεῖν, precludes the possibility of finding here a reference to the picture of the athletic Agon. But it is difficult to decide whether it is more correct to speak here of a paling or broadening in meaning, or, with Stauffer, of a use "im übertragenen Sinne".[2]

The juxtaposition of ἀγωνίζεσθαι and πολεμεῖν in Sir 4:28 finds its best parallel in *II Maccabees* where athletic terms are regularly used in a broader sense. Thus ἀγών itself[3] is three times used for contests in battle (10:28, 14:18, and 15:9). The verb likewise stands three times for action in battle. Twice Judas Maccabaeus exhorts his men to γενναίως ἀγωνίσασθαι (8:16, and 13:14: μέχρι θανάτου περὶ νόμων, ἱεροῦ, πόλεως, πατρίδος, πολιτείας). In 15:27 Judas and his men are pictured as ταῖς μὲν χερσὶν ἀγωνιζόμενοι, ταῖς δὲ καρδίαις πρὸς τὸν θεὸν εὐχόμενοι. The verb γυμνάζειν appears once in the sense to trouble or harass in military encounters—10:15: Ἰδουμαῖοι ... ἐγύμναζον τοὺς Ἰουδαίους. All these passages reflect a development in the use of the terminology of the games which can be detected already in earlier Greek authors, namely their transference into the sphere of warfare.[4] It is doubtful whether the Greek reader was always reminded of the tense efforts of the athletes in the sports-

---

[1] In addition note the use of ἀγωνιᾶν; for יֵרֵא in Dan 1:10 (Th. has φοβοῦμα instead of ἀγωνιῶ) and in Esth 5:1; for דָּאַג in Sm. Jer. 38 [45] : 19; for חָרֵד in Al. I Bas 4:13.

[2] TWNT I, p. 135.

[3] The regular meaning 'athletic contest' occurs in 4:18, the reference to the πενταετηρικὸς ἀγών in Tyre. In 14:43 the word means as much as mental anguish: Razis, attempting to stab himself, misses his stroke διὰ τὴν τοῦ ἀγῶνος σπουδήν (cf. also 15:18: R ὁ ... κείμενος αὐτοῖς ἀγών, and LXX Esther 4:17k where Esther flees to the king ἐν ἀγῶνι θανάτου). The related ἀγωνία shows a similar meaning, denoting agony of mind before an impending threat or disaster, but never fear in general (II Macc 3:14 and 16, 15:19). The verb ἀγωνιᾶν (II Macc 3:21; cf. LXX Esth 5:1e) has the same colouring.

[4] Cf. the references to Josephus below.

arena, but it is at least certain that the words ἀγών and ἀγωνίζεσθαι carried with them, in their transferred use, an emphasis which belonged to their original use in the world of athletics. In all instances, and this is especially clear from II Macc 13:14, the struggle which is fought bears a decisive character, and in so far can be compared to the final spurt of the runner before the goal, or to the last summoning of strength by the wrestler or pancratiast.[1]

Our efforts to trace a traditional use of the Agon metaphor or picture in hellenistic philosophy are for the first time rewarded in the LXX when we come to the *Wisdom of Solomon*, a book which otherwise shows, like Philo, Aristobulus and IV Maccabees, a knowledge of Greek philosophy.[2] The two passages 4:2 and 10:12 belong to the strongest arguments[3] for the view that the work was originally written in Greek.[4]

Following on the thesis in 4:1a, "childlessness is better with virtue", verse 2 reads:

παροῦσάν τε μιμοῦνται αὐτὴν
καὶ ποθοῦσιν ἀπελθοῦσαν·
καὶ ἐν τῷ αἰῶνι στεφανηφοροῦσα πομπεύει
τὸν τῶν ἀμιάντων ἄθλων ἀγῶνα νικήσασα.

The wisdom literature elsewhere pictures wisdom itself as a crown (Sir 6:31 and 15:6) or as granting man a crown of glory (Prov 4:9).

---

[1] The 'character of the decisive' is also to be seen in the use of ἀγωνίζεσθαι in Sir 4:28, I Macc 7:21 and Theod. Dan 6:15 cited above, and can even be observed in the way in which ἀγωνία/ἀγωνιᾶν are used; cf. note 3 supra.

[2] The passages most frequently referred to are 8:7, the four cardinal virtues of Stoicism, 8:19f., the preexistence of the soul, and 9:15, the body as the burden of the soul; cf. O. Eissfeldt, Einleitung in das AT, Tübingen [3]1964, pp. 815f., A. Bentzen, Introduction to the OT, Copenhagen 1958, II p. 235, Schürer, III pp. 507f., J. Fichtner, Weisheit Salomos (HAT 2. Reihe, 6), Tübingen 1938, pp. 8f.; Fichtner nevertheless rightly emphasises that Greek philosophical terms and phrases are placed in the service of genuinely biblical contexts and ideas.

[3] Cf. J. Reider, The Book of Wisdom (Dropsie College Edition of Jewish Apocryphal Literature), New York 1957, p. 27 notes 129 and 131, with reference to wisdom 4:2. The Agon metaphor is surprisingly missing from Pfeiffer's list of images in Wisdom (op.cit., p. 333).

[4] This view is accepted by most scholars who place the work in Alexandria, probably in the first half of the first century B.C.; see S. Holmes, CAP I, pp. 520f., K. Siegfried, KAP I, p. 479, Fichtner, op.cit., p. 8, Schürer, op.cit., p. 508, and Pfeiffer, op.cit., p. 327.

Here the image is changed in so far as virtue herself bears the crown or victor's laurels. In addition the last line quite clearly shows that the στεφανηφοροῦσα also belongs to the picture of the Agon. It is therefore beside the point to regard the crown or garland here as a general symbol of joy and festivity as elsewhere in the LXX, e.g. Wis 2:8, Sir 1:9, 6:30, 15:6 and Jud 15:13.[1]

The hellenistic origin of the picture of virtue's Agon and victory is not only supported by the similar image in IV Macc 17:15,[2] but also by the phrase τῶν ἀμιάντων ἄθλων.[3] It would seem highly probable that one should see in this phrase the traditional contrast between the sage's contest for virtue and the 'unholy' athletic contests as we have observed it in the diatribe and in Philo, a contrast which is then transferred to the prizes in both contests.[4]

The second relevant passage occurs in the section 10:1—11:1 where the protective role of wisdom in history, from Adam to Israel's wandering in the desert, is related. Among the number of the righteous who have experienced her guidance and protection is Jacob (10:10-12):

---

[1] O. Zöckler, Kurzgefasstes Kommentar zu den heiligen Schriften (AT Abteilung IX), München 1891, p. 367, and A.T.S. Goodrick, The Book of Wisdom, London 1913, p. 137. More to the point in view of the context of 4:1 and 9 is Fichtner's reference to Proverbs 16:31, "The hoary head is a crown of glory" (op. cit., p. 20).

[2] Already C.L.W. Grimm, Kurzgefasstes exegetisches Kommentar zu den Apokryphen des Alten Testaments VI Lieferung, Leipzig 1860, p. 201, cites examples in Plato and Epictetus. Note esp. Philo Migr Abr 6.

[3] The nominative must here be ἄθλον = prize, not ἄθλος = contest, since the latter next to ἀγών hardly gives a sensible meaning. Grimm, op.cit., p. 99, refers the ἄθλοι to the "einzelnen Kämpfen, Leiden und Verfolgungen als Momenten und Entwicklungen eines einzigen grossen Lebenskampfes". Goodrick, op.cit., p. 137, interprets the noun as "the struggles of the virtuous life unstained by selfishness or sin", maintaining that this understanding is more in accordance with the philosophical idea of life as a warfare. But this is surely pressing a Stoic content into the metaphor which is absent in the text.

[4] Fichtner, op.cit., pp. 20f.: "ἀμίαντος, weil rein von allem, was die irdischen 'Siegespreise' der Gottlosen befleckt". Grimm and Goodrick, though rejecting this understanding, paraphrase correctly as follows: —"Siegespreise, an welchen kein Makel und keine Ungerechtigkeit des Kämpfenden haftet, wie häufig an den Belohnungen irdischer Sieger" or, "perfect rewards, unstained by unfairness of winning or savage passions on the part of the competitors".
—The γέρας ψυχῶν ἀμώμων in Sap 2:22 hardly contains a reference to the athletic image, but it is just possible that the Stoic use of πόνοι can be seen in 3:15.

διεφύλαξεν αὐτὸν ἀπὸ ἐχθρῶν
καὶ ἀπὸ ἐνεδρευόντων ἠσφαλίσατο·
καὶ ἀγῶνα ἰσχυρὸν ἐβράβευσεν αὐτῷ,
ἵνα γνῷ ὅτι παντὸς δυνατωτέρα ἐστὶν εὐσέβεια.

The references in the first two lines are most probably to Laban
(Gen 31:24) and Esau (Gen 27:41), although the ἐνεδρεύοντες could
also refer to the Canaanites in their anger at the slaughter of the
Shechemites (Gen 34:30).[1] Quite clear, however, is the picture in the
last two lines. The Agon meant is the πάλη of Jacob with the angel
at Pniel (Gen 32:24ff.), a contest in which, according to the author
of these lines, Wisdom played the part of βραβευτής.[2] That the
author of Wisdom had the Greek septuagintal text in mind is
suggested by the words ἐνισχύσας μετὰ θεοῦ καὶ μετὰ ἀνθρώπων
δυνατός in LXX Gen 32:29b, which find their echo here in ἰσχυρός
and δυνατωτέρα.[3] Furthermore the view that Jacob was victorious
in his wrestle with the angel at Pniel is to be explained on the basis
of LXX Gen 32:29b and Hosea 12:5 (καὶ ἐνίσχυσεν μετὰ ἀγγέλου καὶ
ἠδυνάσθη).

For our purposes it is vital to note two points. In the first place
it will be remembered that Jacob also appears in the writings of
Philo of Alexandria as the athlete of God par excellence. Having
found this same motif in Wisdom one can with some justification
assume that the picture of Jacob in this role, on the basis of the
Genesis account, was familiar in Hellenistic Jewish circles, at least
in Egypt. The picture thus gained is further established when it is
borne in mind that the Agon as it appears in Philo is essentially an

---

[1] Reider, op.cit., p. 137, Goodrick, op.cit., p. 233. Goodrick sees the possibility of a third reference, namely to the Jewish legend in Jubilees 37f. where
there is a long account of the strife between the sons of Essau and Jacob.
Essau is killed and his sons made to pay tribute (cf. also Test XII Patr. Jud
4 and 9). Goodrick removes the difficulty that there is no mention of 'liers in
wait' by referring this to another legend.

[2] The general meaning of ἐβράβευσεν is clear despite the difficulty in translating. Holmes has "guided him to victory" = Zöckler's "führte ihn .....
hindurch", Siegfried translates "leitete für ihn [siegreich]", while Fichtner,
Reider and Goodrick have "decided for him". Is it necessary to find here,
with Goodrick, a further instance of Pseudo Solomon's ignorance of Greek!
The references adduced by Grimm are quite to the point, especially to
Josephus Ant 14, 183: πολέμου ῥοπὰς βραβεύει τὸ θεῖον; cf. also Bell 1,215.

[3] Fichtner, op.cit., p. 39. —"Pseudosalomo zieht aus der Erzählung die
Lehre, dass die Frömmigkeit nicht nur nichts von Menschen zu befürchten
habe, sondern Gott selbst überwinde" (Grimm, op.cit., p. 201).

Agon of piety or godliness.[1] Consequently it is hardly accidental that the word εὐσέβεια which appears only here in Wisdom, occurs within the context of the Agon metaphor. This phenomenon is further illuminated by an analysis of IV Maccabees where the Agones of the Jewish martyrs are fought on behalf of εὐσέβεια.

3. Fourth Maccabees and the Jewish Pseudepigrapha

The Fourth Book of Maccabees, like Philo, clearly shows a good knowledge of Stoic philosophy. But, as in the case of Philo, one should rather speak of a correction of the principles of Stoicism in the adoption of its thought and language, than simply of a fusion of Jewish piety with Stoic moral philosophy.[2] The Stoic elements of IV Macc have often been examined[3] so that it will suffice to concentrate on the main theme of the book and its demonstration by means of the Agones of the Jewish martyrs under Antiochus Epiphanes.

The recurring theme runs: "Pious reason rules supreme over the passions".[4] However not only the characteristic definition of reason as εὐσεβής, but also the use of λογισμός and πάθη in IV Macc already distinguishes this theme from the central tenet of the moral theory of the Stoa. Reason is here not the rational principle in man as an emanation of the world-soul, but rather the activity of thinking and

---

[1] The proximity of Wisdom 10:12 to the Genesis account and the general context forbid us to see here a reference to the more developed concept of the moral Agon as found in Philo. The πόνοι in verses 10f. simply refer to Jacob's years of service with Laban (the word occurs relatively frequently in Sirach and Wisdom in the general sense of toil) and not to the πόνοι of the Stoic sage.

[2] According to C. C. Torrey (The Apocryphal Literature, Yale 1945, p. 104), "the book is a fine example of the way in which a treatise in Hebrew theology could wear with ease and grace a dress made in the Greek schools. ... Its author consciously assumes the attitude of a champion of the study of philosophy". However Wolfson, Philo II, pp. 271f., and M. Hadas, The Third and Fourth Books of the Maccabees, New York 1953, pp. 171f., rightly see in IV Macc a refutation, or at least a correction, of Stoicism rather than a synthesis. A. Deissmann KAP II, p. 151, speaks of a Stoic influenced Judaism rather than of a Jewish-modified Stoicism, but Grimm goes too far with his "eine Verschmelzung stoischer Moral mit mosaischer Gesetzesstrenge" (Kurzgefasstes exeg. Handbuch zu den Apokryphen des AT, IV Lieferung, Leipzig 1847, p. 288).

[3] See esp. Torrey, op.cit., p. 104, J. Freudenthal, Die Flavius Josephus beigelegte Schrift über die Herrschaft der Vernunft. Breslau 1869, pp. 37ff., Grimm, op.cit., pp. 288f., Pfeiffer, op.cit., pp. 219f., and Schürer III, p. 525.

[4] Cf. 1:1, 7,9,13f., 19 etc.

reasoning, that is, "Denktätigkeit".[1] In addition the definition of
Reason which is given in 1:15 also points to the element of will in
the function of the λογισμός, so that the word can also be rendered
with "Vernunftwillen".[2]

The scope of the πάθη is also not simply that of Stoicism; the
passions and desires are divinely implanted in man (2:21 and 1:20)
and are consequently not to be eradicated but held in check by
reason as their ἀνταγωνιστής (3:5; cf. 1:6 and 3:2). Here for the
first time the metaphor of the Agon is taken up, but the Stoic tenet
which it serves to illustrate is modified at its central point. IV Macc,
with Philo, sees the aim of the Agon in the *control* of the senses and
passions. Consequently the two main catchwords of the diatribe's
moral philosophy, ἀπάθεια and ἀναισθησία, are completely lacking in
this writing—although the martyrs endure torture with true Stoic
apathy (9:17f., 11:25, 15:11ff.).[3]

In the phrase εὐσεβὴς λογισμός it is clearly the adjective which the
author wishes to emphasise. Not the natural reason of the Stoics
but only devout, God-fearing reason can control the senses and
exercise true virtue, that is, reason which is directed by the norm
of the divine Law. The realization of the ideal of ἀρετή and καλοκά-
γαθία is only possible through the Mosaic Law (7:17-23). Even the
four cardinal virtues of the Stoa (1:2-4 and 18, 5:22f.) have their
source in Wisdom which is found in the Mosaic Law (1:15-18, 7:21-
23, 8:7). All of the Law is "rational", even the ritual law scorned
by the Hellenists (5:24ff.).[4]

The apologetical character of the thesis of IV Macc and its eluci-

---

[1] Grimm, op.cit., p. 288, Freudenthal, op.cit., pp. 50f., and A. Schlatter,
Der Märtyrer in den Anfängen der Kirche, Gütersloh 1915, p. 44, who translates "Denkakt".

[2] 1:15: The λογισμός is the νοῦς μετὰ ὀρθοῦ λόγου (Stoic phrase!) προτιμῶν
τὸν τῆς σοφίας βίον ("Geist, der mit rechter Überlegung das Leben der Weisheit sich wählt", Freudenthal, ibid.). The predication of Reason with θεῖος
in 13:16 also sounds Stoic, but can hardly recall the picture of the human
soul as an emanation of the divine world-soul. It probably refers to the Old
Testament concept of man as created in the image of God (Grimm, op.cit.,
ad loc.).

[3] Two other central terms of the Stoa occur only once in IV Macc, ἐγκράτεια
in 5:34, and ἀταραξία in 8:26. Here they have however lost their programmatic significance, since the Agon of the martyr is finally an Agon of godliness.

[4] IV Macc, like Philo, Aristeas and the Sibyllines, seeks to identify the
Law of Moses with the law of nature and reason; cf. G. Bornkamm, "Die
Offenbarung des Zornes Gottes", in: Das Ende des Gesetzes, München 1961,
p. 16, and Pfeiffer, op.cit., p. 219.

dation is seen throughout the so-called philosophical first section of the work. In the last verse of this section (3:18) the tone is set for the following illustration from the evidence of history, especially from the example of the Jewish martyrs. Once again the central concept of the Agon is hinted at—δυνατός γὰρ ὁ σώφρων νοῦς ... καὶ τὰς τῶν σωμάτων ἀλγηδόνας καθ' ὑπερβολὴν οὔσας καταπαλαῖσαι. Since the book also ends in 18:23 with a hint at the Agon metaphor, we can see how the concept of the Agon actually dominates the entire account of the martyrdoms.

In the Cynic-Stoic diatribe and Philo,[1] the Agon is illustrated from the example of certain patron figures, above all Hercules and Jacob. The author of IV Macc follows this tradition by pointing to the relatively recent historical contests of the Jewish martyrs and their πόνοι. Thus the first of them, Eleazar, appearing in the role of a Stoic sage, refuses to eat swine's meat and ὑπέμενε τοὺς πόνους ... καὶ καθάπερ γενναῖος ἀθλητὴς τυπτόμενος ἐνίκα τοὺς βασανίζοντας (6:9f.).

The seven brothers also refuse to adopt the hellenistic way of life and betray the Mosaic Law. They also endure the agonies τῷ τῆς εὐσεβείας λογισμῷ φιλοσοφοῦντες (8:1). Immediately preceding the description of the brutal tortures the Agon motif again appears. After refusing to yield to the tyrant's demands, and defying his threats, the youths cry out: "We through our evil treatment and endurance shall win the prize of virtue (τὰ τῆς ἀρετῆς ἆθλα) and shall be with God, for whom we also suffer" (9:8). As the first son dies in the flames he calls to his brothers: μιμήσασθέ με, ἀδελφοί, ... μὴ μοῦ τὸν ἀγῶνα[2] λειποτακτήσητε ... ἱερὰν καὶ εὐγενῆ στρατείαν στρατεύσασθε περὶ τῆς εὐσεβείας (9:23f.). Here we probably have the same mixture of the athletic and military image as in the diatribe and in Philo, although it is also just possible that the word ἀγών in its present context could have the pale and general meaning of struggle.[3]

---

[1] Probably also in Sap 10:12.

[2] Reading ἀγῶνα with Rahlfs instead of αἰῶνα. The second reading, accepted by Grimm, Hatch and Redpath, and Townshend (in CAP II) who translates "for ever", is colourless and destroys the parallelism with στρατείαν. Deissmann's rendering "Kämpferschar" is also hardly correct, and the best translation is probably "do not desert me in my contest".

[3] It is probably correct to see a hint at the familiar military metaphor already in 3:5, reason as man's σύμμαχος, and in 7:4: Eleazar ἐνίκησεν τοὺς πολιορκοῦντας, his tormentors.

The force of the image in 11 :20ff. is quite clear. In his agonies the sixth youth cries out: Ὦ ἱεροπρεποῦς ἀγῶνος ... ἐφ'ὃν διὰ τὴν εὐσέβειαν εἰς γυμνασίαν πόνων¹ ἀδελφοὶ τοσοῦτοι κληθέντες οὐκ ἐνικήθημεν .. καλοκἀγαθίᾳ καθωπλισμένος² τεθνήξομαι ... The adjective ἱεροπρεπής (cf. ἱερὰ στρατεία in 9:24) is no doubt a reflection of the familiar contrast between the vain contests of the athletes in the games and the heroic struggle for virtue on the part of the sage. However in IV Macc, as in Philo, this is a fitting and genuine epithet, since the martyrs die in the cause of God's holy Law. In the words of the seventh son, the tyrant is guilty of slaying the servants of God καὶ τοὺς τῆς εὐσεβείας ἀσκητάς (12:11),³ of murdering τοὺς τῆς ἀρετῆς ἀγωνιστάς (12:14).

In the reflections on the heroism and endurance of these "champions of Virtue" (13 :1-14 :10) there occur two passages in which the presence of the athletic metaphor is open to doubt. The youths are reported as having encouraged each other with the words: "Let us not fear him who thinks he kills" (cp. Mat 10:28). "For great struggle and peril of soul (μέγας γὰρ ψυχῆς ἀγὼν καὶ κίνδυνος) awaits in eternal torment those who transgress the ordinance of God" (13 :14f.). The Agon as a struggle in suffering, is a meaning which would be consistent with that found elsewhere in IV Macc; but it is questionable whether the author had the athletic image in mind. The word may be used in an almost colourless sense as in the important phrase of Plato in Phaedrus 247B: ἔνθα δὴ πόνος τε καὶ ἀγὼν ... ψυχῇ πρόκειται,⁴ only with the added emphasis on suffering. Whichever the case may be, it is certain that the future Agon of the transgressor is contrasted, as in 9:1-9, with the present Agones of

---

¹ "Schmerzensreiche Übung" (Deissmann), not "competition in torments" (Townshend). The element of competition is as little present here as it is in 17:12. It is also going too far to take the phrase itself as a designation for martyrdom (E. Stauffer, TWNT I, p. 775).

² Again the mixed metaphor; cf. 13:16: "armed with divine reason's mastery of the passions".

³ Cf. 13:22: ἐν νόμῳ θεοῦ ἄσκησις. In view of the dominance of the Agon motif which runs through IV Macc it would seem correct to see in ἀσκητάς a reference to the athletes (as in 12:14). Townshend's "the followers of righteousness" destroys the metaphor. Cf. also ἐξασκεῖν in 5:23, 13:24.

⁴ Cf. p. 26 supra, and Euripides, Or. 847: ψυχῆς ἀγῶνα τὸν προκείμενον πέρι, similarly Dion. Halic. VII 48 (τὸν ὑπὲρ τῆς ψυχῆς ἀγῶνα τρέχει), and Plutarch Romulus 21c. See also ἀγών in the sense of "Gewissenskampf" in Papyri Fiorentini 36,26 (4.cent.): ὁ περὶ ψυχῆς ἀγών, and Oxyrhynch. Pap. 1409,22 (3.cent.): τῆς ψυχῆς τὸν ἀγῶνα ἕξει (F. Preisigke, Wörterbuch der griech. Papyrusurkunden, Berlin 1925, s.v.).

the champions of godliness. For the first there awaits eternal punishment in flames (9:9), for the second the rewards of virtue (9:8). In the second passage we read that all seven youths did not bulk at the prospect of death but πάντες ὥσπερ ἐπ' ἀθανασίας ὁδὸν τρέχοντες ἐπὶ τὸν διὰ τῶν βασάνων θάνατον ἔσπευδεν (14:5). Although Hadas understands the passage as an athletic metaphor, the use of the noun ὁδός instead of δρόμος[1] and the apparent parallelism between τρέχειν and σπεύδειν rather speak for the assumption of a relatively colourless image in this instance. The character of the Agon in IV Macc as an Agon of endurance in suffering suggests the image of the wrestler, boxer or pancratiast who suffers blows standing directly over against his opponent, rather than that of the runner who strains forward toward the goal.

The acclamatory form of lauding the Agon of the martyrs, noted already in 11:20f., is again used for the mother in 15:29 and 16:14 and for her sons in 16:16. In the first of these three verses —ὦ μῆτηρ ἔθνους, ... καὶ τοῦ διὰ σπλάγχνων ἀγῶνος ἀθλοφόρε[2] —the Agon refers to the ἔνδοθεν πόνοι as distinguished from the ἔξωθεν πόνοι (cf. 18:2). In the second, we again meet with the military image —ὦ μῆτερ δι' εὐσέβειαν θεοῦ στρατιῶτι πρεσβῦτι καὶ γύναι, διὰ καρτερίαν καὶ τύραννον ἐνίκησας. If the traditional character of the metaphor and its frequency in this writing is recognised there is no need to consider this "a bold apostrophe for a woman".[3]

The third and most important passage (16:16) is placed on the lips of the mother who exhorts her sons Ὦ παῖδες, γενναῖος[4] ὁ ἀγών, ἐφ' ὃν κληθέντες ὑπὲρ τῆς διαμαρτυρίας τοῦ ἔθνους ἐναγωνίσασθε προθύμως ὑπὲρ τοῦ πατρῴου νόμου. Since the reading μαρτυρίας (A) in 12:16 is probably to be rejected in favour of ἀριστείας (א), the present phrase with διαμαρτυρία represents the first approach in meaning to that of the word μαρτυρία,[5] as signifying the bearing of witness in blood.[6]

All the passages mentioned up to this point contain little more than hints or allusions to the athletic image. The situation is different in 17:11-16 which follows on vv. 8-10 where the martyrs are

---

[1] As in Ps 118 [119]:32, 18 [19]:6, Jos 23:14; cf. however Philo Agric 177: ὥσπερ τοὺς δρομεῖς ... ὁδοῦ τῆς πρὸς εὐσέβειαν, and II Clem 7:3.

[2] Cf. also 18:23: τῇ ἀθλοφόρῳ μητρί.   [3] Hadas, ad. loc.

[4] Often used in IV Macc for the heroism of the martyrs; cf. 6:10: καθάπερ γενναῖος ἀθλητής.

[5] Cf. Mart Pol 1:1, 13:2, 17:1.

[6] See the final chapter on the post-Pauline picture of the Agon.

celebrated with a fitting epitaph. This passage has rightly been characterised as "almost a Pindaric ode in effect"[1]

> "For truly it was a holy Agon in which they contended. For on that day virtue, proving them through endurance, set before them (ἠϑλοϑέτει) the prize of victory, incorruption in everlasting life. The first to contest (προηγωνίζετο) was Eleazar, the mother of the seven sons also joined in the contest (ἐνήϑλει), and the sons contended (ἠγωνίζοντο). The tyrant was their opponent (ἀντηγωνίζετο), and the world and the life of man were the spectators. Godliness won the victory, crowning her athletes (ἀϑλητὰς στεφανοῦσα). Who but wondered at the athletes of the divine law? Who were not amazed at them?"[2]

The traditional character of the Agon image can also be easily illustrated in this last large complex. The favourite antithesis between the 'holy' and 'profane' contests again comes to light in the qualification of the Agon as holy (v. 11),[3] and verses 14 and 16 suggest the popular Stoic picture of the sage in his struggle with fate and his passions as a spectacle (ϑέατρον) for gods and men.[4] The personification of ἀρετή as the ἀϑλοϑέτης of the Agon also fits into the traditional picture of the sage's contest for virtue.[5]

---

[1] Hadas, op.cit., ad loc.

[2] E. Stauffer (TWNT I, p. 136 with note 8; cf. also his NT Theology, Appendix I note 11) has pointed out that the martyrs of III Macc awaited their end with the beasts in the hippodrome before the city of Alexandria, a site which seemed especially fitting πρὸς παραδειγματισμόν (III Macc 4:11; cf. 5:46 and 6:16). Thus he concludes that a comparison between the contests of the athletes and the martyrs' contests in suffering was already suggested by the fact that the tortures took place on the very same scene as the athletic games. Consequently we are to see a mingling of image and reality. This argument is hardly applicable to the Agones of IV Macc. In the first place their is no hint in the work itself that the martyrdoms took place in a stadium or hippodrome, nor were they suffered at the hands of wild beasts. On the contrary, according to 5:1 Antiochus held judgment "on a high place" —not necessarily the gymnasium in 4:20 —surrounded by his soldiers, who then used fiendish implements of torture like wild beasts (9:26ff.). In the second place Stauffer overlooks the fact that the author of IV Macc is here using a standard metaphor.

[3] Cf. already 9:23f. and 11:20ff. supra.

[4] Cf. also 15:20 and Epict. Diss. II 19,25, III 22,59, Seneca De Prov. 2,9 and Ep. 64,4-6, and the discussion on I Cor 4:9 in the final chapter.

[5] Θεοσέβεια is not personified as a "Kriegsherrin" in v.15 as Grimm (ad loc.) would have it, maintaining that "das Bild des gymnischen Kampfes streift sonach über in das des kriegerischen". The verb νικᾶν here simply means 'won the victory', and is in fact already used in 11:20 in close con-

The above analysis heavily supports the view presented by Wendland and Norden, and now generally accepted by scholars, that the writing reveals the formal and stylistic characteristics of the diatribe, as an edifying or monitory essay or discourse.[1] Whether IV Macc represents a real synagogal sermon[2], a public address[3], or a treatise,[4] is here immaterial for our purposes. More important is the observation that the work gives us an insight not only into the struggle of orthodox Mosaism "um die Bewahrung des Gesetzes gegenüber hellenistischer Aufklärung",[5] but also into the discussion between Jewish piety and hellenistic popular moral-philosophy, a discussion which was carried on with the latter's own terminology and with its own formal instrument, the diatribal form of address.[6]

The terms ὑπομονή and πόνος belong already to the stock vocabulary of the picture of the Agon in the diatribe where the moral athlete is required to remain unmovable in enduring the toils of pain or the blows of fortune. In IV Macc these words acquire a new tone

nection with the Agon image. A. Dupont-Sommer, Le quatrième livre des Machabées, Paris 1939, p. 151, refers at this point to a Jewish tombstone showing victory crowning a nude youth, and suggests that the young man may represent an athlete of the Law (cf. Frey, Corpus Inscriptionum Iudaicarum I, Rome 1936, 1.121).

[1] P. Wendland, Philo und die Kynisch-Stoische Diatribe, pp. 2ff., E. Norden, Die antike Kunstprosa, Leipzig 1923, pp. 416ff. More recently C. C. Torrey, op.cit., pp. 103f., M. Hadas, op.cit., p. 98 and 101, and most recently U. Luck in RGG IV, cols. 622f. P. Riessler, Altjüdisches Schrifttum ausserhalb der Bibel, Augsburg 1928, p. 1313, also recognizes the diatribe form in IV Macc, but is hardly correct in suggesting that the author may have belonged to Essenic circles on the basis of the rejection of hypocrisy in 6:17ff., and the emphasis on 'Nächstenliebe' and 'Feindesliebe' in 2:8ff. The first-mentioned passage rather supports the conclusion that the author stands closest to Pharisaism with his praise of minute faithfulness to the ceremonial law.

[2] Maintained by Freudenthal, op.cit., p. 4-36, and Schlatter, op.cit., p. 43 (delivered on the festival of Chanuka). A. Dupont-Sommer, Le quatrième livre des Machabées, Paris 1939, regards the work as a synagogue-sermon held in 117/18 A.D. on the site of the martyrs' tombs in Antioch to commemorate the day of their death; so also M. Hadas, op.cit., p. 103-115.

[3] Schürer III, p. 524 and Townshend, op.cit., p. 653.

[4] Grimm, op.cit., p. 286, regards the writing as a treatise meant to be read (so also Torrey, p. 104), the oratorical form being only external; cf. also Deissmann, op.cit., p. 151.

[5] Luck, op.cit., col. 623.

[6] Townshend (p. 654) wrongly sees in IV Macc only a positive evaluation of hellenistic philosophy—"How better could the Jewish Hellenistic Philosopher steel the hearts of his brethren than by holding up to them the self negating virtues of Stoicism ...".

parallel to the new emphasis on the Agon as a struggle of suffering
in martyrdom. Victory in the Agon means endurance (ὑπομονή) of
pain until death.[1]

Here we have the *beginnings of the standard vocabulary of the
Christian martyrdom*.[2] Already in IV Macc there is a decided tendency for the word Agon to become a designation for suffering itself.

The contest of the martyrs is also a contest against the tyrant
who seeks to force them to deny the Law of their fathers by means
of suffering. This point is also expressed in the terms of the Agon
image in 17:14 where the tyrant appears as the "antagonist".
Consequently victory over the pangs of suffering also includes the
victory over the godless ruler.[3]

The occasional hellenistic tone[4] with which the goal of the Agon
of martyrdom is expressed should not mislead us. In the language
of popular moral philosophy the author can picture the martyrs as
suffering and fighting in the cause of ἀρετή or καλοκἀγαθία.[5] But
this "virtue" is little more than ὑπομονή or εὐσέβεια itself. It is the
last word which really characterises the Agon in IV Macc.[6] In the
second place, since piety or godliness is based on the Law (5:18ff.),
the Agon is also a struggle on behalf of the divine Law.[7] And thirdly,
since God is the giver and upholder of this Law, the writer can even
say that the faithful suffer *on behalf of God himself*.[8] It is He Who
has called or summoned them to the Agon[9]—they are not free to
take up or drop the struggle at their own whim like the Stoic sage—
and it is God Who grants them the reward of immortality (18:23).
Within this context πίστις πρὸς θεόν (15:24, 16:22; cf. 17:2) means

---

[1] Cf. the frequent phrase πόνον (πόνους) ὑπομένειν, 5:23, 6:9, 7:22, 16:19;
πόνος becomes a synonym for βάσανος, eg. 16:1, 17:7 and 10.

[2] The theme of martyrdom is older than IV Macc (cf. Stauffer, NT Theol.,
Appendix I, and Strathmann in TWNT IV, p. 489), but here we have the
first coupling of this tradition with the athletic metaphor.

[3] Cf. 1:11, 8:2, 16:14; also the victory over the tormentors in 6:10, and
7:4.

[4] An echo of the Stoic paradox, the sage is not only free but also a king,
also occurs in 14:2, 2:23, 7:23.

[5] Ἀρετή in 1:8, 7:22, 9:18, 10:10 etc.; καλοκἀγαθία in 1:10.

[6] Eusebius (H.E. X 6) rightly characterises the contents of 'Pseudo-
Josephus' as Agones ὑπὲρ τῆς εἰς τὸ θεῖον εὐσέβειας—the noun occurs over
fourty times, the verb εὐσεβεῖν five times, also θεοσέβεια in 7:6 and 22, 17:15.
In 12:16 martyrdom is the fulfilment or perfection of piety.

[7] Cf. 6:27, 13:9, and 17:16.

[8] Cf. 9:8, 16:19, and 10:20.

[9] Cf. the phrase ἀγὼν ἐφ' ὃν κληθέντες in 11:20, and 16:16.

steadfast faithfulness (the German 'Treue') to God in suffering, not belief in God.

We again discover the Agon image in the *Testament of Job*. If we can rely on the latest studies on this work, the Testament represents a pre-Christian Midrash on the canonical book of Job, originally composed in Aramaic at the beginning of the first century B.C., and translated into Greek soon thereafter.[1]

The application of the image is new in as far as the contest which it characterises is limited to a personal Agon between two combatants, Job and Satan. In Chapter 4 God warns Job of the suffering which Satan will inflict on him: ἔσῃ γὰρ ὡς ἀθλητὴς πυκτεύων καὶ καρτερῶν πόνους καὶ ἐκδεχόμενος τὸν στέφανον. The second and fuller simile appears in ch. 27. Job, tempted by his wife to curse God, sees Satan lurking behind her. When challenged to come out and fight openly, he yields the victory to Job: ἐγένου γὰρ ὃν τρόπον ἀθλητὴς (παλαίων —conj. James) μετὰ ἀθλητοῦ, καὶ εἰς τὸν ἕνα κατέρραξεν. There follows a description of two athletes, probably pancratiasts, contesting the last stage of the struggle on the sand of the ring, and finally the application: οὕτω καὶ σύ, Ἰώβ, ὑποκάτω ἧς καὶ ἐν πληγῇ· ἀλλ' ἐνίκησας τὰ πλευτρικά μου (παλαιστρικά?) ἃ ἐπήγαγόν σοι.

The moralism of the Stoic picture is here completely absent. Instead, the religious lesson of endurance under trial of faithfulness to God, taken over from the canonical Job,[2] gives the Agon an emphasis which is parallel to that of the struggles of the faithful in IV Macc. Job, it is true, does not have to endure the trial to the point of death. Nevertheless the keynote is still μακροθυμία (ch. 27) and ὑπομένειν μέχρι θανάτου (ch. 5).

There is little in the use of the simile here to suggest its philosophic origins.[3] However the traditional character of the simile

---

[1] K. Kohler, in: Jewish Encyclopedia VII, cols. 200-202, Riessler, op.cit., p. 1333, Pfeiffer, op.cit., pp. 70f., and Torrey, op.cit., pp. 141f. M. R. James, in: Apocrypha Anecdota II, Cambridge 1897 (= Texts and Studies V 1), pp. xciiiff. considers the book a Midrash, but from the hand of a Christian Jew as late as the 2. or 3. cent. A.D. Schürer III, pp. 406f. views the whole work as a Christian product, but the relationship of Test Job to LXX Job makes this unlikely.

[2] Ὑπομονή (11 times in IV Macc) occurs only LXX Job 14:19, but the verb appears 14 times (15 times in IV Macc).

[3] One could at the most see in Job a parallel to the 'athlete' in the diatribe striving to overcome the setbacks of fortune (cf. the other title of the Test., James p. lxxxi, which calls Job ἄμεμπτος καὶ πολύαθλος). But the πόνοι (cf. 5, 24, and 26) are here not moral endeavours but sufferings inflicted by

should be obvious. The question still remains whether the image was original to the Semitic form of the Testament or added to it in the process of paraphrasing[1] the original into Greek. James notes the two passages here in question, plus the picture of the storm-tossed merchant in ch. 18, as similes reflecting the influence of Greek literature.[2] But there is no need to question the possibility of their adoption into Semitic thought and language. The use of πόνοι is here non-philosophical, and occurs in LXX Job seven times. The other possibility would be to view the similes as insertions from a later Christian hand.[3] But the passages fit into the narrative so perfectly that we are entitled to regard them as Jewish and most likely pre-Christian.

In the *Testaments of the Twelve Patriarchs*[4] the command to resist the devil, and the assurance of his flight in defeat, occurs repeatedly —Test Is 7:7, Dan 5:1, Naph 8:4 (taken up in James 4:7). More important, however, is Test Asher 6:2 where we find an allusion to a contest between the "spirits of deception" and men. The text is corrupt.[5] The best attested reading speaks of the "twofaced", i.e. the hypocrites, μιμούμενοι τὰ πνεύματα τῆς πλάνης καὶ κατὰ τῶν ἀνθρώπων συναγωνιζόμενοι, while the variant is an injunction to hate the spirits of deception κατὰ τῶν ἀνθρώπων ἀγωνιζόμενα. Yet in both cases the underlying though of a struggle between Satan and men, parallel to the picture in the Testament of Job, is the same. This is a theme which is reflected not only in the NT (cf. the πάλη against

---

Satan. Even the military simile in ch. 37 is hardly related to the image in the diatribe. The point is Job's faithfulness to God, not his fight against misfortune.

[1] James, op.cit., p. xciv.

[2] Ibid, p. xcvi.

[3] That such echoes of the NT do exist in the work cannot be denied — Bousset/Gressmann, op. cit., p. 45, call it a Jewish legend "in leichter christlicher Bearbeitung". The phrase στέφανον ἀμαράντινον κομίσεις in ch.4 (I Pet 5:4; cf. Jam 1:12, Rev 2:10) is such an addition, not so the picture of the children of Job crowned in glory in ch.40 (also 44).

[4] That the Testaments were written in either Hebrew or Aramaic cannot be seriously doubted since the work of R. H. Charles, The Greek Versions of the Testaments of the Twelve Patriarchs, London 1908, esp. pp. xxiiiff.; cf. the same author in CAP II, pp. 282ff., Schürer III, pp. 339ff., Torrey, op.cit., p. 131, and Pfeiffer, op.cit., pp. 64f. The discovery of the Qumran scrolls has supported rather than destroyed the argument for the pre-Christian origin of the Testaments (see the summary of latest research in Eissfeldt's Einleitung in das AT, pp. 858ff).

[5] Charles, op.cit., p. 179.

the Devil and his powers in Eph 6:10ff.), but one which became particularly frequent in the post-NT literature.[1]

On the other hand it must be admitted that the verse contains neither simile nor metaphor. The verb συναγωνίζεσθαι no doubt represents a Semitic original simply denoting struggle or striving.[2] The same applies to Test Jos 2:2, where Joseph, recounting his struggle against the advance of Potiphar's wife, says: ἠγωνισάμην πρὸς γυναῖκα ἀναιδῆ ἐπείγουσάν με παρανομεῖν μετ' αὐτῆς. The thought of an Agon was hardly present in the original text, as it probably was in Test Job 4 and 27. But when it is remembered that Philo uses the athletic image for the struggle of Joseph against this woman,[3] it appears possible that the idea of a contest was at least suggested here to the reader of the Greek text. It is worth noting that the lesson of this Testament is not only found in the word σωφροσύνη but also in ὑπομονή, in proving oneself δόκιμος under the trial of temptation (2:7, 10:1f.).

However indecisive these passages in the Testaments may be, we are on surer ground in the seventh chapter of *IV Ezra*. In describing the life of the soul after death the author writes: "Of those who have kept the ways of the Most High this is the order when they shall be separated from this vessel of mortality (quando separari incipient a vaso corruptibili)... The first order is that they have striven much and painfully to overcome the innate evil thought (cum labore multo *certati sunt* ut vincerent cum eis plasmatum *cogitamentum malum*) that it might not lead them astray from life unto death" (7:88 and 92).[4] The Greek philosophical background shines through clearly — the typical body-soul dualism again appears, and behind the words 'labor' and 'certor' one can suspect πόνος and ἀγωνίζεσθαι. Yet the

---

[1] Cf. the final chapter.

[2] The καταγωνίζεσθαι in Reuben's wry warning against the wiles of women in Test Reub 5:2 is equally pale: "Women are evil, children. If they have no power or might over a man, then they seek to allure him through enticement. καὶ ὃν διὰ τοῦ σχήματος οὐκ ἰσχύουσιν καταγοητεύσασθαι (v.l. καταγωνίσασθαι = ליכלת, Charles), τοῦτον δι' ἀπάτης καταγωνίζονται. One is reminded of the word of Antiphon the Sophist (Diels II 357,15): μεγὰς γὰρ ἀγὼν γάμος ἀνθρώπωι. (!)

[3] Cf. supra p. 41.

[4] Translation according to Box, in CAP II, text according to R. L. Bensly/ M. R. James, The Fourth Book of Ezra. The Latin version edited from the MSS with an Introduction, Cambridge 1895 (= Texts and Studies III), p. 34.; the text of Fritzsche, Libri Apocryphi Veteris Testamenti, Leipzig 1871, p. 610 (= VI 63ff.), has 'pugnaverunt' and 'sensum malum'.

naming of the opponent as the 'cogitamentum malum' (sensus malus) introduces exactly that modification of the traditional philosophical conception of the Agon which one would expect in a Palestinian writing from the end of the first century of our era. For here the Stoic πάθη are replaced by the יֵצֶר הָרָע of Rabbinic theology.[1] Furthermore, that the author conceived of the whole of life as an Agon to be fought by every man is clearly shown in 7:127f.: Hoc est cogitamentum certaminis quod certabit qui super terram natus est homo, ut si victus fuerit, patiatur...; si autem vicerit, recipiet quod dico.[2]

An immediate parallel to IV Ezra occurs in *Syriac Baruch* 15:7f.: Mundus iste enim est eis (sc. iustis) agon et molestia in labore multo; et ille ergo qui futurus est, corona in gloria magna.[3] The oft-noted similarities between the two apocalypses suggest that, also at this point, we are entitled to find a theme common to them both. Charles[4] relates the cited passage to Baruch 48:50, 51:14, IV Ezra 7:3-14, Ps 90:10, Rom 8:18 and II Cor 4:17, where the life of the righteous in this world is full of suffering and tribulation, the future full of glory. But the passage is even more closely related to IV Ezra 7:92 and 127f. in as far as the Agon motif again appears, once more with 'labor multus', but with the added element of the crown of glory (cf. I Pet 5:4). Perhaps the same picture lies behind the βραβεῖα as the merits of the righteous in Greek Baruch 12.[5]

The conclusions to be drawn from the passages cited from the Ezra and Baruch Apocalypses are obvious. At this point it is immaterial whether they were first written in Hebrew or Aramaic. For the certainty of an original Semitic form illustrates how deeply the

---

[1] The same theologoumenon is suggested in 14:34, by 'cor malignum' in 3:21f., 26, 7:48, 'malignitas radicis' in 3:22, 8:53, and 'granum seminis mali' in 4:30. For the Rabbinic doctrine of the 'two impulses' see J. C. Porter, The yeçer hara, a Study in Jewish doctrine of sin, New York 1901, Strack-Bill., Exkurs 'Der gute und der böse Trieb', IV, 1 pp. 466ff., Bousset/Gressmann, op.cit., pp. 402ff., Pfeiffer, op.cit., p. 65, Ellis, op.cit., pp. 59ff., Davies, op. cit., pp. 20ff. (plus Appendix C pp. 332f.), and A. Juncker, Die Ethik des Apostels Paulus I, Halle 1904-19, pp. 68ff.

[2] Bensly-James, op.cit., p. 38, Fritzsche, op.cit., p. 613 (= VII 57).

[3] Latin version according to Fritzsche, ibid., p. 661.

[4] CAP II, p. 491.

[5] Cf. James, Apocrypha Anecdota II, Cambridge 1897, p. 93. In the Sibylline Oracles note also the typically Greek phrase ψυχὰς γυμνάζοντες (III 230) and the active use of συναγωνιᾶν = συναγωνίζεσθαι, to strive together with, in III 710ff.

concept of an Agon of life was assimilated even by Palestinian Judaism.

4. Josephus

Up to now none of the studies on the Agon image have examined the material offered in the works of Flavius Josephus. That the number of relevant passages is small is not surprising since Josephus writes as an historian and not as a moralist or interpreter of the Scriptures, as does Philo. The majority of the passages which use the terms borrowed from the sphere of the games reflect a use often noted, namely, their application to military life and to the contests of warfare.

Nevertheless there are enough references in Josephus to point to the Agon tradition traced up till now. In Ap. 2.217f. the prizes at the games, high honours for the agonistically minded Greek, are contrasted with the reward for those who live in accordance with the law: "τοῖς μέντοι γε νομίμως βιοῦσι γέρας[1] ἐστὶν οὐκ ἄργυρος οὐδὲ χρυσὸς οὐ κοτίνου στέφανος ἢ σελίνου καὶ τοιαύτη τις ἀνακήρυξις. No; each individual... is firmly persuaded that to those who observe the laws and, if they must needs die for them, willingly meet death, God has granted a renewed existence and, on the revolution of the ages, the gift of a better life".[2]

Although the Greek striving for acclamation and honour is rejected, the terminology of the games, especially when applied to the rewards for piety toward God, is still retained. This is best seen in Ant 8.208 where Jeroboam is exhorted: φύλαττε τὰ νόμιμα, προκειμένου σοι τῆς εὐσεβείας καὶ τῆς πρὸς τὸν θεὸν τιμῆς ἄθλου μεγίστου τῶν ἁπάντων", the prize being that of becoming as great as was David.[3] In Ant 6.160 the paradoxical choice of David as king receives the

---

[1] Usually in the general sense of reward in Jos, but γέρας νικητήριον in Ant 11.35. For the following passages in Josephus the author is indebted to the Institutum Iudaicum Delitzschianum in Münster/Westphalia where a complete concordance to the works of Josephus is in preparation.

[2] Translation according to H.St.J. Thackeray, Vol. I, p. 380 of the LCL edition, London 1926ff.

[3] On the connection between εὐσέβεια and τιμή see also Ant 11.120 — through the cult and the life of piety God receives the honour due to Him; cf. Ap 2.192: "τοῦτον (sc. θεὸν) θεραπευτέον ἀσκοῦντας ἀρετήν, for this is the most saintly manner of worshipping God". Cf. A. Schlatter, Wie sprach Josephus von Gott, in: BFChTh, Gütersloh 1910, pp. 77f., where Schlatter (note 2), also points out the use of the athletic image before Paul's time.

explanation (= I Sam 16:7b): "I (i.e. God) do not make the kingdom a prize (ἔπαθλον) for comeliness of body but for virtue of the soul". The terms used for the prize vary (in addition ἆθλον εὐσεβείας in Ant 16,95, εὐσεβείας ἀγωνίσματα in 17.150, and τῆς ἀρετῆς ἔπαθλα in Ant 4.182; cf. also Ant 1.14: for those who do God's will and do not transgress the law γέρας εὐδαιμονία πρόκειται παρὰ θεοῦ), but in each case the roots of the metaphor are the same.

The above usage conforms to that of Hellenistic Judaism in that, as in Philo and IV Macc, the image is closely connected with the concept of εὐσέβεια. Further points of contact with Philo, though certainly not indicating dependence, may be observed. Philo calls the Essenes ἀθληταὶ ἀρετῆς,[1] and pictures them largely in the colours of Stoic encratism. Josephus records that the Essenes turn from the pleasures as evil and regard as virtue ἐγκράτειαν καὶ τὸ μὴ τοῖς πάθεσιν ὑποπίπτειν (Bell 2.120).[2] The entrants into the order are required to swear terrible oaths to honour (εὐσεβεῖν) God, to preserve justice to all men, not to harm anyone, and μισήσειν ἀεὶ τοὺς ἀδίκους καὶ συναγωνιεῖσθαι τοῖς δικαίοις (2.139). To fight the battle of the just may, it is true, simply mean to assist them against the unjust, but the verb can just as well denote participation in the Agon which the righteous, that is, the members of the community, contend for sanctity.[3] Again, Philo pictures the wandering of the Israelites in the desert as an Agon given up by some but won by others.[4] A similar picture, without the moral allegorization of Philo, appears in Josephus in Ant 3.15: Moses suggests that it is to test (δοκιμάζειν) their manhood and fortitude (ἀρετή and καρτερία) that God is exercising (γυμνάζειν) them with trials. Finally, in a passage which

---

[1] Omn Prob Lib 88, cf. supra p. 42 note 2.

[2] In Ant 6.296 Josephus makes a Nabal a Cynic living ἐκ κυνικῆς ἀσκήσεως, taking the LXX's καὶ ὁ ἄνθρωπος κυνικός (MT "and he was of the house of Caleb", כָּלֵב = dog) in a technical philosophical sense (I Bas 25:3).

[3] The discipline or ascetic training of the order is called an ἄσκησις in 2:150, and ἀσκεῖν is used for their particular cultivation of sanctity in 2.119. It is just possible that the term ἄσκησις here, and elsewhere as the practical exercise and training in morals afforded by the Mosaic Law (ἄσκησις τῶν ἠθῶν in Ap 2.171-173, ἄσκησις ἀρετῆς in Ant 1.6), still has a ring of its original use in the sphere of athletics. The original connection is clear in Ant 15.270 γυμνικαὶ ἀσκήσεις, and Ap 2.229 ἀσκεῖν σώματα πρὸς κάλλος, but the word is also used generally for the cultivation of a virtue or art—cf. Thackeray, A. Greek Lexicon to Josephus (incomplete), Paris 1930, s.v. For the philosophical use of the word see Windisch, TWNT I, pp. 492ff.

[4] Congr. Erud 164f.

reminds of Philo's Agon of wickedness in Abr 40 (cf. Agric 111ff.), Josephus describes king Baasha as a champion of iniquity (I Kings 15:34). "Like those who have a prize held out before them (προκειμένων αὐτοῖς ἄθλων) and in their earnest effort to obtain it do not leave off striving toward it, so too Basanes... every day ὥσπερ ἀθλητὴς κακίας τοῖς περὶ ταύτην πόνοις προσετίθει." (Ant 8.302).

The technical athletic/philosophical use of πόνοι, seen in the last passage, is once more observed in Ap 2.228: the changes of rule in Asia have inflicted ordeals and labours (ἄθλους καὶ πόνους) on the Jews which demanded more endurance than that demanded of the Lacedaemonians.

The above material is significant in that it again emphasises the possibility of the adoption of the athletic image without the moralism of its traditional philosophical use. The image, used in a religio-ethical sense, is here only occasional, and is far more closely related to Jewish parallels than to the purely hellenistic. Nowhere is there more than a hint at the Cynic-stoic attitude to life as such as an Agon—despite the adoption of traditional words and phrases.[1]

In addition Josephus and the whole field of Greek literature, as well as the papyri, provide a multitude of uses of the athletic image, as well as of pale athletic terminology, which are completely unrelated to the traditional philosophical use of the image. The most frequent application, namely in a military sense, has already been noted for II Macc, but is much older, having been often used by the Greeks for the contests of warfare between the states themselves and their common enemies.[2] The whole range of terms is employed for a similar purpose by Josephus: ἀγών and ἀγωνίζεσθαι (usually with an accompanying adverb, especially the familiar γενναίως), together with its compounds, ἀγωνιστής and ἀνταγωνιστής, as well as γυμνασία / γυμνάζειν and ἀσκεῖν / ἄσκησις for the training of troops.[3] Here one can generally still speak of a metaphor and not

---

[1] At the most one could point to the 'Stoic' advice of Vespasian to his soldiers to meet good fortune with sobriety and to remain cheerful when contending with reverses (ἀναπαλαίων τὰ σφάλματα, Bell 4.42); cf. Marc. Aurel. 7.61.

[2] E.g. Plato Leg. V 729D (ἀγῶνες πολεμικοί = Ep Arist 14), XI 920E, Tim. 19C, Repub. 403Eff. (πολεμικοὶ ἀθληταί), Herod. 9.60.1, 8.102, Appian Bell. Civ. 1.10, Thucyd. 7.61.1ff., Diod. Sic. 13.14.1ff., Plutarch Aratus 1044D, Philop. 362C; for later references see Preisigke, op.cit., and Ditt. Syll. 434/5, 10 etc.

[3] For references see Thackeray, op.cit., s.v.

simply of a pale or colourless usage. Occasionally the image is stated explicitly,[1] as in Bell 4.88ff. where the Roman troops are trained καθάπερ ἀθλητὰς ... τῶν ἀγώνων (cf. Ant 13.327 and 17.259), or in Bell 6.133 where Titus supervises the fighting of his men looking down on them as an ἀγωνοθέτης from the fortress of Antonia.

The image is, however, certainly paler in the frequent use of ἀγών / ἀγωνίζεσθαι, and related words for strife, contention, and legal issues and speeches.[2] In many instances the terms can denote little more than intense striving and utmost exertion,[3] but even in a pale usage the phraseology of the games is still retained, especially the almost technical phrase ἀγών / ἆθλον πρόκειται[4] (cf. Hebr. 12:1).

---

[1] Also in Plato Laches 182A, Repub. 403Ef., Diod. Sic. 15,5, Aristotle Eth. Nic. III 8.1116b.6 etc. In Josephus note also Ant 12.304 —the Agon is for the ἔπαθλα of ἐλευθερία, πάτρις, νόμοι and εὐσέβεια; ἔπαθλα with ἀγωνίζεσθαι also in 12.409.

[2] Apart from the numerous other references in the lexica note in Josephus, Bell 1.574,633, 2.15,30,83,245, 16.8,71,200, 17.81,92,103, 19.141; note on the other hand Ant 17.47.

[3] In Josephus cf. Ant 2.159: "striving (ἀγωνιζόμενος) by any means to mollify and appease his wrath". 'Αγών in the sense of mental struggle or anxiety only appears in Vita 30.

[4] Ant 19.92; 16.313, 18.173, 19.131, Ap 1.53. The references to the completely colourless use of ἀγωνίζεσθαι in Preisigke and Dittenberger are very late for our purposes, and not of much significance for a study of Paul's language.

CHAPTER FOUR

PALESTINIAN JUDAISM AND THE GAMES

The development of the Agon image and terminology as traced up till now can rightly be called a tradition in as far as its use, even by Hellenistic Judaism and the pseudepigraphical writings of Palestinian Judaism, continually betrays its Greek origins. However, it should be noted that the passages in IV Ezra and the Syrian Baruch apocalypse, while presenting the typically Greek thought of life as an Agon, do not contain a conscious comparison from the games. In these instances one can only speak of a pale, non-metaphorical, use of 'agon'.[1]

That we should not expect a positive use of the athletic image on Palestinian soil is only to be expected when one surveys the attitude of the Palestinian Jews, and especially of the Rabbis, to the games and allied Greek institutions. While the Jew in the hellenistic diaspora felt more free to enter the Greek theatre and stadium,[2] the situation in Palestine itself was different.

In the first place the fostering of athletic contests[3] and gymnasia[4]-

---

[1] The use of the loan word אֲגוֹן (= ἀγών) in Jelamdenu, Emor, also reveals a pale military sense (cf. J. Levy, Neuhebräisches und Chaldäisches Wörterbuch über die Talmudim und Midraschim, Leipzig 1876, p. 20, and M. Jastrow, A Dictionary of the Targumim, The Talmud Babli and Jerushalmi, and the Midrashic Literature, New York 1950, p. 11); the lexicographers also cite a possible occurrence of אֲגוֹנְיָא (= ἀγωνία) in Tanch. Mishpatim 92a, but the text is not certain.

[2] Philo himself reports having attended an ἀγὼν παγκρατιαστῶν and the performance of a tragedy by Euripides (Schürer II, p. 60 and S. Krauss, Talmudische Archäologie III, p. 119). In addition note the inscription reserving a place for the Jews in the theatre at Miletus (A. Deissmann, Licht vom Osten, Exkurs IV) and the inscription from Berenice in Cyrenaica set up εἰς τὸν ἐπισημότατον τόπον τοῦ ἀμφιθεάτρου (CIG III, 5361, lines 26f., in Schürer III, p. 80). The famous letter of Claudius to the Alexandrians in 41 A.D. (Tcherikover and Fuks, Corpus Papyrorum Judaicarum II, Cambridge/ Mass. 1960, no. 153 lines 88ff.) orders the Jews not to intrude themselves into the games (γυμνασιαρχικοῖς ἢ κοσμητικοῖς ἀγῶσιν) since they enjoy what is their own. But the order could presuppose previous participation.

[3] Cf. the πενταετηρικὸς ἀγὼν in Tyre in II Macc 4:18ff., originally founded by Alexander the Great (Schürer II, p. 47).

[4] The Hellenizers erected a gymnasium in honour of Antiochus on the acropolis of Jerusalem κατὰ τὰ νόμιμα τῶν ἐθνῶν, I Macc 1:14, II Macc 4:9-17,

institutions which went directly against the national and religious sensibility of the Jews—had been a major weapon of the program of hellenization under Antiochus Epiphanes. But the greatest introduction of these foreign practices came under Herod the Great. Not only in Caesarea did he build a theatre and amphi-theatre and institute quinquennial games with great prizes.[1] Even in Jerusalem itself he erected such buildings, and, as in Caesarea, celebrated showy πενταετηρικοὶ ἀγῶνες in the muses, athletics and chariot racing, attracting champions from neighbouring countries with the promise of munificent prizes.[2] In addition he endowed other Palestinian cities with theatres, gymnasia, stadia and other public buildings of this nature,[3] and also sponsored the Olympic games which were declining for want of funds.[4] The judgment of Josephus on these innovations as being κατὰ τοὺς Ἰουδαίους ἔθους ἀλλότρια[5] can be taken as representing the common feeling of the majority of the Jews. Four reasons are suggested for this attitude. The gymnastic athletes contested naked, and the games themselves were consecrated to Caesar[6]—in imperial times the public games in the provincial cities were connected with the Caesar-cult. But it was above all the cruelty of the gladiatorial contests also introduced by Herod which were condemned as a destruction of honoured customs.[7] In addition the trophies gave special cause for offence since they were mistaken for images.[8]

Nevertheless, the material gathered by Schürer[9] shows that the imperial times saw an amazing growth of these foreign institutions even within Palestine—thus the even more radical renunciation in the Rabbinical literature. But here the polemics are directed more against the frivolity of the theatre and the cruelty and impiety of the 'venationes'.[10] Only rarely does an illustration taken from the

---

and IV Macc 4:20. Antiochus also wanted to introduce the Dionysia in Jerusalem, and a palaestra is mentioned in II Macc 4:14.

[1] Bell 1.415, and Ant 16.137f.

[2] Ant 15.268ff.

[3] Cf. Schürer II, p. 61; Bell 1.430 reports that the king was himself proficient ἐν ταῖς γυμνασίαις.

[4] Bell 1.426f, and Ant 16.149.

[5] Ant 15.268.

[6] Ibid and 16.138.

[7] Ant 15.274; many Jewish prisoners perished in the arena at the end of the Jewish war (Bell 3.539, 7.23f, 37f, and 96).

[8] Ant 15.276.

[9] Schürer II, p. 47-52, and 60f.

[10] See Strack-Bill. IV 1, Exkurs 15B, pp. 401ff.: "Stellung der alten Syna-

athletic games appear, and the isolated cases which may be noted[1] are in no way related either to Paul's use or to the traditional philosophical use in the diatribe. Thus at this point the rejection of the Rabbis can not be immediately paralleled with the protests of the Stoic diatribists.[2]

Nevertheless one passage does deserve mention, namely, the prayer of Nehoniah ben Ha-kana (first generation of the Tannaim) recorded in b. Berach. 28b and its parallel in j. Berach. 4.7d. Only j. Berach. contains a certain allusion to those "who sit in the theatre and circus", but the polemic against the vain efforts of the athletes or contestants is the same in each instance. "I labour and they labour, but I labour and receive a reward and they labour and do not receive a reward; I run and they run but I run to the life of the future world (אני רץ לחיי העולם הבא) and they run to the pit of destruction" (b. Berach).[3] As in the diatribe we have here a polemic against the futile games plus a positive adoption of the athletic image. However the use of the picture is in no way related to that of the diatribe, but lies closer to the use of רוּץ and דֶּרֶךְ in the OT, and to those passages which speak of running the ways of God's commandments (Ps 119:32) or of hastening to do good or evil (Prov 1:16, Is 59:7).[4] In addition the OT also speaks of the time of salvation when even the nations which have not known God will run to, and be collected in Zion (Is 55:5, 2:2, and Tobit 14:7).

---

goge zu den heidnischen Spielen", and T. Bergmann, Jüdische Apologetik im neutestamentlichen Zeitalter, Berlin 1908, pp. 16-20. The Talmud does not deny that Jews also attended the theatre and circus (cf. S. Krauss, Talmudische Archäologie III, p. 119) but this only increased the Rabbis' attacks on this practice.

[1] Ibid III, pp. 402ff. on I Cor 9:25.

[2] Cf. J. Bergmann, Die stoische Philosophie und die jüdische Frömmigkeit, in: Judaica, Festschrift zu Hermann Cohens siebzigstem Geburtstag, Berlin 1912, p. 157, who points to the rejection of gladiatorial contests, common to both Stoics and Rabbis.

[3] j. Berach. 4.7d in W. Bacher, Die Agada der Tannaiten, Strassburg ²1903, I, p. 55 —cf. also the use of רוּץ noted supra, p. 49.

[4] Cf. supra, pp. 50., and W. Michaelis, TWNT V, pp. 47ff. for the דֶּרֶךְ / ὁδός motif in the OT.

B

THE ATHLETIC METAPHOR AND TERMINOLOGY IN PAUL

PRELIMINARY REMARKS

The material here placed under special examination is limited to the occurrences of the express athletic image and the terms which suggest this image.[1] The passages which immediately come into consideration are the following. The picture of the athletic contest, in its various forms, is most extensively developed in I Cor 9:24-27 (στάδιον, τρέχειν, βραβεῖον, ἀγωνίζεσθαι, ἐγκρατεύεσθαι, στέφανος, πυκτεύειν). Phil 3:12-14 provides the second largest complex, although the metaphor is only explicit in v. 14 (σκοπός, βραβεῖον). The same picture of the runner (τρέχειν) appears again in Gal 2:2, 5:7, Rom 9:16 and Phil 2:16. In Phil 1:27-30 (συναθλεῖν, ἀγών), Col 1:29-2:1 (ἀγωνίζεσθαι, ἀγών) and 4:12f. (ἀγωνίζεσθαι, πόνος, v.l ἀγών!), the presence of the image is reasonably assured by the plurality of terms, while in other instances where only one term occurs

---

[1] Not considered are the passages in which a reference to the games or metaphorical termini has been postulated but remains extremely hypothetical. Eidem (pp. 144ff.) rightly rejects a reference to the broad-jump in II Cor 10:13ff. More recently C. Spicq (L'Image Sportive de II Cor 9:7-9", in: Eph Th Lov 1937, pp. 209-229) has attempted to show the presence of an image from the wrestling ring in II Cor 9:8f. His argument, which is indebted to imagination more than to proof, runs as follows: The image of the earthen vessels (v. 7) suggested the athletic image since the contestants were accustomed to rub themselves in with oil and dirt before the contest. The grimy crust which the sweat of the contest formed was afterwards so thick as to give the athletes the appearance of earthen vessels! Paul's thought then shifts from the weakness and fragility of the Apostle as an instrument of God to the picture of the athlete prepared for the contest through the power within him (pp. 215ff.). The various verbs in vv.8ff. then describe the various stages in the wrestling match. However Spicq's attempt to prove that these verbs have a technical athletic sense is not convincing. All are more easily understood as picturing in general terms the trials and afflictions of the Apostle. The passage is thus certainly a commentary on Paul's missionary Agon, but most certainly not Paul's most genuine sporting metaphor, as Spicq maintains (p. 228).
—There is little point in again going into the meaning of θηριομαχεῖν in I Cor 15:32. The verse, though a metaphor from the Roman 'Venationes', does, however, reveal an aspect of what Paul means when speaking of his work as an Agon. On the passage cf., apart from the commentaries, Eidem, pp. 148ff., BAG s.v., and the literature cited there.

one may ask whether a conscious metaphor is intended. The passages here concerned are I Thess 2:2 (ἀγών), Rom 15:30 (συναγωνίζεσθαι), Phil 4:3 (συναθλεῖν) and Phil 4:1 and I Thess 2:19 (στέφανος). Less important and pale in use are βραβεύειν in Col 3:15 and καταβραβεύειν in Col 2:18. Of secondary significance is the image of the θέατρον in I Cor 4:9, although the passage must be considered in so far as it is connected with the idea of the Apostle's Agon.[1]

As in any work on Paul the problem of the genuineness or authenticity of the so-called Deutero-Pauline letters here asserts itself.[2] The problem is not so acute in the case of πάλη (v. 12) within the large military metaphor in Eph 6:10ff. In the first place the meaning of the word is rather colourless in its present context. Secondly, its use does not betray an immediate relationship to the Agon passages of the 'accepted' letters of Paul, but rather to his use of the military image.

Not so simple, however, is the *question of the Pastoral Epistles*. Already the frequency of the image demands that special attention be given the following passages —I Tim 4:7-10 (γυμνάζειν, γυμνασία, ἀγωνίζεσθαι), 6:11f. (ἀγωνίζεσθαι, ἀγών), II Tim 2:3ff. (ἀθλεῖν, στεφανοῦν) and 4:6ff. (ἀγών, ἀγωνίζεσθαι, δρόμος). Two other factors make it necessary to draw these passages into the present examination. Although they show a further development, an almost technical use of the image, they are still closely and directly related to the Agon in the acknowledged epistles of Paul. In the second instance II Tim 4:6-8 belongs to the noted personal elements in the Pastorals, containing as it does an autobiographical statement which is reminiscent of similar words of Paul in Acts 20:24. It can, of course, easily be argued that both passages have been placed into the mouth of the Apostle. But considering the popularity of the image in Paul's own writings, Acts 20:24 could well be a reminiscence of actual words of Paul, and II Tim 4:6ff. a genuine autobiographical statement.[3]

---

[1] The use of θέατρον in the diatribe in connection with the Agon of the sage further demands a consideration of I Cor 4:9 (cf. also the use of θεατρίζεσθαι in connection with the athletic image in Hebr 10:33). Attention must also be given to recurring words and phrases within the Agon passages, such as κοπιᾶν (with ἀγωνίζεσθαι in Col 1:29, I Tim 4:10; with τρέχειν in Phil 2:16), εἰς κενόν (Gal 2:2, Phil 2:16), and ἐγκόπτειν (Gal 5:7 and I Thess 2:18).

[2] Despite the opinion of many scholars, the present writer feels free to accept the authenticity of Colossians.

[3] P. N. Harrison, The Problem of the Pastoral Epistles, Oxford 1921, pp.

A thorough discussion of the whole problem of authorship is here out of place, and if the Pastorals are included in the present study this is done on the working hypothesis that the relevant passages contain genuinely Pauline thought, or at least closely reflect it.[1] The study will itself show whether this hypothesis is correct or not.

Finally two other groups of passages also require consideration, the extra-Pauline occurrences of the athletic image or terms in the NT, especially in Hebrews,[2] as well as the instances where the military image appears.[3] The references in both groups are only noted to the extent to which they parallel or clarify Paul's use of the Agon image.[4]

The interpretation of the Pauline use of the athletic metaphor has till now been burdened with a false use of analogy both with the military metaphor and with the thought of the diatribe. Whether Paul's usage is directly traced back to that of popular moral philosophy or not, the result is that he has often been understood as representing the traditional concept of life as an Agon, more specifically, as a moral Agon.

A few references to older and more recent works will soon bear out this point. The false analogy is clearest in the statement of *W. M. Ramsay*[5] who cites Lightfoot with approval: "Both Paul and Seneca 'compare life to a warfare, and describe the struggle after good as a contest with the flesh'". Speaking of the Stoics, *R. H.*

87-135, reckons II Tim 4:6ff. amongst the genuine Pauline fragments contained in the Pastorals (cf. M. Dibelius, Die Pastoralbriefe [HNT], Tübingen ³1955, p. 4, and W. Michaelis, Einleitung in das NT, Bern ³1961, p. 249).

[1] Both Schlatter and Jeremias have made strong arguments for the apostolic origin of the Pastorals, and most recently E. E. Ellis, Paul's Use of the Old Testament, p. 9, has concluded that "all in all, the weight of evidence favours the genuineness of the Pastorals".

[2] Cf. Hebr 10:32ff. (ἄθλησις, θεατρίζεσθαι), 11:33 (καταγωνίζεσθαι), 12:1-4 (τρέχειν, ἀγών, ἀνταγωνίζεσθαι), 5:14, 12:11 and II Pet 2:14 (γυμνάζειν); also Jude 3 (ἐπαγωνίζεσθαι), Lk 13:24 and John 18:36 (ἀγωνίζεσθαι), and Lk 22:44 (ἀγωνία).

[3] Note esp. Rom 6:13, 7:23f., 13:11ff., I Cor 9:7, II Cor 2:14, 6:7, 10:3ff., Eph 4:8 (Ps 68:18), 6:10ff., Col 2:15, I Thess 5:4ff., I Tim 1:18f. (an important parallel to the Agon passages in the Pastorals), II Tim 2:3ff. (in connection with the athletic metaphor) and Phil 2:25 and Philem 2 (also important for an understanding of the Apostle's Agon).

[4] The most complete work in this area is also given by Eidem, ch. IV "Krig och krigsmän", pp. 188ff. Cf. also A. von Harnack, Militia Christi, Tübingen 1905, and the excurses in the commentaries of Dibelius and Schlier on Eph 6:10ff., as well as Oepke in TWNT V, pp. 300ff.

[5] St. Paul the Traveller and the Roman Citizen, London 1895, p. 354.

Pfeiffer[1] also writes, "life, as the early Christians likewise knew, was a race to be won, a battle to be fought..., after undergoing severe athletic training." According to *W. A. Beardslee*[2] "in Paul's letters the moral struggle is not infrequently pictured in the form of an athletic contest", an image which is supposed to emphasise the idea of progress and growth of character and strenuous moral exertion. He also finds in Paul metaphors which are "references to life as a 'conflict'",[3] and cites with approval *J. Weiss*[4] who sees in the figure of the prize fighter the ideal of testing and experience. Weiss treats I Cor 9:24ff. under the heading 'education and training', that is, he only treats the passage in connection with Pauline paraenesis and the moral Agon.[5] A similar generalisation may be found in the otherwise excellent work of *W. D. Davies*.[6] Paul had to become "the father of his converts in life as well as in faith, their trainer in 'the race' or 'boxing contest' of the Christian discipline". The recent work of *W. Schrage*[7] also simply sees in Paul's use of the Agon image an instance of his paraenetic emphasis that "der Christ ist noch Kampfgebiet... und zum Kampf gerufen".

A more correct emphasis is given by *A. Schlatter*[8] when he characterises the "Wettkampfgedanke" as describing "das christliche Streben nach seiner Notwendigkeit und Tüchtigkeit". By means of this image Paul impresses on the Christian community "dass sie die ihr verliehene Kraft zu betätigen und sichtbar zu machen und darauf einen entschlossenen Willen zu richten habe, mit dem tiefen Ernst, dass dies die Bedingung ihrer Rettung sei". *Lydia Schmid*,

---

[1] Op.cit., p. 141.

[2] Op.cit., p. 68.

[3] Ibid, although Beardslee also notes that "Paul most frequently applies the athletic metaphors to himself", and that "the metaphor suggests the incompleteness of the present situation"—two correct observations, though the Agon is still primarily understood as a moral struggle.

[4] Earliest Christianity, New York 1959, p. 577 (Urchristentum, Göttingen 1917, pp. 449f.).

[5] A more correct emphasis follows (ibid); Paul "feels himself to be a field soldier of the Lord ... His life is a struggle (ἀγών) ... his work is a campaign in the service of God".

[6] Paul and Rabbinic Judaism, London 1955, p. 112 with note 6.

[7] Die konkreten Einzelgebote in der paulinischen Paränese, Gütersloh 1961, p. 31 with note 74. Cf. also A. Schweitzer, The Mysticism of Paul the Apostle, London ²1953, p. 296 (Die Mystik des Apostels Paulus, Tübingen ²1954, p. 288) who relates I Cor 9:27 to the crucifying of the affections and lusts in Gal 5:24.

[8] Die Theologie der Apostel, Stuttgart 1922, p. 297f. with note 3.

Schlatter's pupil, also sees in the thought of exertion and application of divinely granted strength the central emphasis of the Agon image in Paul. But Schlatter still comes very close to a false view of the Christian Agon when he cites I Cor 9:24 as an instance of the application of the picture to the moral struggle of the Christian. The misunderstanding of I Cor 9:24ff. is graver when *A. Juncker*[1] cites the passage, with others, to illustrate how Paul describes the inner life of the Christian as a battle field on which σάρξ and πνεῦμα continually wrestle with each other: "So ist und bleibt seine Sittlichkeit eine Sittlichkeit des Kampfes und steht somit noch nicht auf dem Gipfel idealer Vollendung." The real point of I Cor 9:24ff. is thereby missed. The same characteristic error noted above appears clearest in Juncker's statement that the thought of training, self-discipline and abstinence are to be seen in "the repeated description of the Christian life as a contest for the heavenly prize".[2]

It has frequently been observed that Paul most frequently applies the Agon image to his own person.[3] But even here the Agon is still often limited to the moral struggle of the Christian as exemplified, supposedly, by the Apostle's own behaviour. When *W. Wrede*, for example, writes that Paul "war der Läufer in der Rennbahn, der nach dem Kleinod jagt",[4] he still pictures the Agon as a moral struggle. Paul testifies in this picture to the "deep moral earnestness" of his "menschlich-sittliche Individualität".

That a strong paraenetic element is retained in all of Paul's Agon passages cannot be denied. But the above characterisations are guilty of ascribing an emphasis to Paul which is not found in his use of the metaphor, but is largely transplanted over to him from the traditional use of the image or from the motifs which the image of the games suggested to the Greek mind. The last error is illustrated to perfection in the work of L. Schmid who needlessly involves herself in a wide comparison between Pauline and hellenistic, speci-

---

[1] Die Ethik des Apostels Paulus, (Halle, I 1904, II 1919), I p. 212.

[2] Op.cit., II, p. 127, citing I Cor 9:24ff. and Phil 3:12ff. The former passage is again understood as speaking of the necessity of strenuous moral exertion (II, p. 95), while much the same emphasis is given to the second reference (I, p. 204).

[3] Seen also by L. Schmid and E. Eidem. But they have also failed to emphasise that it is thereby Paul the Apostle and his missionary activity which is above all characterised.

[4] W. Wrede, Paulus, Religionsgeschichtliche Volksbücher, Tübingen 1907, p. 21.

fically Stoic, ethics, since she also sees in the apostle's use of the image an 'Auseinandersetzung' with the Greek spirit and ethical ideals connected with the image.

Since I Cor 9:24ff. contains the most elaborate application of the athletic image in Paul's letters, and also because most misinterpretations have centred around this passage, we commence the exegetical examination at this point.

CHAPTER FIVE

THE APOSTOLIC AGON FOR THE GOSPEL

1. The Self-Apology of the Apostle in I Cor. 9:24-27

The interpretation of this passage has often suffered from the outset by treating the verses as a separate unit of general Pauline paraenesis. Form-critical considerations would seem to support the view that they should be dealt with as a complete and independent unit. In his extensive work on the subject Martin Dibelius has shown that the form of NT paraenesis reveals, amongst others, the following two characteristics. The content is often not specifically Christian in origin, but rather reveals traditional material adopted by the Christian writers. The Stoa, and its literary medium, the diatribe, contributed much of the paraenetic material in the NT epistles.[1] In the second place the paraenetic sections usually fit very loosely into their present context[2] without adhering strictly to a logical sequence of thought, rather giving general injunctions which are already familiar to the readers.

It may be asked whether both these rules can be applied to our present passage. The above study of the tradition of the athletic image can hardly leave any room for doubt that I Cor 9:24ff., at least formally, carries on this tradition. The antithesis between the στέφανος φθαρτός and στέφανος ἄφθαρτος in v.25 certainly repeats a familiar contrast (whether applied to the Agon itself, or to the prizes to be won) which has been often noted in the examination.[3]

---

[1] M. Dibelius, Der Brief des Jakobus (KEK), Göttingen [10]1959, pp. 3-10, and his Formgeschichte des Evangeliums, Tübingen [3]1961, pp. 239ff.

[2] Although this applies primarily to those cases in which we find chains or series of paraenetic injunctions where a connecting theme is completely lacking; cf. Jakobusbrief, p. 7.

[3] Cf. esp. Philo Migr Abr 6—even Pindar has not succeeded in making the wreath of glory ἄφθαρτος. The victors in the games are not those remembered in history. Note also Wis 4:2, I Pet 5:4 and J. Berach. 4.7d, and Seneca Ep. 78.16: "What blows do athletes receive in their face ... Yet they bear all the torture from thirst of glory. Let us also overcome all things, for our reward is not a crown or a palm branch or the trumpeter proclaiming silence for the announcement of our name, but virtue and strength of mind and peace acquired ever after". It is difficult to say whether the antithesis still contains

In addition the theme of ἐγκράτεια which has programmatic significance in the diatribe's picture of the sage's Agon, is also introduced
in v.25 as the central point of the image. Even a change of pictures,
as in v.26, is not foreign to the parallels in the diatribe or in Philo.
Finally it is also possible to see in the introductory οὐκ οἴδατε in
v.24 one of the many forms of litotes popularly used by the diatribal
writers to introduce an argument or injunction.[1]

The last point already suggests that vv.24-27 belong more
directly to 9:1-23 than to 10:1ff.[2] which continues the discussion on
eating meat offered to idols. The second passage continues with a
new motif (cf. πειρασμός 10:13) from the OT desert-wandering
tradition. The γάρ in 10:1 is simply a loose conjunctive pointing
to 9:24-27 as the transitional section between the two larger passages.

However such formal considerations do not alone justify the
treatment of these verses as a separate unit of general paraenesis.
J. Weiss has argued that Paul is often led beyond the practical
purpose in hand "in the creation of pictures which have a meaning
all of their own, and like independant mosaics project themselves
out of the context".[3] Yet even if we agree reservedly with J. Weiss,
and also with H. Lietzmann who remarks that our passage shows

---

the original polemical tone of the Stoic and Cynics, but it is at least certain
that the verses cannot be understood as revealing Paul's general attitude to
sport, as in J. Hering, The First Epistle of St. Paul to the Corinthians, ET:
London 1962, p. 83: "the author would not have made this comparison if he
had been strongly averse to sport".(!) Nor can we say that Paul shows "a
readiness to admire whatever was innocent and beautiful in human customs,
when he wrote (sc. I Cor 9:24ff.) to his converts in Corinth" (F. W. Farrar,
The Life and Work of St. Paul, London 1896, p. 699). Nor does the character
of the image allow us to make any conclusions as to the relationship of the
Corinthian Christians to the games, as does Schlatter, Paulus der Bote Jesu,
Stuttgart ³1962, p. 284. In all probability the Christians ceased to attend the
'sacred games', but these verses are anything but a practical directive in the
Christian's attitude to them.

[1] Cf. Epict. III 24,31: οὐκ οἶσθ', ὅτι στρατεία τὸ χρῆμά ἐστιν; in Paul also
in Rom 6:16, 11:2, I Cor 3:16, 6:3.9.15.16.19, 9:13; also τί οὖν in Rom 3:9,
6:15, etc. A similar formula is found with the use of ἀγνοεῖν in Rom 6:3, 7:1,
etc., and of τί ἐροῦμεν in Rom 3:5, 4:1, etc.; cf. Bultmann, TWNT I, p. 117,
and Der Stil der paulinischen Predigt und die kynisch-stoische Diatribe
(FRLANT), Göttingen 1910, pp. 13 and 65.

[2] E.g. Robertson and Plummer, I Corinthians (ICC), Edinburgh ²1914,
pp. 193ff., P. Bachmann, Erster Korintherbrief (KNT), Leipzig ³1921, pp.
327ff., Eidem, pp. 106f, and Farrar, op.cit., p. 699.

[3] J. Weiss, Earliest Christianity II, p. 406, without, however, referring to
I Cor 9:24ff.

that the strength of Pauline rhetoric does not lie in his use of images,[1] it cannot be denied that Paul's images never stand as isolated units, but always serve to illustrate a specific point in hand, even though the logical connection between argument and illustration is often difficult to ascertain. In the second instance the formula οὐκ οἴδατε does not mark the advent of a new train of thought, but, as already in v.13, introduces a new argument or illustration into a train of thought already begun.

The last point already suggests that vv.24-27 belong more directly to 9:1-23 than to 10:1ff.[2] which continues the discussion of the problem of eating meat offered to idols, begun already in 8:1. The γάρ in 10:1 is simply a loose conjunctive pointing to 9:24-27 as the transitional section between the two larger passages.

An *analysis of chapter* 9 shows the following context for vv.24-27. In 9:1ff. Paul abruptly diverges from the direct discussion of Christian liberty and self-restraint 'concerning food offered to idols', and points to his own behaviour as an Apostle in order to illustrate the principles of freedom and abstention.[3] The question around which this illustration revolves is Paul's refusal to allow himself to be maintained by the gifts of the Corinthian congregation, in contrast to the practice of the other Apostles. Paul answers the reproaches of the Corinthians, who no doubt saw in his action an offensive sign of weakness, by categorically stating his claim to liberty of action as an Apostle of Jesus Christ. In vv.3ff. he begins not an apology of his apostleship as such, as in II Cor 10-13, but rather a defence of his right to freedom of action as an Apostle.[4] In the first place Paul states his rightful claim to maintenance by pointing to the rights of the other Apostles (vv.4-6), using the

---

[1] Lietzmann-Kümmel, An die Korinther I, II (HNT), Tübingen [3]1949, p. 43.

[2] By connecting vv.24-27 with 1:1ff. Bachmann gives our passage a completely false tone, as can already be detected from the heading which he gives to 9:23-10:22: "Die Sorge für das eigene Heil als Norm des Freiheitsgedankens" (op. cit., p. 327). Not Paul's own salvation, but the course of the Gospel, is that which determines the point of vv. 24ff.

[3] The break between 8:13 and 9:1 is admittedly very sharp, but the contents of chapter 9 do not justify the conclusion that the chapter "opens up a new subject without any transition" (Héring, op.cit., p. 75). Héring incorrectly sees here a resumption of the defence of Paul's apostleship (chs. 1-4) and assigns ch.9 to a second letter. The apparent looseness in connection does not merit the application of any "Teilungshypothese" at this point.

[4] The catchword in vv.1f. is ἐλεύθερος, not ἀπόστολος.

analogous picture of the soldier, viner and shepherd who have a claim to the fruits of their labours (v.7), the proof from scripture (vv.8-10), the example of those serving in the temple (v.13), and finally by referring to a verbum Domini (v.14).

Having established his rights Paul immediately renounces them on the principal that nothing is to hinder the course of the Gospel (vv.11-13). Here already in v.12b appears the catchword πάντα which is again taken up in vv.22bf. (cf. also v.19): *everything for the sake of the Gospel.* In vv.15-18 there follows the reason for his renunciation of the support of the congregation. Paul's work of evangelization is not the result of a voluntary decision on his part. He has been pressed into service by his Lord: ἀνάγκη γάρ μοι ἐπίκειται.[1] Consequently as a slave of the Lord he has to fulfil his will (i.e. εὐαγγελίζεσθαι) without any claim on reward.

In vv.19-23 the Apostle explicates the principle; of his own will he renounces his personal liberty in the interests of his missionary task. The principle itself is formulated in v.22b with the repetition of the adjective 'all': τοῖς πᾶσιν γέγονα πάντα, ἵνα πάντως τινὰς σώσω. His renunciation of personal liberty is conditioned alone by his concern to place everything in the service of the Gospel. These words offer the central point of the whole chapter, and are in turn an explanation of the ἀνάγκη in v.16. And just as the thought of divine compulsion there included the thought of the Apostle's own salvation (οὐαὶ γάρ μοί ἐστιν ἐὰν μὴ εὐαγγελίσωμαι), so also in v.23 the apostle's self-restriction in all things (πάντα) for the sake of the Gospel includes, at the same time, the condition for his own share in its blessings. Paul cannot separate his apostolic commission from his own salvation. The two go hand in hand.

Verses 24-27 now follow as the crowning conclusion to 9:1-23, and in particular as an explanation of v.16, so that to separate them from what precedes is to completely miss the point of the athletic image. From our analysis of the entire chapter it is clear that the *central point of the image must lie in* πάντα ἐγκρατεύεται *in v.25.* Consequently it is false to assign an independent (metaphorical) weight to individual features of the image.

---

[1] E. Käsemann is hardly right in interpreting ἀνάγκη in the sense of fate, in "Eine paulinische Variation des 'amor fati'", ZThK 56, 1959, pp. 135-154. Paul's compulsion results from his call and obligation to the Lord in his service, in contrast to his freedom from any obligation over against men, that is, apart from delivering to them the Gospel (cf. Rom 1:14).

This applies above all to the several components of the image, as it is developed in v.24, which serve to unfold the picture before its actual application to Paul's own person in vv.26f. The introductory character of these verses, and the intention of Paul, is misunderstood, if it is asked what the Apostle may have meant by the στάδιον and the βραβεῖον when translated into terms of the Christian life. The stadium and the victor's prize are simply necessary features of the image, without any independent weight of their own.

Only an allegorizing interpretation which assigns to v.24 independent importance can see a problem in the εἷς δὲ λαμβάνει τὸ βραβεῖον. Thus Origen is forced to equate εἷς with the Christian church, and thereby destroys the very significance of the word.[1] W. Bousset, on the other hand, is equally wrong in finding, as in v.25, a contrast between the race in the stadium and the Christian 'race' —"In the contest only one can win the prize; but many hope to win the heavenly prize of victory. Nevertheless all are to run as if only one can receive the prize".[2] The failure to realize that the centre of vv.24f. is not to be found in the picture of the Agon itself but in the idea introduced with the verb ἐγκρατεύεσθαι has also lead A. Ehrhardt to grapple with the same non-existent problem. On the basis of an Orphic fragment he seeks to prove that "Paul was here referring to a popular conception of man's religious task on earth as a struggle before the face of the Godhead, who had himself arranged the contest for him".[3] The Orphic quotation with its plural, κατὰ τῶν ἀγωνιζομένων οἱ στέφανοι, indicates that more than one crown is to be won in this contest. Paul, according to Ehrhardt, avoids the misunderstanding which could arise from the εἷς in v.24, by adding v.25 which replaces τρέχειν with ἀγωνίζεσθαι, thus referring to the popular conception of the Agon.[4] Apart from the

---

[1] "It is the Christian Church that runs, and there is a prize for each one of its number. But the prize is not in all cases the same: God gives to each according to his merit" (cf. Robertson-Plummer, op.cit., p. 194). The συγκοινωνός in v.23 already prevents a misunderstanding of the εἷς!

[2] W. Bousset, Die Paulinischen Briefe (SNT II), Göttingen ³1917, p. 117.

[3] Arnold Ehrhardt, "An unknown Orphic writing in the Demosthenes scholia and St. Paul" (ZNW 1957, pp. 101-110), p. 109.

[4] Ibid. In actual fact the early practice at the games was to offer more than one prize, and where only one was offered, other placings were also acknowledged. In Iliad 23 all competitors receive a prize, naturally of graded value. In the chariot races and dramatic contests in later times it was still honourable to occupy second place (Meier, in Pauly-W. I, cols. 847 and 851). In Agric 121 Philo applies this latter point to the moral Agon. In Lucian

questionability of relating v.25 to the Orphic fragment, there appears here the same error of assigning independent importance to the introductory picture of the Agon, thereby failing to recognize that the tertium comparationis is only to be found in the continuation of v.24.

The purpose of the image in v.24 is the following: Paul, by pointing directly to the example of the runners in the arena[1] who exert all their strength and energy to become the "one", *sets the stage for the theme of* ἐγαράτεια which follows. All the endeavours of the athlete are in vain if he has not trained his body and abstained from all that may in any way harm his physical condition. Consequently (v.25) he is prepared to exercise self-control "in all things" in view of the goal.[2]

In v.25 alone lies the point of comparison.[3] It is only by isolating the two verses that commentators have concluded that the major stress lies on the necessity of the application of the Christian's total strength, of maximum endeavour in the struggle to attain to the heavenly prize.[4] This conclusion is only possible by falsely subordinating the *central* theme of ἐγκράτεια, and by raising the *preparatory* picture of the striving runner and the *complementary* image of the victor's crown to a position of independent importance. Not the thought of maximum exertion but rather the theme of self-restriction (as developed in vv.19-23) dominates in Paul's mind.

Thus πάντα ἐγκρατεύεται in v.25 directly takes up the catchword sounded in vv.12b, 19, and 22bf. and provides an illustration of the

---

Anach. 10ff. we also find the statement that only one gains the prize. However not the one prize but the glory of participation is the main thing.

[1] Certainly not, either in v.24 or 25, to a popular conception of man's religious task on earth as an Agon (against Ehrhardt).

[2] For the concrete details of the role of ἐγκράτεια in preparation for the games, see Bachmann, op.cit., p. 326 note 2, Weiss, op.cit., p. 247, and Eidem, p. 100.

[3] Thus it is not incongruous that the idea of ἐγκράτεια appears after the image of the race itself (Lietzmann-Kümmel, op.cit., ad loc.), since the conditions of the race dictate the necessity of self-discipline. Nor is ἐγκράτεια equated with the race itself—against W. Straub, Die Bildersprache des Apostels Paulus, Tübingen 1937, p. 90.

[4] Thus for Bachmann (op.cit., p. 325) the Agon image shows "wie notwendig energische Anspannung aller Kräfte zu jeder irgend möglichen Leistung auch auf dem Boden des Heilslebens sei". Schlatter, op.cit., p. 284, also sharply separates v.24 from 25 by differentiating between two lessons: persevering endeavour to the end (24), and selfrestriction in view of the goal (25); similarly Héring, op.cit., p. 83.

Apostle's principal: *everything* for the sake of the Gospel—including
the right use of his liberty in the renunciation of his rights. With
the ἐγὼ τοίνυν in v.26 follows the application of the image to his own
person, and therewith the goal of the illustration.

Before examining the application of the image in v.26f. it is
necessary to turn to the difficult phrase in v.24b: οὕτως τρέχετε ἵνα
καταλάβητε. These words, together with the ἡμεῖς in v.25b have
provided the immediate point of departure for understanding the
whole section only as a piece of paraenesis relating to the common
Agon of all believers for the prize of salvation. The verb τρέχετε,
accepted by all as an imperative, threatens to destroy the thesis
that the entire section stands primarily in the service of Paul's
apology of his apostolic freedom of action. It is not merely the
alternating between images which provides the chief problem of the
passage. The main difficulty is posed by the shift between image and
application. The problem is already contained in the change of
persons in the three verses which appear to provide an application—
second person plural (τρέχετε) in v.24b, first person plural (ἡμεῖς)
in v.25b, and finally first person singular (ἐγώ) in v.26f. Here, as
much as anywhere in the letters of Paul, one is called to read between the lines and to fill in the connecting thoughts which Paul,
in his compressed style, flits over or presupposes.[1]

If τρέχετε is understood as an imperative—and no commentator
seems to have considered any other alternative—the connection
between the picture of the Agon and the theme of 'enkrateia', as has
been drawn above, would seem to be impaired, since the image in
v.24 thereby receives an independent significance, while in actual
fact its real purpose is to prepare the way for the following. The
most obvious way out of the problem would be to take the verb as
indicative in form. The meaning would then be: So you are running
in order to receive the prize.[2] Various considerations might seem to

---

[1] Straub (op.cit., p. 90) concludes his analysis of the difficulties of this
whole passage with the words: "So verrät der kurze Abschnitt ein unruhiges
Hin und Her zwischen Bild und Sache, wobei man fast unter dem Eindruck
steht, die Stelle sei unter starker Ermüdung, jedenfalls mit geringer Form-
kraft diktiert worden. In der Eile konnte die Fülle der Gedanken auf knapp
bemessenem Raum nicht mehr ohne störende Unebenheiten in der Wieder-
gabe veranschaulicht werden". These same problems prompt Lietzmann's
judgement on the section, cf. supra p. 83f.

[2] An even smoother reading would be gained if one could understand
τρέχετε as impersonal, i.e. "one runs in such a way that one may win". The

support this interpretation. The verb is also used in the indicative for the Christian's life in faith in Gal 5:7: ἐτρέχετε καλῶς,[1] and there is good reason to assume that Paul could presume a familiarity with this figure of speech from earlier use by himself, both in the Galatian and Corinthian congregations. In the second place the verb which is required in v.25b —where Paul includes himself in the picture[2] — is the indicative ἐγκρατευόμεθα, not an imperative. Finally the unity and smoothness in the progression of thought in the four statements which make up vv.24f., is better preserved with the indicative. Thus οὕτως refers back to the preceding picture[3] of the runner straining for the goal, while the adversative δέ, which is to be emphasised at the beginning of the following sentence, points to the incompleteness of the previous thought in its application. Consequently this short and abrupt phrase has the function of a connecting member in the chain of thought which reaches its goal in the theme of 'enkrateia'.

Even if the indicative tense is preferred—the question must still be left open—it can hardly be denied that these first two verses also includes an injunction. This is quite clear in the case of v.25b where the sense is: If the athlete forgoes all for the glory of a corruptible crown, how much more cause have we to renounce all in view of the incorruptible crown (cf. I Pet 5:4, ἀμαράντινος ... στέφανος) which awaits us.[4] Nevertheless, both the wider context of ch. 9

---

phrase thus understood would complete and complement the foregoing image, not apply it. But this translation poses a grammatical problem since the impersonal or indeterminate use of the verb in the second person is excluded from the present indicative and only found in the subjunctive and optative (signifying potentiality), and future (cf. E. Schwyzer, Griechische Grammatik II, München 1950, p. 244, 3a[b]). Had Paul meant to give the verb impersonal sense, he would have used the third person singular.

[1] Cf. also Rom 9:16.

[2] It is a feature of Paul's writings that he usually includes himself and his readers when speaking of the gifts of salvation through Christ, e.g. Rom 5:1-11, 6:3-11, 8:31-37, Gal 3:13, 23-25, 5:1.

[3] Weiss (op.cit., p. 249 note 3) is probably right in taking οὕτως in the sense of οὖν/itaque. In Paul's writings the adverbial use of οὕτως usually requires a correlative (e.g. καθάπερ, Rom 12:4; καθώς, II Cor 1:5; ὥσπερ, Rom 5:12; and ὡς, as in our passage in vv.26f. This connective use of οὕτως finds immediate parallels in Rom 1:15 and 6:11.

[4] Whereas βραβεῖον purely refers to the prize of the athlete, στέφανος (like βραβεῖον in Phil 3:14) is definitely metaphorical. As noted in the first section of this work, the thought of the prize or crown is subordinated in the purely hellenistic use of the Agon motif (cf. however, Sen. De Prov. 2.3ff. and Epict. III 15.2) but plays an important role in the same motif in the Hellenistic Jewish literature (e.g. Sap 4:2, IV Macc 17:15, Test Job 4, Philo Leg All II

and the culminating application of the principle of 'enkrateia' to Paul's own self and the nature of his mission underscores the fact that the central point of our section does not lie in these first two introductory verses.

Paul commences the appropriation of the athletic metaphor to himself with two images which run parallel to each other in formulation. The first, that of the runner, stresses his consciousness of the goal which determines his actions and conduct. The word ἀδήλως[1] certainly does not mean 'unsure of the goal', whereby Paul would then mean to say: I do not run uncertain of reaching the goal which lies before me.[2] Rather, as the Vulgate rendering 'in incertum' indicates, the meaning is: I do not run as one who has no fixed and certain goal.[3] Not the doubt of attaining to the goal, but rather the high goal itself, determines the manner of Paul's running and his 'enkrateia' (v.27).

Secondly, Paul turns to the picture of the boxer in order to reintroduce the principle of self-restriction and selfnegation, which he then concretely develops in v.27. The problem as to whether the phrase ἀέρα δέρων signifies the failure of the pugilist to make his blows tell or his actions in carrying on the mock contest of a shadow-boxer (σκιαμαχία), cannot be answered by reference to antique parallels. Both uses can be adduced,[4] so that commentators have had to attempt to decide the issue from the context alone. In the first case[5] the emphasis would be on the effectiveness of Paul's efforts to subdue and counter his opponent, in the second,[6] on the earnestness of the task in hand, an earnestness which again is conditioned by the goal. The context at first sight seems to support

---

108 and III 74; also Apoc Baruch 15:8). The nature of the crown is not further qualified as in I Thess 2:19, II Tim 4:8, James 1:12, I Pet 5:4 and Rev. 2:10.

[1] Τρέχειν (οὐκ) ἀδήλως may be a term. tech. (Weiss, ad loc.).

[2] Against Schlatter, op.cit., pp. 285ff.

[3] So already Bengel: "Scio quod petam et quomodo". Eidem, op.cit., p. 99, also prefers the objective 'without clear goal' to the subjective 'with-out certainty of reaching the goal', and emphasis which fits as little into the present context as in Phil 3:14: κατὰ σκοπὸν διώκω. Lietzmann-Kümmel, op. cit., ad loc., refer to Epict. II 15.20 for a similar thought from the diatribe.

[4] Cf. K. L. Schmidt, TWNT VI, pp. 916f., and W. Foerster, TWNT I, p. 165, 27ff., and the commentaries.

[5] Accepted by the majority of interpreters, e.g. Weiss, Eidem, Schlatter, and H. D. Wendland in NTD.

[6] Preferred by Bachmann. Farrar, op.cit., p. 699, also sees a reference to the shodow boxer.

the first interpretation since v.27 contains the—surprising—statement of an opponent. On the other hand the second interpretation better preserves the parallelism between οὐκ ἀδήλως and οὐκ ἀέρα δέρων. The possibility that both ideas are contained in the one phrase is enhanced by a passage in Philo where they also appear combined. Philo compares the man struggling against suffering and fate with the boxer or pancratiast who avoids the blows of the other "and thus compels the opponent to strike into empty air (κατὰ κενοῦ φέρειν τὰς χεῖρας) so that he carries on something like a shadow-fight (σκιαμαχία)".[1]

In v.27 we finally receive an indication of what the necessity of 'enkrateia' means for Paul himself. That the σῶμα is not to be regarded as the opponent in the contest in v.26b is indicated by the sudden change of image. Strictly speaking v.26b pictures the boxer in the course of the bout, while v.27a obviously reintroduces the thought of 'enkrateia' (and thus returns to the theme of the whole section) which belongs to the preparation for the contest. The metaphorical weight of the two verbs ὑπωπιάζω[2] and δουλαγωγῶ is not to be pressed too far. The first word literally means to strike under the eye, thus to beat black and blue, while the second signifies to make a slave or treat as such. The opinion of J. Weiss who takes the two verbs together as an example of a "Hebraizing parallel double-expression" supports the view that the image of the boxer is here left behind.[3] For the verb δουλαγωγεῖν hardly fits into the language of the actual contest. If the two verbs are taken together in the complementory sense of 'mortify and subject',[4] there results the picture of the athlete who does all to discipline himself and to keep his body under rigorous control, in order that it might serve and not hinder his progress to the goal. Despite the view of Weiss and Eidem,[5] Bachmann is quite right in saying: "Davon, dass der

---

[1] Philo, Cher 81.

[2] Ὑπωπιάζω is textually far better attested (Alexandrian tradition and Western text) than ὑποπιάζω = crush down, which would suggest the picture of the wrestler. The second reading was probably inserted later for the harsh and drastic ὑπωπιάζω; cf. the notes of Weiss, p. 249, and Bachmann, p. 327.

[3] J. Weiss, "Beiträge zur paulinischen Rhetorik", in: Theologische Studien, Festschrift für B. Weiss, Göttingen 1897, p. 169.

[4] Cf. Liddell-Scott, s.vs. Bachmann also points to another transferred (and non-athletic) use of ὑπωπιάζω in Aristoph. Pax 541—used of cities 'battered' in war. In Luke 18:5 the word implies 'wear out/harass'.

[5] Their interpretation is all the harder to understand since they agree that the image of v.26 is left behind in v.27.

Leib als Gegner dargestellt wäre, dem der Kampf gilt, ist keine Rede".[1]

If the vv.26 and 27 are thus separated we have a parallel to the development of thought in vv.24ff. The central tertium is not the full application of energy and the development of strength necessary to reach the goal,[2] but rather the necessity of self-renunciation in view of the goal. Verses 24 and 26 are both introductory, both stress the idea of the aim and purpose which dictate the necessity of 'enkrateia'.

We are now in a position to be able to examine the nature of Paul's 'enkrateia' in connection with the meaning of σῶμα. This is in turn only possible if we are clear on the nature of the Apostle's goal. The immediate answer is to see the end of all Paul's endeavour in the final clause μήπως ... ἀδόκιμος γένωμαι. But this phrase itself omits—or silently includes—a thought which is demanded by vv. 19-23. A feature of this section is the repeated final use of expressing the goal of all Paul's missionary endeavours: ἵνα ... κερδήσω (vv.19, 20 and 22), ἵνα ... κερδάνω (v.21), and ἵνα ... σώσω (v.22). The same underlying urgency appears in the negative final clauses: ἵνα μή τινα ἐγκοπὴν δῶμεν τῷ εὐαγγελίῳ (v.12), and εἰς τὸ μὴ καταχρήσασθαι τῇ ἐξουσίᾳ μου ἐν τῷ εὐαγγελίῳ (v.18). Everything he does under the divine 'necessity' which rests upon him is done for the sake of the Gospel. Only then does Paul point to the final significance of this for his own person with the final clause ἵνα συγκοινωνὸς αὐτοῦ γένωμαι (v.23; cf. v.16c).[3]

It is in the service of this all-important goal, the free, unhindered, and therefore effective course of the Gospel, that Paul renounces his apostolic rights. And it is in the same context that v.27 is to be understood. It is therefore completely incorrect to equate the appearance of σῶμα here with σάρξ[4] (cf. σῶμα τῆς ἁμαρτίας, Rom 6:6,

---

[1] Robertson-Plummer, op.cit., ad loc., also state that the body is not the antagonist, but is only subjected in so far as it hinders Paul's progress to the goal. The reference of Strack-Bill. (III p. 405) to Aboth 4:1 with its subjection of the יֵצֶר הָרָע is quite beside the point.

[2] Against Bachmann it must be said that he reads too much into v.26 in seeing an emphasis here on "energische Anspannung ... in bildlicher Form".

[3] It is not only foreign to Paul's thought, but above all far removed from the context to see in the ἵνα (μή πως) γένωμαι of vv.23 and 27 a tone of doubt in the certainty of his own salvation, a thought which then prompts him to use the illustration of the athlete in order to point to the necessity of extreme exertion in striving after the goal of salvation —against Eidem, op.cit., p. 102.

[4] Cf. Bousset, op.cit., p. 117, who finds it characteristic that Paul's own

and σῶμα τῆς σαρκός, Col 2:11), thereby relating Paul's words to the general struggle of the Christian against sin. The significance of δουλαγωγῶ is not to be gained from Rom 6:6 (τοῦ μηκέτι δουλεύειν ... τῇ ἁμαρτίᾳ)[1], but from ἐδούλωσα in v.19. Similarly the word σῶμα equals ἐμαυτόν in v.19.[2] It is comprehensive and all-embracing in that it points to the Apostle's body and everything included in his physical life, his hopes, plans, ambitions, desires, comforts and pleasures—all these are subjected to the one goal, the effectiveness of the Gospel which he preaches. K. H. Rengstorf correctly defines the present use of δουλαγωγῶ, and at the same time aptly summerizes the whole section, when he writes: "Paulus gebraucht das Wort I K 9,27, neben ὑπωπιάζειν, um auszudrucken, dass sein σῶμα mit allem, was das leibliche Leben einschliesst, nachdrucklich und vollkommen seinem Amt untergeordnet ist und ein Recht zur Existenz nur so weit hat, als es ihn bei der Ausrichtung seines Amtes mindestens nicht hindert".[3]

The somewhat harsher term ὑπωπιάζω allows us to think of the physical privations to which Paul subjects his body in the process of labouring for the Gospel. It thus closely corresponds to κολαφιζόμεθα in I Cor 4:11 where the Apostle speaks of the hunger, thirst and nakedness, the hard manual labour necessary to support himself, the derision, slander and persecution which he suffers for the Gospel (cf. also II Cor 4:8f. and 11:23-28). In these words there is no trace of an ascetic mortification of the body, of self-castigation carried out for its own sake. Ἐγκράτεια does not assume the importance of an independent virtue, as in the Stoic diatribe. Nor does it serve a purely self-centred goal,[4] Paul's own salvation, but stands

---

body should appear as the opponent in the boxing contest. (!) "Der Hauptsitz, der Kern der Sünde ist ihm die Sinnlichkeit. Daher Kampf gegen die Sinnlichkeit eine Hauptaufgabe des Christenlebens". But where in the whole passage is there a hint of this?

[1] Against Robertson and Plummer, op.cit., ad loc., Nor is the reference of Weiss (op.cit., p. 248) to the phrase πράξεις τοῦ σώματος θανατοῦν in Rom 8:13 any more to the point.

[2] Cf. R. Bultmann, Theologie des NT, §17 (ET: London 1956, p. 194): "In not a few cases soma can be translated simply "I" (or whatever personal pronoun fits the context); thus I Cor 13:3; 9:27; 7:4, ... or Phil 1:20 ..." cf. the further evidence of K. Grobel, "Σῶμα as 'Self, Person' in the Septuagint", in: Neutest. Studien für Rudolf Bultmann, Berlin ²1957, pp. 52ff.

[3] K. H. Rengstorf, TWNT II, p. 283, 22ff.; see also Schlatter's closing remarks (op.cit., p. 286).

[4] W. Grundmann here deserves to be quoted in full (TWNT II, p. 340, 4ff.): "'Ἐγκράτεια hat hier aber keine asketische Tendenz im Sinn der ver-

in the service of his apostolic commission which places him under the obligation of doing all and renouncing all 'ινα πάντως τινὰς σώσω (v.23).

If the final phrase with μήπως still moves within the same theme it is easier to provide an answer to the question as to whether v.27b contains a continuation of the athletic metaphor in the words κηρύξας and ἀδόκιμος, or whether they are to be understood without any reference to the previous image. According to the first possibility Paul considers himself a herald summoning others to the Agon, and concludes with the thought, it would be terrible if the herald himself did not stand the test of the contest which he has proclaimed.[1] The function of the herald at the great public games was to call out the names of the competitors before the contest and the names of the victors afterwards, but also to proclaim the laws and conditions of the games and the qualifications required from the candidates.[2] The last function can hardly be intended, since ἀδόκιμος,[3] if a metaphor is at all present, must refer to the final outcome of the contest and not to the exclusion from it through lack of qualification. Any competitor could be barred from participation as a slave or criminal, but not through lack of 'enkrateia' (v.27a), which belonged to his personal preparation and not to the laws of the games. Nor can the second function of the herald be implied, for Paul could hardly have allowed himself the bold thought of himself proclaiming the names of the saved at the Judgement. True, Philo frequently uses κηρύσσειν / κήρυγμα in his picture of the moral Agon. He who has won in the 'holy contests' against the opposing vices goes out from them a crowned and proclaimed victor (στεφανωθεὶς ἐκηρύχθη).[4] Noah is crowned as a victorious agonist and celebrated with a κηρύγματι λαμπροτάτῳ when it is said of him that

---

dienstlichen Askese, sondern besagt: um des Zieles willen, dem er zustrebt, um des Auftrags willen, den er hat, um der Aufgabe willen, die er erfüllen muss, enthält er sich aller Dinge, die Ärgernis geben und schaden könnten. Nicht um seinetwillen und um einer Heilsnotwendigkeit willen, sondern um der Brüder willen, vollzieht er das ἐγκρατεύεσθαι''. The central concern of Paul in vv.24-27 is here better reproduced than in all the commentaries!

[1] Thus Bousset, op.cit., p. 117; similarly Farrar, op.cit., p. 699, who translates: "lest perchance, after making proclamation to others, I myself should prove to be a rejected combatant". Bengel, Heinrici (I Kor [KEK], Göttingen ⁷1888), Schmiedel, Bachmann, and Robertson and Plummer, also see here a continuation of the athletic imagery.

[2] Cf. Field, pp. 174f., and G. Friedrich, TWNT III, pp. 684,4ff., 696,34ff.

[3] A 'vocabulum agonisticum' according to Bengel (cf. Philo Cherub 22).

[4] Praem Poen 52; cf. also Agric 112.

he pleased God (Gen 6:9).[1] But in all cases Philo is interested in the κηρυχθείς and not in the κῆρυξ himself.

The only alternative is to take κηρύξας, if metaphorical, as signifying the office of summoning to the contest. But this interpretation poses the difficulty of having to explain how Paul can then speak of himself, the κῆρυξ, as also receiving the prize. The heralds at the games sometime vied amongst themselves in a special contest on the programme,[2] but this fact hardly lies behind Paul's words. The reference to Sueton. Nero 24: "Victorem autem se ipse (sc. Nero) pronunciabat qua de causa et praeconio ubique contendit" (cf. also Demetr. De Elocut. 260), has been rightly rejected as irrelevant to the present question.[3]

Two considerations, Paul's stereotype use of κηρύσσειν and δόκιμος / ἀδόκιμος, and the theological scope of our passage, speak decidedly against the assumption that the athletic metaphor is here continued.[4] The verb κηρύσσειν is used throughout Paul's letters as a terminus technicus designating his own missionary proclamation and that of others. The content of this proclamation varies: "the word of faith" (Rom 10:8 and 14f.), "Christ crucified" (I Cor 1:23), Christ raised from the dead (I Cor 15:11ff.), "Christ Jesus" (II Cor 1:19 and 4:5; ct. Phil 1:15 and Rom 16:25), "Jesus" (II Cor 11:4), "the Gospel" (Gal 2:2, Col 1:23 and I Thess 2:9), and the proclamation of freedom (Gal 5:11; cf. vv.1 and 13). All these formulae may be subsumed under the one heading: Paul 'proclaims' the Gospel of the crucified and risen Christ. Over against this fixed usage it appears impossible that Paul could regard his proclamation as summons and challenge "to moral achievement, discipline and struggle"![5] Parallel with Paul's kerygma there runs a didactic and paraenetic concern, but the kerygma itself, as the preaching of

---

[1] Abr 35; cf. also Spec Leg II 246, Agric 112, Praem Poen 6.

[2] E. N. Gardiner, Greek Athletic Sports and Festivals, London 1910, p. 139, and Friedrich, op.cit., p. 686,13ff.

[3] Cf. Field, ibid, and Eidem, p. 104.

[4] In any case the picture of the contest itself is already left behind in v. 27a. It is even unlikely that we here have a "sleeping metaphor" (Eidem, p. 105). The office of the herald in antiquity extended far beyond his activities at the games.

[5] Weiss, op.cit., p. 249: "Paulus habe dies Wort (sc. κηρύξας) gewählt, weil es zugleich an seine missionarische Verkündigung mit ihren mannigfaltigen Aufforderungen zu sittlicher Leistung, Zucht und Kampf erinnerte". Cf. also Robertson and Plummer, ad loc.: "Paul not only summons men to the good ἀγών. He also is a competitor".

divine grace in Jesus the Christ, is not to be confused with a summons to a moral Agon. This would be to convert Paul into one of the numerous itinerant morality-preachers of his day.[1] In any case, as we have seen, v.26f. deals with Paul's own Agon and his own selfrenunciation in the service of the Gospel, not with an ethical struggle common to all believers.

If a conscious metaphor is missing in the word κηρύξας the same must apply to the following ἀδόκιμος. This conclusion is further supported by the theological use of this term, and δόκιμος, elsewhere in Paul. Without reference to a concrete image these words suggest the motif of divine testing and the necessity of steadfast and faithful probation under trial, both always seen in connection with the thought of divine judgment and the necessity of rendering account.[2] This is best seen in II Cor 13:5ff. But the specific thought which underlies ἀδόκιμος here in v.27b, the necessity of Paul having to give account of his own stewardship of the Gospel with which he has been entrusted, is best understood in connection with I Thess 2:4: δεδοκιμάσμεθα ὑπὸ τοῦ θεοῦ πιστευθῆναι τὸ εὐαγγέλιον. Paul's fear is that, having once been found δόκιμος to proclaim the Gospel, he might nevertheless be found ἀδόκιμος at the Judgment through failure to carry out his commission as expected of him. Thus the δοκιμή of Paul in I Cor 9:27 is not identical with that in which all believers have to prove themselves.[3] The thought of this last clause is not: lest I myself should fail the test into which I have summoned others, but rather: lest even though I have proclaimed the Gospel to others, I should nevertheless be rejected. The emphasis lies on the great claims which the Gospel makes on his own person, and is therefore not to be reduced to the weak and general aphorism: "Practise what you preach".[4]

---

[1] Field's grammatical observation (ibid) is also to the point. Had Paul meant to retain the athletic image we would rather expect ἄλλους κηρύξας instead of ἄλλοις κηρύξας.

[2] Cf. W. Grundmann, TWNT II, pp. 26off., for the twin ideas of "Prüfung" and "Bewährung" contained in these words.

[3] This is not the sense of the contrast between ἄλλοις and αὐτός.—It may here already be noted that I Thess 2:4 stands immediately after the mention of Paul's Agon for the Gospel. But a conscious athletic metaphor is not to be pressed into this word, nor into the following δεδοκιμάσμεθα. The situation may be otherwise in Jam 1:12 where the occurrence of δόκιμος in connection with the following στέφανος may well call into mind the athletic image (cf. however, Dibelius, Jakobusbrief [KEK]. Göttingen ¹⁰1959, p. 86).

[4] The antique parallels here adduced by Schlatter and Weiss ad loc., are

On the basis of the above analysis of I Cor 9:24-27 an answer can now be given to *the problem* which the passage poses. Do these verses serve a primarily *paraenetic purpose, or* do they still stand within the framework of the Apostle's *self-apology* in the earlier verses of ch.9? The answer given by the commentaries and most of the references to this passage is almost unaminously the following: Paul here presents himself merely as a "Spezialfall" in order to illustrate a paraenetic concern expressed in vv.24f. "Der ganze Abschnitt ist nicht um seinetwillen geschrieben, sondern um jener Ermahnung willen".[1] According to Eidem, Paul presents himself as a type of the man who is conscious of the goal and who trains for the spiritual race. Underlying the whole section is the silent exhortation μιμηταί μου γίνεσθε.[2] Again, the Apostle points to himself and his own behaviour as a model and example for the ethical struggle of the Christian.[3]

Not only the wider context, but also the relevant verses themselves, forbid the above generalisations. Paul is not concerned with impressing on his readers the necessity of a Christian moral Agon. Rather, his *immediate concern is to defend his apostolic actions* and the principle of self-negation demanded by his special office. In this sense it is completely impossible to equate the Agon of Paul with that of every believer by seeing in the Apostle a particular instance of a general rule.[4] The point may be clarified by once more stating the relationship between vv.24f. and vv.26f. The first two verses have a preparatory or introductory function leading up to the theme of 'enkrateia'. The underlying thought is: the goal dictates the necessity of renouncing all that may hinder progress to it. The final two verses do not offer a further illustration of this general rule as

consequently irrelevant. The thought uppermost in Paul's mind is not his own relationship to the message of the Gospel, but rather the consequences of his indebtedness to preach it.

[1] J. Weiss, op.cit., p. 248.

[2] Eidem, pp. 102f.

[3] Heinrici, op.cit., p. 266: "Paulus stellt seine eigene ethische Kampfweise (als Läufer und Ringer) den Lesern als Muster hin"; similarly Bousset, op. cit., p. 117. Schlatter and Wendland (in NTD) also stress Paul's character as "Vorbild", but fortunately without emphasising a common moral contest, i.e. keeping in mind Paul's unique situation.

[4] Nor is the statement of goal in vv.25 and 27 immediately parallel since the final μήπως clause includes, as we have seen, two thoughts which are inseperable for Paul —the faithful enactment of his ministry and his personal salvation.

it applies to the life of every Christian, but rather provide an application to the concrete situation of Paul as an Apostle: If self-
renunciation is necessary for the athlete, so also for the believer who
is running towards the incorruptible crown. But how much more
does this not apply to him who has been entrusted with the commission to proclaim the Gospel? Seen in this light vv.24f. do not
receive an independent paraenetic weight,[1] but serve the climax of
the entire passage and chapter, vv.26f.—not vice versa.

The phrase 'independent paraenetic weight' has been deliberately
used. Thereby it is already admitted that the entire section has a
decidedly *monitory emphasis*. The primary motive for the use of the
image is determined by the context of ch.9, the self-apology of the
Apostle, but this chapter itself stands within the context of the
question of eating meat offered to idols (8:1ff.). In this question the
guiding lines which are laid down are those of Christian liberty
together with the application of the law of love—ἵνα μὴ τὸν ἀδελφόν
μου σκανδαλίσω (8:13). Paul then points to his own apostolic ministry as a parallel—but not identical—situation, which is also
characterised by freedom on the one hand, but the necessity of self-
renunciation (here the concrete matter of the support of the congregation) on the other —ἵνα μή τινα ἐγκοπὴν δῶμεν (9:12). The
concrete situation is in both instances not the same, the immediate
goal is not identical,[2] the Agon of Paul is not that of every Christian;
but the eventual necessity for *restriction of personal liberty* is a rule
which applies in both cases.[3] Here one can speak of Paul as an example, not in reference to a common Christian moral Agon. Thus
simply to see in the passage a general characterisation of the
Christian life as an Agon is to miss the point and purpose of Paul's
use of the image. Verse 25 certainly pictures the believers as in a
race. This thought will have to be further considered (cf. Part B
ch. II infra). But for the present it must be stressed that this verse
does not provide the key to the whole passage.

---

[1] This would not even be the case if τρέχετε were still to be taken as an
imperative (a possibility which cannot be completely ruled out). We would,
however, then be entitled to see in the word a further trace of traditional
form behind the passage.

[2] Wendland, op.cit., ad loc., thus distinguishes between the "eschatalo-
gisches Ziel" and the "rechte Zurüstung zum apostolischen Dienst"!

[3] If this, and not maximum exertion, is the point of Paul's words, the
problem of work-righteousness does not even arise.

2. "LEST I RUN OR HAVE RUN IN VAIN"

Two features of I Cor 9:24-27, the characterisation of the Apostle's work as a 'running' together with the final clause, find a parallel in Gal 2:2: μή πως εἰς κενὸν τρέχω ἢ ἔδραμον, which again corresponds to Phil 2:16: ὅτι οὐκ εἰς κενὸν ἔδραμον οὐδὲ εἰς κενὸν ἐκοπίασα. These external similarities justify the question whether the relationship between the three passages is not even deeper, whether further lines of connection can be traced in order to gain a fuller picture of the Apostle's Agon.

It can hardly be doubted—setting aside for the moment the question of the exact weight of κοπιᾶν in Phil 2:16—that the verb τρέχειν in both instances is meant to recall the picture of the athletic runner, and is consequently to be understood as a conscious metaphor. The fuller development of the image in I Cor 9:24ff. together with the recurrence of the metaphorical use of the word in Rom 9:16 and Gal 5:7,[1] and already the repetition of the verb in Gal 2:2, suggest that Paul had a concrete image in mind which he did not need to develop further. The one word sufficed to imply the image and its point. It is true that τρέχειν is frequently used in a pale figurative sense in Greek literature,[2] also in the LXX,[3] without reference to the games. On the other hand it has been shown that the picture of the runner is also used to illustrate the Agon of the sage in the diatribe and in Philo,[4] possibly also in IV Macc 14:5, so that we may assume that the language of popular moral philosophy again shimmers through at this point.[5]

The double occurrence of the phrase εἰς κενὸν τρέχειν may well indicate that the expression represents a standard phrase. Although the relatively frequent εἰς κενόν[6] does not make the verb any more

---

[1] Cf. also II Thess 3:1, Phil 3:14 (διώκειν), II Tim 4:7 = Acts 20:24 (δρόμος). The image is clearest in Hebr 12:1.

[2] Cf. Liddell-Scott, s.v.

[3] Cf. above pp.49ff.

[4] Cf. above pp. 31 and 40 with note 6.

[5] It is impossible to say whether the quotation of Phil 2:16 in Pol Phil 9:2 is taken as an Agon metaphor. This certainly is the case in the apocryphal Passio Pauli XII, where the phrase is combined with II Tim 4:8: "nunc autem non in vacuum cucurri per multas passiones, nec sine causa patior nam restat mihi corona iustitiae, quam reddet mihi cui credidi ..." (Bonn.-Lip. I, p. 37).

[6] Equal to the classical διὰ κενῆς. The phrase occurs also in II Cor 6:1 and I Thess 3:5, in the LXX in Lev 26:20, Job 39:16, Mic 1:14, Hab 2:3, Is 29:8,

concrete,[1] it certainly fits well into the picture of the runner and his eventual success or failure in the race.

However, the similarity in theological thought which underlies I Cor 9:26ff., Gal 2:2 and Phil 2:16, provides the decisive argument for establishing the metaphorical weight of τρέχειν in the last two passages. In each case Paul appears as the ἀγωνιστής of the Gospel, and in each case the thought of the goal is uppermost in his mind, together with the thought of his possible failure to reach the goal.

This is especially clear in *Gal* 2:2 where the activity circumscribed by τρέχειν is to be understood on the basis of the preceding phrase τὸ εὐαγγέλιον ... κηρύσσω. The context of the passage is as follows. Paul's work in the Galatian congregations is threatened with disruption through the work of legalists who in particular maintain that circumcision (5:2f., 6:12f.) and the observation of cultic times and seasons (4:10)[2] is still necessary for salvation. With particularly this question of circumcision in mind (2:3-5), Paul stresses the unity of the Kerygma which he preaches to the heathen with that which the authorities in Jerusalem proclaim. He relates how he went up to Jerusalem under divine revelation to present his Gospel for scrutiny and recognition, with the result that his mission to the uncircumcised received the full acknowledgement of the other leading Apostles (vv.6ff.).

The short account of the journey to the mother congregation is concluded with the μήπως clause. It is at this point that the exegetical difficulties set in. Is this a final clause, an indirect question, or an expression of implied apprehension? Commentators are agreed[3] that the interpretation of the clause as final in construction is excluded by the indicative tense of ἔδραμον, since the past indicative only stands in final clauses when a hypothetical assumption

---

45:18, 65:23, Jer 6:29, 18:15, 26(46):11, 28(51):58, and in Josephus Bell 1.275 and Ant 19.27 and 96 (also εἰς τὸ κενόν Job 2:9 and εἰς κενά Job 20:18). —The connection with τρέχειν also in Menander Mon. 51: ἀνὴρ ἄβουλος εἰς κενὸν μοχθεῖ τρέχων.

[1] Eidem, p. 140.

[2] Cf. H. Schlier, Der Brief an die Galater (KEK), Göttingen [12]1962, pp. 19ff., and A. Oepke, Der Brief des Paulus an die Galater, (ThHK), Berlin [3]1957, pp. 9f.

[3] For the fuller discussion of this question see Oepke and Schlier, op.cit., F. Sieffert, Galaterbrief (KEK), Göttingen [9]1899, pp. 89ff., T. Zahn, Galaterbrief (KNT), Leipzig [3]1922, pp. 83f., and E. de Witt Burton, Galatians (ICC), London [5]1956, pp. 73ff.

is expressed—here clearly not the case. The second possibility taking μή πως as introducing an indirect question expecting a negative answer, and dependent on ἀνεθέμην, is adopted by Sieffert, Zahn and Oepke,[1] but weakens the effect of Paul's words: I submitted my Gospel to decide the question whether I might be running or had run in vain. These scholars fail to produce conclusive references for the use of μή πως in this construction, since the usual proof from I Thess 3:5 is by no means persuasive, but rather speaks, together with Gal 4:11, for the third and usually accepted understanding which sees in the clause an expression of apprehension after an implied verb of fearing, with the same moods and tenses as used with φοβεῖσθαι.[2] The present subjunctive τρέχω then expresses the fear of continuous fruitless effort into the future, while the indicative ἔδραμον is used since "the fact of having run in the past is no longer dependent on the will of him who fears".[3] The objection of Sieffert and Oepke that this interpretation introduces a false subjective note into Paul's words, rests on an incorrect understanding of the concern which prompted the Apostle's actions (the μήπως clause refers both to ἀνέβην and ἀνεθέμην, and not only to the second verb). He does not express his misgiving as to the legitimacy or soundness of his Gospel.[4] On the contrary, he goes up to Jerusalem certain of the fact that the Gospel which he has received not from man but by divine revelation (1:1 and 12) is the only Gospel possible (1:8f.).[5] The purpose of his journey is to establish and preserve the unity of this one Gospel and the one Church composed of Jews and Gentiles, lest a schism should occur and the fruits of his labour be

---

[1] Zahn, op.cit., and BAG, s.v.

[2] Thus J. B. Lightfoot, St. Paul's Epistle to the Galatians, London [11]1890, H. Lietzmann, An die Galater (HNT), Tübingen [3]1932, and Burton and Schlier, op.cit.

[3] Cf. Schlier, op.cit., p. 67, and Blass-D., §370.2 who also includes Gal 4:11 (μή πως κεκοπίακα) and I Thess 3:5 (μήπως ἐπείρασεν) under this grammatical rule.

[4] Sieffert, op.cit., p. 91, is himself guilty of a subjective interpretation of Paul's fears. For him the Apostle was concerned lest "seine Verkündigung für den beabsichtigten Heilserfolg nicht ausreichend wäre, sondern, um diesen zu haben, durch die Forderung der Beschneidung ergänzt werden müsste". Paul may have feared a decision against his Gospel, but never its incompleteness.

[5] "His concern was not that his Gospel to the Gentiles should conform to the requirements of the Jerus. authorities, but that they should understand and agree with him in his interpretation of the Gospel" (G. S. Duncan, Epistle of Paul to the Galatians [MNTC], London 1955, ad loc.).

destroyed by the clash between two conflicting Gospels. "His fear is grounded not on a doubt of the truth of his Gospel, rather the conviction that the disapproval of his work by the leading Apostles would seriously interfere" with his running, his labour.[1]

That Paul's fear lest he should be running in vain is related to his entire apostolic work is further evident in *Phil* 2:16 where the verb τρέχειν[2] is paralleled or complemented by the verb κοπιᾶν. In a short study A. von Harnack has shown that Paul favours the word-group κόπος / κοπιᾶν to express his own strenuous missionary labours and those of others in the Christian congregation.[3] The striking fact that the verb appears three times in the NT in connection with an athletic term (with ἀγωνίζεσθαι in Col 1:29 and I Tim 4:10) has led Lightfoot to see in κοπιᾶν a continuation of the Agon metaphor, signifying the labour which is spent in training for the race.[4] Four considerations serve to disprove this theory. 1. Our linguistic examinations have clearly shown that πόνος / πονεῖν, and not κόπος / κοπιᾶν, serve as technical terms for the labours of the athlete—and sage—whether in training or in the course of the contest itself. Harnack is right in noting this colouring of πόνος in I Clem 5:4, and in concluding that Paul avoided the word for the very reason that it had this profane ring.[5] 2. Further, Harnack has taken up the thoughts of A. Deissmann[6] in seeing in Paul's use of κοπιᾶν a reminiscence of his hard manual work at his trade as a tent maker. It is on this background that the Apostle introduced the word into the Christian vocabulary "für die Missions- und Gemeindearbeit im Hinblick auf die schwere Handarbeit, die er leistete und die ihm

---

[1] Burton, op.cit., p. 72.

[2] J. J. Wettstein, Novum Testamentum Graecum II, Amsterdam 1752, p. 272, strangely applies the word to Paul's long journey to reach Philippi: longum iter Hierosolymis per totam Macedoniam.

[3] A. von Harnack, "Κόπος (κοπιᾶν, οἱ κοπιῶντες) im frühchristlichen Sprachgebrauch", ZNW 27 (1928), pp. 1ff.; cf. also F. Hauck, TWNT IV, pp. 827ff.

[4] J. B. Lightfoot, St. Paul's Epistle to the Philippians, London 1910, p. 118. The author further refers to Ign Pol 6:1: συγκοπιᾶτε ἀλλήλοις, συναθλεῖτε, συντρέχετε, and to Anthol. Pal. III, p. 166, ed. Dübner (cf. BAG, τρέχω 2a): μὴ τρέχε, μὴ κοπία. A further parallel is offered in II Clem 7:1: ἀλλ'οὐ πάντες στεφανοῦνται, εἰ μὴ οἱ πολλὰ κοπιάσαντες καὶ καλῶς ἀγωνισάμενοι (cf. the same author, The Apostolic Fathers II, London ²1889, p. 351, on Ign Pol 6:1).

[5] Harnack, op.cit., p. 4. In Paul's letters the word is only found as a textual variant to Col 4:13.

[6] Licht vom Osten, pp. 265f. (ET: Light from the Ancient East, pp. 316f.).

mit seinem Missionswerk sozusagen zusammenfloss".[1] 3. The connection of κοπιᾶν with the athletic image in Phil 2:16, Col 1:29, I Tim 4:10, Ign Pol 6:2 and II Clem 7:1, is therefore certainly secondary (the connection in the last passage could also be conditioned by the NT passages). 4. Finally—a point which Harnack fails to give due attention—it is also possible that Paul's use of κοπιᾶν, especially in connection with the phrase εἰς κενόν, is influenced by septuagintal language. The phrase appears, admittedly in a completely different sense, three times in LXX Job,[2] but is even more relevant in Is 49:4 where the Ebed Jahweh says: κενῶς ἐκοπίασα καὶ εἰς μάταιον καὶ εἰς οὐδὲν ἔδωκα τὴν ἰσχύν μου, and in 65:23 where the eschatological blessings of Israel are promised: οἱ δὲ ἐκλεκτοί μου οὐ κοπιάσουσιν εἰς κενὸν οὐδὲ τεκνοποιήσουσιν εἰς κατάραν.[3]

Whether we are to see in Paul's use of κοπιᾶν a reminder of his manual labours or a reflection of the LXX is finally unimportant for our purposes.[4] Both explanations exclude the possibility of seeing in the word in Phil 2:16 a continuation of the athletic metaphor begun with τρέχειν—the second verb explains the meaning of the first so that τρέχειν, like κοπιᾶν, becomes a comprehensive term for the entire missionary labours of the Apostle. The term suggests, however, more than mere labour or effort, since the thought of the goal is always prominent.

Phil 2:16 follows a short paraenetic section (vv.12ff.) which concludes with the summons to the Philippians to shine as lights in

---

[1] Harnack, op.cit., p. 5. The original use of the word is then best seen in I Cor 4:12 (cf. also Eph 4:28).

[2] Job 2:9 = Test Job 24 (of child-bearing), 39:16 (of the ostrich laying her eggs in the sand), and 20:18 (of the rich man). —The combination of τρέχειν and κοπιᾶν in Prov 4:12 and Is 40:31 is here irrelevant since the sense is in both cases far removed from Paul's metaphorical use.

[3] Cf. also LXX Jer 28(51):58: οὐ κοπιάσουσι λαοὶ εἰς κενόν, Is 30:5: μάτην κοπιάσουσι, and Ps 126(127):1: εἰς μάτην ἐκοπίασαν (cf. Herm Sim IV 4:8). The phrase 'to labour in vain' is also found in the Rabbinical writings; cf. Strack-Bill. III, p. 220, note 1.

[4] It must be said that Deissmann carries his thesis too far, i.e. on the colouring of κοπιᾶν, when he writes: "The frequent references to 'labour in vain' are a trembling echo of the discouragement resulting from a width of cloth being rejected as badly woven and therefore not paid for" (op.cit., p. 266, ET: p. 316). Similarly Harnack (op.cit., p. 5): just as the worker's life depends on reward or wages so as not to have toiled in vain, so also for the Apostle this striving and care is the chief thing. On the day of judgment he must show profit and as a persecutor show in addition an "überschüssige Leistung als καύχημα".

the world, holding fast to the Word of life. Verse 16 expresses the consequences of their faithfulness or lack of faithfulness for Paul's own person. If he is able to present his congregations blameless before the judgment seat of Christ he may glory in the fact that he has not run or laboured in vain. This καύχημα is not a boasting in meritorious effort but the sign of the completion of a divinely assigned commission.[1] Not his rigorous labours, but rather the faithfulness of the Philippians is the cause of his boasting (cf. also II Cor 1:14: "We are your cause for boasting as you are also ours in the day of the Lord", and 7:4). That the *Gospel* has borne fruit through him will be his pride at the return of Christ, but only this day will reveal whether *his work* for the Gospel has been in vain or effectual (I Cor 3:10-15).[2] Since Paul is certain of the effectiveness of the Gospel itself, it is only a falling away from the "Word of life" that will rob him of his pride, forcing him to stand before the Judge with empty hands.

Once the connection is seen between Paul's use of τρέχειν as a picture of his apostolic work and the accompanying thought of the final day on which he will have to render account of his commission, it appears possible that the use of στέφανος in two passages complements the picture of Paul as a runner of the Gospel. In *Phil* 4:1 the readers are addressed as his χαρὰ καὶ στέφανος, and in *I Thess* 2:19 as his χαρὰ ἢ στέφανος καυχήσεως (as his δόξα and χαρά in v.20). A. Deissmann has concluded from the explicit reference to the παρουσία of the Lord in the second passage that the picture of the crown is to be understood on the background of the custom of presenting the sovereign with a golden crown at his παρουσία (as a technical expression in the East for the arrival or visit of the king or emperor).[3] This explanation is quite inapplicable since, as Deissmann himself observes, the gift of the crown was made to the ruler himself, whereas Paul claims the faithful as his own crown on the day of the Lord. E. Lohmeyer emphasises the use of the image

---

[1] E. Lohmeyer, Der Brief an die Philipper (KEK), Göttingen [12]1961, p. 110. Similarly Bultmann, TWNT III, pp. 650ff. "Er soll seine Leistung an der ihm gestellten Aufgabe messen" (p. 651).

[2] Here the aorists ἔδραμον and ἐκοπίασα are spoken from the standpoint of the 'day of Christ'.

[3] Deissmann, op.cit., p. 315, ET: p. 373, with reference to I Thess 2:19. For this custom see further U. Wilckens, Griechische Ostraka aus Aegypten und Nubien, Leipzig 1899, pp. 295-302 (in the LXX in I Macc 10:29, 11:35, 13:27 and 39, II Macc 14:4).

of the crown in connection with martyrdom, as in the Apocalypse and the early Christian martyr acts.[1] This explanation—reflecting the writer's understanding of the entire epistle to the Philippians as conditioned by the predominating thought of martyrdom—is also artificial since Paul's στέφανος as the symbol of his joy and pride is not the reward of martyrdom, but of his apostolic work. Any reference to the crown of the Mysteries is for the same reason out of place.[2]

More certain is the influence of the LXX in these two passages. A similar thought is found in Prov 12:4, 16:31 and 17:6 (a wife, old age, and children as a man's crown), and the phrase στέφανος καυχήσεως in I Thess 2:19 also appears in Prov 16:31, Ez 16:12 and 23:42.[3] However the *picture of the crown in the NT is always prospective* and not retrospective, seen more as a promise and possession of the future than as a present reality.[4] This point is quite clear in I Cor 9:24f., and also in II Tim 4:8 where the Agon image is explicitly developed, but also applies to the two present passages. In this respect Gal 2:2 and Phil 2:16 are again significant since they indicate the same double characteristic. In both instances Paul is able to declare in the present situation that his 'running' has as yet not been in vain, the criterion for this judgment being on the one hand the fact that his 'free' Gospel has not been nullified by the binding introduction of the Law, and on the other hand the clear

---

[1] Lohmeyer, op.cit., p. 164. The concrete image suggested by the crown in Rev is difficult to ascertain. G. Hirschfeld also here would like to see a reference to the agonal wreath ("Νίκη τοῦ δεῖνος", in Philologus 50, Göttingen 1891, pp. 43off.). He points to two late inscriptions from Asia Minor which he suspects to be of Christian origin, and which depict victory (probably in martyrdom) with palm fronds and crowns and, in one case, also a goal post (cf. Phil 3:14 σκοπός). But this reference is too uncertain to allow a definite conclusion.

[2] R. Reitzenstein, op.cit., pp. 42ff. The use of the image is interesting in the Odes of Sol 1, 5:12, 9:8f. and 17:1 (cf. J. Rendell Harris, The Odes and Psalms of Solomon, Cambridge ²1911, p. 23 and 90, and Harris and A. Mingana, The Odes and Psalms of Solomon II, Manchester 1920, p. 207). Here the OT image of Jahweh as the crown of Israel (Is 28:5) and the role of the crown in the mysteries appears to be united; cf. e.g. Apul. Metam. XI 24, the mystic appears as 'sol invictus' with a crown, and Tert. De Cor. 15, the 'miles' of Mithra says "Mithras is my crown".

[3] The variant reading (A and Tert.) ἀγαλλιάσεως is best explained on the basis of στέφανος ἀγαλλιάματος in Sir 1:11, 6:31, 15:6.

[4] Harris and Mignana, op.cit., p. 209. This applies also to Jam 1:12, I Pet 5:4 and Rev 2:10. According to these authors the NT crown is to be understood as the 'corona militis'.

proof of the faith of the believers he has won. But the final judgment on his work will only be given on the day of the Lord.[1] This twofold emphasis can also be noted in the metonymical use of στέφανος in Phil 4:1 and I Thess 2:19. Through their faith the Apostle's converts are already a source of honour and joy for him, just as they in turn can glory in Paul (II Cor 1:14). But by their continual faithfulness they ensure for him a crown on the day when the final word will be spoken on his apostolic work (cf. especially ἐλπίς and παρουσία in the second passage). The present includes the futuristic sense of the words.[2]

In view of the many spheres of religious, social, political and military life in which crowns, wreaths and garlands were used in antiquity[3] it is impossible to ascertain with certainty the exact colouring of στέφανος here. The frequency of the athletic image in Paul, plus the applicability of the picture of the victor's crown to that of Paul himself as a runner for the Gospel, can only suggest a reference to the ἀγῶνες στεφανῖται as possible, if not probable.[4] Nothing in the immediate context allows us to say more. It is doubtful whether one may legitimately take ἐγκόπτειν in I Thess 2:18 as a term from the games, as does G. Stählin.[5] Further, the occurrence of συναθλεῖν in Phil 4:3 can hardly be related to the image of the crown in v.1. On the other hand it is wrong to question a relationship between Paul's use of τρέχειν as a designation of his own work and the pale use of στέφανος, by contending with E. Eidem that, even when Paul compares himself with an agonist he does not think of the congregations as his crown of victory, but rather of his personal participation in salvation as the beckoning prize.[6] This

---

[1] Schlier, op.cit., R. Bring, Commentary on Galatians, ET: Philadelphia 1961, and R. Bultmann TWNT III, p. 652, are therefore right in referring also Gal 2:2 to the parousia.

[2] Eidem, pp. 128ff., also Vincent, Philippians (ICC), on Phil 4:1.

[3] A summary of all these in W. Grundmann, TWNT VII, "Verwendung des Kranzes", pp. 617-622.

[4] Eidem, p. 129, grants that the pale use of στέφανος in connection with the parousia may have taken on concrete features for Paul and therefore regained its agonal colouring. Conybeare and Howson, The Life and Epistles of St. Paul II, London 1852f., p. 204, express themselves less cautiously: Both passages refer to "the Joy and exultation of the victor … This subject illustrates the frequent use of καύχησις by St. Paul". A. Oepke and G. Heinzelmann (NTD) also see in I Thess 2:19 and Phil 4:1 respectively a reference to the victor's crown; also M-M, s. στέφανος.

[5] G. Stählin, TWNT III, p. 855, 14ff.

[6] Eidem, p. 131 together with note 4. Nor is J. E. Frame (Thessalonians,

applies neither to Gal 2:2 nor to Phil 2:16, nor does it character-
ise the picture of the crown in I Cor 9:24f. In every case the Apostle's own personal position before the divine Judge is inseparably
united with the judgment which will fall on his apostolic labour.
The picture of the Agon in the Pastoral Epistles provides no
exception, as we shall see.[1] The image and the accompanying
thought of the crown, whether applied to Paul himself or to Timothy, is also to be understood as referring to the Agon for the Gospel. The evangelist's personal share in the blessings which the Gospel proclaims is inseparably connected with his obligation to preach
the same.

With the last observation a basic point of contact between I Cor
9:24f., Gal 2:2 and Phil 2:16 is indicated. The customary interpretation of τρέχειν has seen in the verb little more than an emphasis
on the necessity for strenuous effort and exertion.[2] This emphasis
is certainly strong, as proved by the appositional κοπιᾶν. For this
reason it is unlikely that Paul's use of τρέχειν is primarily influenced
by the LXX's use of the word for the activity of the courier or of
the prophet, as in Jer 23:21: οὐκ ἀπέστελλον τοὺς προφήτας καὶ αὐτοὶ
ἔτρεχον (cf. also Hab 2:2 and Is 52:7). The negative sense of this
sentence in Jeremiah makes a direct reference to it in the words of
Paul unlikely, despite the temptation to draw an analogy between
ἀποστέλλειν and Paul's own title of ἀπόστολος.

However the significance of the verb is not exhausted with the
one observation, the stress on exertion and toil. All three passages
clearly illustrate the goal of Paul's running, testifying to the fear
which continually accompanied Paul's toil, the fear that his running
might be in vain despite all his toil. In the first case it is his own
person and his own interests which may impede the Gospel, in the
second the threat of the introduction of the Law as the condition
for salvation, and in the third the possibility of unfaithfulness on
the part of the Philippians. If in each case Paul can still his fears,
this is not indicative of his trust in the independent efficacy of his
own exertions on behalf of the Gospel, but rather an expression of

---

ICC) correct in assigning the crown to the Thessalonians: "As he looks
forward to the day of Christ, when the Christian race is over, and the Thessalonians receive the triumphant wreath, he sees in them his hope and joy and
in their victory his ground for boasting".

[1] For the detailed discussion of the Pastorals see infra.
[2] Schmid, pp. 32 and 49, and Eidem, p. 140.

confidence in the effectiveness of the divine grace operative in his apostleship.[1]

Because the picture of the runner always stresses the connection between present effort and future results, the thought of the goal is immediately suggested—and also underlies the qualifying εἰς κενόν. But the goal is not to be confused or identified with the reward. *The immediate goal is always the unhindered effectiveness of the Word*.[2] Only in respect to the divine approbation of the Apostle's efforts towards this end does the thought of reward appear, that is, only in connection with his faithfulness to his commission.

A word on the use of τρέχειν in II Thess 3:1 may be briefly added as an appendix to this chapter. Here the Word itself is personified as a runner: προσεύχεσθε ... ἵνα ὁ λόγος τοῦ κυρίου τρέχῃ καὶ δοξάζηται. Apart from the difficulty of imagining the picture suggested if a conscious athletic metaphor is meant,[3] a reference to Ps 147:4(15) here suffices to explain the pale image—ὁ ἀποστέλλων τὸ λόγιον αὐτοῦ τῇ γῇ, ἕως τάχους δραμεῖται ὁ λόγος αὐτοῦ. The same image and thought is found in Philo, Mut Nom 42: κοῦφον γὰρ ὁ λόγος καὶ πτηνὸν φύσει, βέλους θᾶττον φερόμενος καὶ πάντῃ διᾴττων, and is applied to Wisdom in Sap 7:24: πάσης γὰρ κινήσεως κινητικώτερον σοφία, διήκει δὲ καὶ χωρεῖ διὰ πάντων διὰ τὴν καθαρότητα.[4] Irrespective of the question of authorship, II Thess 3:1 provides a parallel to Paul's words with τρέχειν expressing his dominating concern for the free course of the Gospel. The tertium is here the swift progress of the Word—if an image is intended it is that of the herald in his urgency.

---

[1] Cf. A. Oepke, TWNT III, p. 660, in connection with Paul's use of κενός with reference to his own work: "Aus allen diesen Stellen spricht ein starkes Verantwortungsbewusstsein gegenüber der Grösse der göttlichen Gabe und der durch sie gesetzten Aufgabe, aber ein noch stärkeres Vertrauen zu der Gnadenmacht Gottes, die normalerweise den Erfolg verbürgt".

[2] How greatly this concern overrides all else is reflected also in Phil 1:12 —even his sufferings and imprisonment serve the προκοπή of the Gospel.

[3] This is assumed by J. S. Howson, The Metaphors of St. Paul, London ³1883, p. 139, and J. E. Frame, Thessalonians (ICC), Edinburgh, pp. 290f.

[4] Cf. Harris, op.cit., p. 96 with reference to Ode 12:5: "For the swiftness of the Word is inexpressible, and like its expression is its swiftness and force". A similar personification of the Word in its progress in Ps 18(19):5 (Rom 10:18) and in Is 55:11 (Acts 12:24). Possibly Bengel had Ps 147 or Is 52:7 in mind when he related the running of Paul in Gal 2:2 to that of the Gospel: cum celeri victoria evangelii (ad Gal 2:2).

3. Contending for the Faith – the Pale Athletic Termini

The isolated occurrences of terms in Rom 15:30, Phil 1:27-30, 4:3, Col 1:29-2:1, 4:12f., and I Thess 2:2, pose the following two questions. 1. What is their metaphorical character, and 2. how do they fit into the picture of the Agon as sketched up to this point?

In every instance there is a comparative lack of evidence for the assumption of a conscious athletic metaphor. Thus the use of the relative terms in a pale transferred sense denoting intense striving, struggle, or conflict, as already noted in both secular and septuagintal Greek, must be taken into account. This also applies to the cases where there occurs a reduplication of Agon termini as in Phil 1:27-30, Col 1:29-2:1 and possibly Col 4:12f. (πόνος!). On the other hand the frequency of these terms, though variating, already speaks against the assumption of a completely colourless and unrelated use.

An immediate link with the findings of the last chapter is found in *Col* 1:29-2:1. Here it is the verb ἀγωνίζεσθαι which accompanies κοπιᾶν as an all-inclusive characterisation of the Apostle's missionary work which consists (v.28) of proclamation, exhortation and teaching. As in I Cor 9 the striking repetition of πᾶς stresses the all-embracing claims of the Gospel and the high goal of the Apostle's endeavours. And once again the eschatological goal of Paul's work is in the foreground, since παραστήσωμεν is certainly to be understood as referring to the day of Christ.[1]

As at Phil 2:16, Lightfoot also here considers κοπιᾶν to be a reference to the labour of the athlete in training, and therefore a fitting introduction to the following verb ἀγωνίζεσθαι.[2] The arguments against this view, as stated above, also apply here. Again it must be pointed out that the second verb is qualified by the first, and not vice versa,[3] so that both verbs designate the intense labour

---

[1] Cf. E. Lohmeyer, Die Briefe an die Philipper, an die Kolosser und an Philemon (KEK), Göttingen ¹²1961, p. 89.

[2] J. B. Lightfoot, St. Paul's Epistle to the Colossians and to Philemon, London ⁸1886, p. 171. The use of 'agon' in 2:1 certainly refers back to the related verb in 1:29, but does not make a conscious athletic metaphor any more probable in this passage. —P. Ewald, Die Briefe des Paulus an die Epheser, Kolosser und Philemon (KNT), Leipzig ²1910, p. 350, objects to the simple translation 'sich bemühen' for κοπιᾶν, but his 'mich müde plage' assigns to the word a stronger sense than otherwise found in Paul.

[3] Lohmeyer, op.cit., p. 89 note 2, sees in Sap 9:10 and Sir 51:27 the roots of Paul's use of κοπιᾶν.

and efforts of Paul toward the one goal, "to present every man perfect in Christ". Consequently the translation 'striving' is to be preferred to any reference to struggle or conflict.[1] In support of this view we may note the phrase εἰς ὅ (cf. εἰς τοῦτον ... κοπιῶμεν καὶ ἀγωνιζόμεθα in I Tim 4:10) which determines both verbs, expressing the thought of the goal as does the infinitive in Lk 13:24 (ἀγωνίζεσθε εἰσέλθειν διὰ τῆς στενῆς θύρας) and ἵνα in John 18:36 (οἱ ὑπηρέται ἂν οἱ ἐμοὶ ἠγωνίζοντο, ἵνα μὴ παραδοθῶ).[2] Although a conscious reference to the athletic Agon is hardly present, it is interesting to observe how the use of the verb ἀγωνίζεσθαι still carries with it its original colouring, the striving after a specific aim or goal.

All commentators are agreed that ἀγών in 2:1 takes up the verb in 1:29, providing a closer application to the present concrete relationship between Paul and the Colossians and Laodiceans. Two considerations, Paul's absense from his readers (2:1 and 5) and his imprisonment, have prompted most scholars to see here a reference to the Apostle's inner struggles on behalf of his readers,[3] with the thought of prayer (cf. ὑπὲρ ὑμῶν) predominant.[4] These observations are correct in so far as they allow that the appearance of the noun goes one step further that the preceding related verb in 1:29. Whereas the verb refers to the intensity of all Paul's labours in the service of the Gospel, the noun introduces the added thought of conflict and struggle against opposition, a new side to his Agon which arises out of his position as a prisoner (4:10).[5]

---

[1] Straub, op.cit., p. 28: "ἀγωνίζεσθαι ist offenbar kaum noch bildhaft empfunden worden und entspricht unserem 'sich sputen'".

[2] For similar constructions with ἀγωνίζεσθαι expressing purpose, see F. Preisigke, op.cit., s.v., and I Clem 35:4: ἀγωνισώμεθα εὑρεθῆναι ἐν τῷ ἀριθμῷ τῶν ὑπομενόντων, and Barn 4:11: φυλάσσειν ἀγωνιζώμεθα (parallel to the foregoing μελετῶμεν) τὰς ἐντολὰς αὐτοῦ.

[3] Cf. Cremer-Kögel, Wörterbuch der ntl. Gräcität, Gotha 1915, p. 75: Agon designates the "Sorge und Mühe, die der Apostel innerlich empfindet, und die ihm seine 1:28 genannte Lebensaufgabe bereitet"; cf. BAG, s.v.: 'care, concern', Liddell-Scott, s.v., 'mental struggle and anxiety'. T. K. Abbott, Ephesians and Colossians (ICC), Edinburgh 1897, ad loc., also sees in the verb only a reference to inner struggles.

[4] Lightfoot, op.cit., p. 171: "the inward struggle, the wrestling in prayer, is the predominant idea as in 4:12"; cf. also Bengel, ad. loc.: Paul's Agon is a "certamen solicitudinis, studii, precum, quibus sarcio ea, quae praestare non possum, absens". A. Schlatter, Die Theologie der Apostel, p. 297, also sees here an Agon of prayer.

[5] Against Lietzmann-Greeven, An die Kolosser, Epheser, an Philemon (HNT), Tübingen ³1953, p. 25: "ἀγωνιζόμενος wird 2:1 mit ἀγών wieder auf-

Against the usual interpretation it must be said that there is no reason to assume that Paul here means to describe only an inner struggle. Any reference to I Thess 2:2 or to Phil 1:30 for this meaning of 'agon' is invalid. Paul is more than anxious or concerned for his readers. His Agon is immediately related to his active wrestling on their behalf "so that (ἵνα) their hearts may be comforted, being knit together in love".

To this extent the reference of F. Field to Plutarch Tit. Flam. 16.1[1] and to I Clem 2:4 (ἀγὼν ἦν ὑμῖν ἡμέρας τε καὶ νυκτὸς ὑπὲρ πάσης τῆς ἀδελφότητος—cf. ἱκετεύειν in v.3) and Col 4:12 are to the point, and suggest that the thought of intercessary prayer on behalf of the faithful is included as a part of Paul's Agon. However, as in Phil 1:30, the present situation of Paul as a prisoner fills the word with a meaning which is already prepared for in v.24 at the beginning of the present section. Here Paul speaks of his παθήματα ὑπὲρ ὑμῶν, that is, his sufferings on behalf of Christ and his Body which serve to complete the tribulations which must be suffered by the faithful between the resurrection and the return of Christ.[2] It is this thought which is prepeated in ἀγὼν ὑπὲρ ὑμῶν. The apostolic activity of Paul does not cease with his sufferings and imprisonment since he also views the latter as serving his Agon for the Gospel.

The inclusion of the thought of suffering brings us closer to the picture of the Agon of the martyrs IV Macc. But the preposition ὑπέρ does not assign to Paul's suffering any vicarious atoning character, as in IV Macc. What is meant thereby is explained in the following verse (2:2). His sufferings serve to comfort those from whom the Apostle is physically separated, for even in them the Christ whom Paul proclaimed when free is still glorified, and the bond between him and the faithful strengthened.

Lohmeyer seizes on these verses to support his thesis that the letter to the Colossians, like that to the Philippians, is permeated with the thought of martyrdom. He already sees in the verb

---

genommen, ist also ebenso zu deuten und nicht auf Kampf, sondern auf Anstrengung zu beziehen".

[1] Πλεῖστον δ'ἀγῶνα καὶ πόνον (!) αὐτῷ παρεῖχον αἱ περὶ χαλκιδέων δεήσεις πρὸς τὸν Μάνιον (Field p. 195). Field also prefers a reference to outer conflict (also E. Stauffer, TWNT I, p. 139), but his suggestion that Paul here borrowed from Is 7:13 (cf. supra p. 52) is not to be followed. —For the regularity of the prepositions ὑπέρ and περί with ἀγών and ἀγωνίζεσθαι, see Ditt. Syll. 317.20, 386.19, 409.33, and Liddell-Scott, and M-M., s.vv.

[2] Cf. Lietzmann-Greeven, op.cit., pp. 22f.

ἀγωνίζεσθαι "ein fast technisches Wort für Begriff und Tatsache des Martyriums", and notes the same for the following noun.[1] The following considerations speak against this view. The phrase εἰς ὅ which summarises the preceding three verbs in v.28 describing Paul's apostolic mission of preaching and teaching speaks against the narrowing down of the Agon to include only suffering. Secondly there is no mention in the entire letter to the Colossians, nor in that to the Philippians, of martyrdom itself, whether in the case of Paul or of his readers. The possibility of death is certainly continuously before his eyes, but he still expresses the expectation in Phil 1:24ff. that he will see his addressees again. Finally, it must be denied that either ἀγών or ἀγωνίζεσθαι are used by Paul as almost technical expressions for martyrdom. Col 2:1, together with Phil 1:30, points towards this development, as does the use of the athletic image in IV Macc. But the final stage is only reached in the early Christian martyr acts after the Martyrdom of Polycarp.[2]

The appearance of the phrase ἐν πολλῷ ἀγῶνι in *I Thess* 2:2 provides a direct analogy to all the texts examined so far. Again it is the proclamation of the Word (λαλῆσαι ... τὸ εὐαγγέλιον) by the Apostle himself and his coworkers which is pictured. The difficulty of ascertaining the exact emphasis of 'agon' is the same as in Col 2:1. Of the three meanings which have been suggested one must be rejected from the outset. From a purely linguistic point of view the translation "in great anxiety or sollicitude"[3] is possible, since the word came to be used more and more in later Greek for deep concern and anxiety. But, despite the testimony of the Vulgate's "in multa sollicitudine" (the Itala leaves the possibility of interpretation open with its literal "in multo certamine"), a picturing of purely inner struggles is made impossible by the context, and in particular by the verb παρρησιάζεσθαι. In Acts the word designates the joyful and fearless courage which accompanied the early proclamation of the Easter message despite, and in the face of, opposition (Acts 9:27f., 13:46, 14:3 and 19:8; also Eph 6:20).[4] Since the same emphasis

---

[1] Lohmeyer, op.cit., pp. 89 and 92.

[2] See the concluding chapter.

[3] Cf. J. E. Frame, Thessalonians (ICC), Edinburgh ³1953, p. 94. His argument for understanding the word as a reference only to inner struggles is falsely founded on the view that Col 2:1 also merely refers to anxiety. The witness of Irenaeus and Chrysostom is also not convincing due to the following argument.

[4] Cf. K. H. Rengstorf, Die Auferstehung Jesu, Form, Art und Sinn der

can be found here it is hard to understand how Paul could have spoken of the boldness of his preaching in one breath, and of his fear and anxiety in the other—unless one avoids the obvious contradiction by an artificial distinction between his external behaviour and inner feelings!

The fact that παρρησιάζεσθαι follows προπαθεῖν and ὑβρίζειν should not lead to the false conclusion that the stay in Thessalonia is pictured as a happy contrast to the sufferings experienced in Philippi (cf. Acts 16:20-24). M. Dibelius, who presents this argument, concludes that the word ἀγών must simply refer to Paul's exertion and effort in preaching in Thessalonia.[1] Lightfoot, consistent with his treatment of all of the Pauline Agon termini, goes to the other extreme and wishes to find in Paul's choice of just this expression (i.e. ἀγών) an emphasis on his strenuous exertion as a spiritual agonist, implying a conscious athletic metaphor.[2] But this is the case as little as in Col 1:29ff., otherwise one must find the use of πολύς rather strange.[3]

That the moment of intense effort is found in every appearance of 'agon' is self-evident, but as in Col 2:1 a further thought is here implied by the word, the thought of the opposition which accompanied the preaching of Paul and his companions.[4] If the account of Acts 17:1-5 is to be regarded as trustworthy—and there appears to be no sound reason why it should not—Paul's stay in Thessalonia

---

urchristlichen Osterbotschaft, Witten/Ruhr [4]1960, p. 20.

[1] M. Dibelius, An die Thessalonicher I & II, an die Philipper (HNT), Tübingen [3]1937, p. 7, with reference to Is 7:13 and I Clem 2:4.

[2] J. B. Lightfoot, Notes on the Epistles of St. Paul, London 1904, p. 20. Similarly W. Hendriksen, Exposition of I and II Thessalonians, Grand Rapids 1955, p. 61: Paul and his companions exerted themselves as athletes aiming for the prize, in order that they might do the will of God and win the Thessalonians.

[3] The plural form in Ditt. Syll. 434/5,10: πολλοὺς καὶ καλοὺς ἀγῶνας ἠγωνίσαντο μετ' ἀλλήλων ... (of political and military struggles between states), and Herodot. 8.102: πολλοὺς πολλάκις ἀγῶνας δραμέονται περὶ σφέων αὐτῶν οἱ Ἕλληνες. The singular does occur in Thucyd. 7.71.1: ὅ τε ... πεζὸς ἀμφοτέρων πολὺν τὸν ἀγῶνα ... εἶχε ...; note also the use of the adjective μέγας in Appian Bell. Civ. 1.10.

[4] Thus correctly BAG, s.v., 'under a great strain or in the face of great opposition' = RSV; W. Bornemann, Die Thessalonicherbriefe (KEK), Göttingen [5 & 6]1894, p. 76: "äussere Anfechtungen und Gefahren", and E. Stauffer, TWNT I, p. 138, who refers the word to Paul's missionary work "umdroht von hundert Gefahren und erfüllt von äusseren und inneren Kämpfen: ἔξωθεν μάχαι, ἔσωθεν φόβοι (2 K 7,5)", assign to the word a wider significance, but the thought of 'fear' is hardly present.

was anything but a happy contrast to the conflicts which he en-
countered in Philippi. In the epistle itself it is likely that 2:14ff.
refers not only to the sufferings to which the Thessalonians themselves have been subjected by the Jewish populace, but also contains
a reminiscence of the initial opposition which it stirred up against
Paul's message (cf. v.16)—according to Acts it was the Jews who
were responsible for his departure. The position of παρρησιάζεσθαι
does not indicate a contrast between Paul's work and its reception
in the two cities. The thought will rather be: Having suffered and
been abused in Philippi, Paul and his companions were nevertheless
bold (took their confidence in God) to preach to the Thessalonians
even though again faced with hostility. It is impossible to judge
from the context what form this conflict took. Most likely the
memory of his verbal conflicts and debates with the Jews was
uppermost in Paul's mind when he wrote these lines, but it is not
therefore necessary to see in 'agon' a legal terminus.[1] Nor is it
necessary to conclude that Paul was subjected to physical harm in
Thessalonia. According to Acts he was able to leave the city un-
touched. In this respect the word is not completely identical in
meaning with 'agon' in Col 2:1 where it includes the suffering of
imprisonment.

A commentary to I Thess 2:2 with its reference to the sufferings
and abuse received in Philippi is found in *Phil* 1:27-30 where Paul
reminds his readers of the Agon which he once fought in their midst
and which they are now to carry on in his absence. The juxtaposition of συναθλεῖν and ἀγών speaks for the assumption of a stronger
metaphor than in the previous two passages. But most English
commentators, beginning again with Lightfoot, have carried this
point too far in finding here not only a clear athletic image, but also
one from the gladiatorial arena. Paul thus pictures the Philippian
Christians as wrestlers of gladiators in the arena of faith (v.27), and
then includes himself in the same image (v.30).[2] German exegetes

---

[1] G. Wohlenberg, Der erste und zweite Thessalonicherbrief (KNT),
Leipzig ²1909, p. 43, note 2. This meaning is well attested (cf. Ditt. Syll. 916.
5, Liddell-Scott, s.v., F. Preisigke, op.cit., s.v., and H.St. J. Thackeray,
Greek Lexicon to Josephus, s.v.), but it is too narrow for the word in its
present context.

[2] Cf. J. B. Lightfoot, St. Paul's Epistle to the Philippians, pp. 105f.: the
believers are condemned to fight for their lives like combatants in the Roman
amphitheatre; J. H. Michael, The Epistle of Paul to the Philippians (MNTC),
London 1928, p. 66: Here "it is the encounters of the arena that are in Paul's

have on the other hand preferred to see in both terms little more than the general idea of struggle with the added thought of suffering.[1] The probability of at least a pale metaphor is enhanced by the variation in terms between συναθλεῖν and ἀγών—unlike Col 1:29-2:1 where a relatively colourless ἀγωνίζεσθαι could easily suggest an equally pale use of ἀγών. From this consideration alone it would be wrong to take both words in a completely colourless sense.[2] On the other hand it is equally false to attempt to draw the concrete features of the picture to which Paul supposedly refers by seeing Paul and the Philippians as gladiators in an arena! In their context the words are sufficiently clear without one having to take recourse to a concrete image. A closer examination of the text shows the advisability of steering this middle path between the two extremes.

Up to 1:16 Paul has spoken of his own sufferings and of the inner bond of faith and prayer which nevertheless still unites missionary and congregation. Turning from his own situation the Apostle directs the attention of his readers to that which is required of them in his absense. They are not to forget their own task by thinking only of his fate.[3] It is in the fulfilment of this task that the unity of the Philippians themselves is to find expression and be further strengthened (2:1ff.), as well as the close bond with the Apostle. For this task they now share in common with Paul. For the Philippians it means presenting a united and unwavering front over

---

mind, as in the rest of the paragraph, but the more serious and bloody contests rather than the merely spectacular and competitive. The Philippian Christians are like a group standing in the arena surrounded by wily fierce antagonists" —similarly p. 73; also F. W. Beare, A Commentary on the Epistle to the Philippians, London 1959, p. 67f.: "His metaphor shifts (sc. from the military image in στήκετε) quickly to the picture of a team of athletes ... engaged in a wrestling match".

[1] Together with the commentaries see Cremer-Kögel, p. 75: "Kampf und Leiden für das Evangelium", and BAG, s. ἀγών: "struggle, fight, only fig. of suffering for the Gospel". Only Schmid, p. 35, finds a conscious metaphor here.

[2] Cf. Straub, op.cit., p. 38, who finds that ἀγών in v.30, as in I Thess 2:2, is "offenbar sehr verblasst und bedeutet nur noch so viel wie Mühe, Not. Schwierigkeit". Caution is here advisable; as we have frequently seen the athletic terms rarely lost their metaphorical colouring even in a pale transferred use. In view of the following 'agon' the verb συναθλεῖν must not be weakened to mean little more than support or assist (cf. Liddell-Scott, s.v., and P. Ewald-G. Wohlenberg, Philipperbrief [KNT], Leipzig ³1927, pp. 97f.).

[3] "Nicht um das Leben des Paulus sollen sie sich sorgen, sondern um den rectus cursus, die προκοπή des Evangeliums oder des Glaubens" (K. Barth, Erklärung des Philipperbriefes, Zollikon ⁶1947, p. 43).

against the attacks of the enemy in their conflict for the Gospel. In his absence they are to continue the very same conflict which Paul once fought amongst them and which he now continues to fight even in captivity. The twofold nature of the Agon remains the same: on the one hand the struggle for the Gospel (συναθλοῦντες τῇ πίστει τοῦ εὐαγγελίου, v.27), and on the other, the suffering which must result from this struggle (πάσχειν, τὸν αὐτὸν ἀγῶνα ἔχοντες, vv.29f.).

It is especially the first aspect of Paul's stress on unity, the need for concerted effort amongst the Philippians themselves, which is expressed in v.27. And it is in this sense that συν- in συναθλεῖν is to be understood, that is, as complementing the preceding phrase "in one spirit and in one mind". They are to stand united in their struggle for the cause of the faith—a demand which by no means presupposes existing rifts in the congregation, but rather stresses the increasing need of concord in the light of the present situation, the situation of persecution.[1] Lightfoot, and especially Lohmeyer,[2] have related συν- to the following πίστει, seen as personified. Apart from the questionableness of such a bold personification, the thought that the believers are to fight on the side of faith is as little possible as an instrumental understanding of the dative πίστει. They are not to fight *with* the faith of the Gospel, but rather *for* it (gen. subj.: the faith which belongs to, and which comes from, the hearing of the Gospel, taking the dative as a dative of advantage or interest in the same sense as in Jude 3: ἐπαγωνίζεσθαι τῇ ... πίστει).

Although the thought of hostility and persecution underlies the whole section, being present already in στήκετε and explicit in the mention of the ἀντικείμενοι, it would be wrong to view the struggle suggested by συναθλεῖν as a head-on frontal battle between the faith, and its enemies, whoever they may be.[3] The purpose of this

---

[1] The same emphasis on unity in συναθλεῖν with συγκοπιᾶν and συντρέχειν in Ign Pol 6:1.

[2] Lightfoot, op.cit., p. 105: "Striving in concert with the faith" (with 'faith' wrongly understood as 'teaching'), and Lohmeyer, Philipperbrief, pp. 75f. The latter objects to the interpretation here presented because the stress on 'together' has already been twice made (cf. the double εἷς), and supports his own understanding with the formal observation that both 'faith' and 'enemies' stand parallel to each other at the end of the two clauses. "Der Glaube [ist] der eigentliche Streiter im Kampf gegen die Widersacher, dem die Gläubigen sich verbunden wissen" (p. 76). —An instrumental dative with συναθλεῖν and συναγωνίζεσθαι is rare; cf. Euseb. H.E. V 18.5: συναγωνίζεσθαι τοῖς τῆς κενοφωνίας λόγοις, βλασφημῆσαι.

[3] The 'opponents', here not specifically identified, must be the enemies

struggle is not the conquest and defeat of the enemy as such, but the spread and growth of faith,[1] the same goal which was set before all Paul's work. In the pursuit of this goal there necessarily arise opposition and even suffering, as in the case of the Apostle himself. Commentators rightly reject an interpretation of συν- which pictures the Philippians as contesting in fellowship with the Apostle; the pronoun μοί which is found in 4:3 (with συναθλεῖν) and in Rom 15:30 (with συναγωνίζεσθαι) is missing. But even though the thought is not explicit it is certainly to be supplied both from the nature of the ἄθλησις in v.27 and from the express mention of the common Agon in v.30.

The verbs στήκειν and πτύρεσθαι[2] do not prove that the struggle meant is only the suffering of persecution for the faith's sake (Lohmeyer). Both words apply equally as well to the offensive of faith (cf. Eph 6:13) as to the defensive over against the attacks of the enemy. In their striving for the faith the believers are to stand firm, are not to be deterred from their one aim, or to be dismayed by suffering, for in their steadfastness alone lies the sign of their victory and the destruction of their enemies. The steadfastness of faith is the victory which Paul holds before their eyes. The word ὑπομονή which figures largely in Pauline paraenesis is not found here, but nevertheless underlies the whole train of thought.

The objection against a onesided understanding of the ἄθλησις in v.27 as the struggle of persecution, shows, at the same time, the falseness of attempting to explain συναθλεῖν in the concrete terms

---

outside of the Christian congregation responsible for its suffering, whether Jews or Gentiles. Paul cannot refer to internal strife caused by heretics (cf. 3:2) since he parallels his own situation with that of the Philippians (cf. M. Dibelius, An die Philipper [HNT], 'Exkurs' ad loc.). Nor is it necessary, for the same reasons, to interpret ἀντικείμενοι from Eph 6:12, "our wrestling is not against flesh and blood" (thus Vincent, Philippians [ICC], p. 68), or to understand them as the ranks of worldliness and sin (thus Lightfoot, op.cit., p. 105, with reference also to I Cor 4:9). Behind the actual physical opponents Paul may, it is true, have seen the powers of Satan striving to overthrow the Gospel.

[1] Thus Barth, op.cit., p. 45, and note 3 above. The onesided emphasis of Lohmeyer's interpretation is best seen in the statement: "Der Kampf ist nichts anderes als das mannhafte Erdulden von äusseren Verfolgungen" (op. cit., p. 75).

[2] The word is used of the shying of timid horses (references in Lightfoot, op.cit., p. 105), but also has a general meaning so that the picture of chariot racing is entirely unnecessary here (cf. Eidem, p. 143).

of a gladiatorial contest. In v.27 it is not merely a matter of standing
on the defensive, or of protecting and guarding the faith, but rather
of a positive offensive for the faith. Already at this point, and not
first at the point of suffering, the believers at Philippi and Paul are
bound together; they share not only a "Schicksalsgemeinschaft", a
fellowship in suffering, but also a common task, the more so since
Paul's absence places on them an added responsibility.

A unity and fellowship in suffering does find clear expression in
v.30. This verse is particularly instructive for an understanding of
Paul's entire apostolic mission as an Agon, not only because—unlike
Col 1:29ff. and I Thess 2:2—the idea of suffering is explicit
(πάσχειν), but also because he regards his experiences at Philippi
and at present in his imprisonment as aspects of one and the same
conflict and contest. It is this fact, namely, that Paul never speaks
of his various Agones but always of his one Agon in its various
aspects, that justifies our speaking of a concept of the Agon in his
letters.

Since the Philippians now share the Apostle's Agon for the faith,
they, like him, must be prepared to suffer—also a sign of God's
grace (v.29). But to read into this expression of fellowship in suffering[1] a fellowship in actual martyrdom is to find more in these verses
than is possible. The Agon which Paul has contested in the past and
which he now shares with his readers contains the added aspect of
suffering in the situation of persecution, but contains more than
this one thought.[2] The dangers to which Lohmeyer's onesided exegesis leads are best seen in his statement that "Martyrien Hohe-
punkte des gläubigen Lebens sind und in ihnen ein 'Zeichen des
Heils' und ein Charisma Gottes liegt".[3] The paradigmatic character of Paul's Agon, including its manifestation in suffering, is certainly emphasised by the double ἐν ἐμοί; but this does not raise martyrdom to an ideal, to the status of the highest goal in the Christian
life.

The last passage has revealed an extension of the Apostle's Agon
to include the striving and suffering of his fellow believers. This

---

[1] On the frequency of Paul's stress on the Christian fellowship of suffering
and comfort, see Dibelius, op.cit., on v. 30 together with the following 'Exkurs' (II Cor 1:6 and I Thess 2:14 cited).

[2] Juncker, op.cit., II p. 31, rightly observes that Paul's Agon of preaching
and suffering are here united. But the second does not exclude the first
aspect.

[3] Lohmeyer, op.cit., p. 79.

point and the interpretation of συναθλεῖν as indicating more than suffering for the Gospel, but rather an active participation in Paul's own wrestling for the spread of the faith of the Gospel, is supported by *Phil* 4:3. In this verse Paul exhorts the two factious women Euodia and Syntyche to unity, at the same time commending them as those who ἐν τῷ εὐαγγελίῳ συνήθλησάν μοι, together with Clement and his other coworkers whose names are written in the book of life. The pronoun μοί and the phrase "in the Gospel", designating the sphere of their labours (cf. Rom 1:9 and I Thess 3:2), clearly assigns to these Christians the role of participants in his own Agon for the Gospel. The same range of interpretations as noted for the above passages has been offered in explanation of the verse. A conscious athletic metaphor[1] must again be rejected as improbable. The appearance of στέφανος shortly before does not speak to the contrary; a strange mixture of pictures would otherwise result. According to v.1 the brethren are pictured as Paul's crown of victory, in v.3 they are pictured as contesting along with him. On the other hand συναθλεῖν should again not be robbed of any colour by being simply equated with συνεργεῖν, and thus taken to mean no more than 'help' of 'assist'. The following συνεργῶν indicates the nature of the struggle which is meant but without the force or intensity of the previous verb.

As in Phil 1:27ff., the thought of fellowship is uppermost in these personal lines. This is already brought out by the threefold repetition of συν- in σύζυγος, συναθλεῖν, and συνεργοί. It is most natural to interpret all three words in the same sense, as expressing participation in Paul's missionary activity. This is quite apparent in the case of συνεργοί, and it is unlikely that we should see anything more in the other two terms. Lohmeyer, consistent with his thesis, relates them to fellowship in martyrdom, in suffering for the faith.[2] But it

---

[1] Thus already Bengel, ad loc.: Alluditur ad athletas victores, quorum nomina cluebant. But such an image would not be suggested by the final phrase ("whose names are written in the book of life") which repeats a familiar Jewish picture (cf. Lohmeyer, op.cit., p. 165 with note 7). —J. H. Michael, op.cit., p. 192, sees behind the verb a metaphor from the arena — Paul and his coworkers fought side by side against opposition.

[2] Lohmeyer, op.cit., pp. 165ff. The reference to Phil 1:27 carries no weight; συναθλεῖν also here refers to more than suffering for the Gospel. It is Hebr which first limits the contest to an ἄθλησις παθημάτων (10:32); cf. Passio Andreae 15 (Bonn.-Lip. II 1, p. 37) where the day of martyrdom is the day of the Apostle's ἄθλησις.—For the other interpretation of σύζυγος as a name, see BAG, s.v., and Barth, op.cit., p. 120.

is surely just in this passage that the wider meaning of the Agon of Paul himself is reflected. The verb συναθλεῖν refers to the help which these coworkers afforded Paul at the founding of the Philippian congregation, toil which no doubt also involved them in the dangerous opposition which always attended Paul's contest for the Gospel.[1] "Das Verbum συναθλεῖν wird nicht nur da gebraucht, wo es sich um einen Kampf mit gleichartigen Gegnern oder um Wettkampf handelt, sondern es drückt jedes Ringen wie gegen Menschen, so mit widrigen Verhältnissen, ja jede mit Eifer und Opfern verbundene Bemühung aus. Sie haben mit und fur den Apostel sich abgerungen".[2] Both the present passage and the record in Acts 16 allow no certain conclusions as to the nature of their struggle with and for Paul. The verb would seem to imply a more active role than the mere acceptance of the Apostle into their homes on the part of these women (Acts 16:15)—perhaps the exercise of their influence with the authorities as in Acts 17:12 is included.

Eusebius offers support for the above understanding of συναθλεῖν. In H.E. III 4.9 he refers to Phil 4:3 as reporting that Clement of Rome was a συνεργὸς καὶ ἀθλητής of Paul. Quite apart from the problematical identification of Clement, it must be remarked that if Eusebius, who otherwise favours the athletic image to picture martyrdom (as well as the frequent use of ἀθλητής for the martyr, cf. especially ἀγῶνα διαθλεῖν VII 12.1 and IX 1.9, προθύμως ἐναθλεῖν VIII 3.1, and μαρτύρων ἀθλήσεις VIII 10.12) here failed to note a reference to martyrdom, it is more than unlikely that we should follow Lohmeyer in doing so.

It is the same thought, the extension of his own missionary Agon to include the active participation of his fellow-believers, which underlies the petition of the Apostle in *Rom* 15:30. About to make his last journey to Jerusalem, he writes: παρακαλῶ δὲ ὑμᾶς ... συναγωνίσασθαί μοι ἐν ταῖς προσευχαῖς ὑπὲρ ἐμοῦ πρὸς τὸν θεόν. The immediate purpose of their prayer is twofold: "that I may be delivered from the unbelievers in Judea, and that my service for Jerusalem"

---

[1] At the most one may say with Vincent (op.cit., ad loc.) that συναθλεῖν indicates an activity attended with danger and suffering (with reference to I Thess 2:2). —The observation of F. W. Beare (op.cit., p. 141) that Paul depicts the struggle for the Gospel as a contest in which they have been pitted along with him 'against principalities and powers ...', Eph 6:12, no doubt applies to the Apostle's conception of his mission, but probably over-interprets the present text.

[2] Ewald/Wohlenberg, op.cit., p. 214, note 2.

(the handing over of the collection for the mother congregation) "may be acceptable to the saints" (v.31). Verse 32 may be taken as expressing the final purpose of v.31 and as also dependent on συναγωνίζεσθαι in v.30. The Roman Christians are to pray for the success and safe issue of Paul's mission to Jerusalem that he may be preserved to come and visit them also.

It is usually correctly observed that the phrase συναγωνίζεσθαί μοι expresses participation in an Agon of Paul himself. But it is in establishing the nature of this Agon that a misunderstanding has arisen. The interpretation of O. Michel best illustrates the usual mistake.[1] He sees in this verse a reflection of the Jewish or Israelitic picture of prayer as a struggle ("Gebetskampf, ἀγών"), as a wrestling with God for the decisions of the future, a wrestling into which others may also be drawn. "Das Bild vom israelitischen Bebets-kampfes stammt aus der Jakobsgeschichte (Gen 32.24ff.), wird aber später immer wieder aufgenommen ... Es bringt zum Ausdruck, dass das Schicksal des Beters ganz in Gottes Hand steht, dass es aber in jedem ernsten Ringen mit Gott erkämpft und durchkämpft werden kann."[2] With this concept of prayer in the background, Paul is represented as requesting his readers to join him in his Agon of prayer.

Two objections must here be made. 1. In the first place even if such an Israelitic picture of prayer can be traced, it is certain that the picture is not that of the Agon, as Michel seems to suggest. At least we have been unable to find this connection in any of the Hellenistic Jewish sources examined in this work. When Sap 10:12 and Philo treat the familiar scene in Gen 32 as an Agon they are not concerned with painting a picture of prayer as a contest with God.

2. In the second place it must be denied that the Agon of Paul in which the Roman believers are to participate is *limited* to an Agon of prayer. The context speaks against this claim. The Apostle is about to travel to Jerusalem conscious of the fact that a twofold struggle

---

[1] O. Michel, Der Brief an die Römer (KEK), Göttingen ¹²1963, p. 373.

[2] Ibid, note 2. Michel cites G. Harder, Paulus und das Gebet, Gütersloh 1936, where, however, only b.Ber. 53b is given as an example of this Jewish concept of prayer (pp. 125f.). Michel further cites Col 4:12 (see further below) in support of his view, as well as Origen: ut adjuvetis me in agone orationum ad deum. In Eusebius H. E. III 23.19 prayer and fasting belong to the Agon of repentance and contrition: καὶ δαψιλέσι μὲν εὐχαῖς ἐξαιτούμενος, συνεχέσι δὲ νηστείαις συναγωνιζόμενος.

awaits him there, on the one side with the Jews who hate him as a deserter of the faith of the Fathers, and on the other side with the Jewish Christians of whose support and acceptance he can not even yet be certain. He is thus about to enter into another phase of his apostolic Agon, and it is with this oncoming conflict in mind that he calls on the Romans to wrestle with him.[1] They are to support him in this struggle by becoming his co-agonists in prayer to God on his behalf. Consequently the verb is to be understood on the basis of Paul's own missionary Agon, and not only on the background of a picture of prayer as an Agon.

In its contemporary usage the verb συναγωνίζεσθαι always means to take part in the Agon of another and can assume the almost colourless sense, to assist or support another.[2] Josephus shows the range of transferred uses possible. The word appears, usually with the dative, in a military context signifying fighting on the same side (Bell 5.311, 7.7 and Ant 5.183), in a legal context meaning to support the claims of someone (Bell 2.15: συναγωνιούμενοι περὶ τῆς διαδοχῆς 'Αρχελάῳ, and 2.83), and in the more pale and general sense to assist or help (the Essenes are reported as having sworn to συναγωνιεῖσθαι τοῖς δικαίοις, Bell 2.139; Moses says πονοῦντί μοι ... συνηγωνίσατο [sc. God], Ant 4.316). In every instance it is participation and assistance in the Agon of someone else which is expressed—in Rom 15:30, therefore, participation through prayer in Paul's ensuing struggle in Jerusalem. This participation does not presuppose identity of action. Thus we are not compelled to see Paul and the Roman congregation bound together only in a common Agon of prayer. The specific way in which the Roman Christians are to take part in the Apostle's contest is, because of the

---

[1] "Das Wort (συναγωνίζεσθαι) ist gewählt in Rücksicht auf die Gegner, von denen der Apostel errettet zu werden begehrt —v.31, nicht wie ἀγωνίζεσθαι —Kol 4.12. An eine Situation wie Gen 32, ein Kämpfen mit Gott, ist weder hier, noch Kol 4.12 zu denken" (Cremer-Kögel, p. 76); also B. Weiss, Der Brief an die Römer (KEK), Göttingen ⁹1899, p. 592: "συναγωνίζεσθαι weist auf den Kampf gegen feindliche und gefährliche Gewalten hin, in dem sich der Apostel befindet und in dem sie ihm zur Seite stehen sollen in ihren Gebeten". Similarly also T. Zahn, Der Brief des Paulus an die Römer (KNT), Leipzig ³1925, p. 604, and K. Barth, Der Römerbrief, Zollikon 1954, p. 518.

[2] J. J. Wettstein, Novum Testamentum II, ad loc.: συναγωνίζεσθαι σημαίνει βοηθεῖν, ἀλλὰ κυρίως ἐν τῷ ἀγῶνι; cf. also BAG and Liddell-Scott, s.v. In Jewish literature the word is only found in Test As 6:2, where the text is however uncertain (supra p. 66).

distance which separates them, in supplication *to* God (πρὸς τὸν θεόν), not in an Agon of prayer *with* or against God.

Rom 15:30 does not justify an examination of a Pauline concept of prayer as an Agon. To do this is to introduce a problem into the text which which is foreign to it. The answers which are offered in explanation of what Paul might mean by speaking of prayer as an Agon certainly indicate the character of prayer, but are not based on the text itself. Common to all—although the words of Michel can easily be misunderstood—is the careful avoidance of speaking in terms of a contest with or against God. Thus the basis of the conflict is seen in man himself, in the necessary struggle within the heart of the praying man himself.[1] Again, it is the zeal and intensity of prayer which the Agon termini in Rom 15:30 and Col 4:12 wish to emphasise.[2] The same emphasis underlies L. Schmid's examination of the Pauline picture of the "Agon of prayer". Having briefly considered the interpretation which we have given the present passage she turns to an explanation of the text whereby "dieses Gebet ... als Kampf bezeichnet wäre".[3] Her treatment suggests that this is the interpretation which is to be preferred. She also rejects the understanding in which God becomes an opponent Who is to be overcome in prayer; the opponent is not God "wohl aber diejenige Macht ..., die sich dem Werk des Christus, das Paulus treibt, entgegensetzt" (Eph 6:10ff.).[4] Because she would like to see both in Rom 15:30 and Col 4:12 a reference to the popular Agon motif, L. Schmid comes to the further conclusion that the "Vergleichsmoment der Anstrengung deutlich auf das Gebet übertragen [ist], und durch die Vermittlung des Bildes der Gedanke deutlich gemacht, dass der Verkehr mit Gott, wie ihn das Gebet darstellt, die äusserste Anstrengung vom Beter fordere, die der des Wett-

---

[1] Cf. Bengel: Orare, agon est, praesertim ubi homines resistunt, and W. Sanday and A. C. Headlam, The Epistle to the Romans (ICC), Edinburgh 1952, p. 415: the Romans "will as it were take part in the contest that he must fight by praying on his behalf to God, for all prayer is a spiritual wrestling against opposing powers. So of our Lord's agony in the garden, Luke 22:48, Mtt 26:42".—Note also their quotation from Origen: Et ideo agon magnus est orationis, ut obsistentibus inimicis, et orationis sensum in diversa rapientibus, fixa ad Deum semper mens stabili intentione contendat.

[2] Eidem, p. 137.

[3] Schmid, p. 38.

[4] Ibid., p. 39. It is probably in this sense that we are to understand Sanday and Headlam when they speak of "a spiritual wrestling against opposing powers".

kämpfers gleiche".[1] In describing this exertion she speaks of "Willensanstrengung", of the "Konzentration des Innenlebens" in which
the eye is directed to God in the earnest longing to know His will,
of the struggle for "Willenseinigung" with God.[2] Such considerations certainly belong to an examination of the nature of Christian
prayer, but just as certainly do not arise directly from the use of
συναγωνίζεσθαι in Rom 15 :30.

A. Schlatter also supposes that Paul here speaks of a "gemeinsamen Anspannung ihrer Kraft im Gebet miteinander". The point
of comparison behind the verb is "das Aufgebot des Willens".
Schlatter proposes the use of the athletic termini in a legal sense as
the background of the text. "Die, die sich mit dem Gefährdeten und
Recht suchenden einsetzten, dass er Recht bekomme und freigesprochen werde, übten das συναγωνίσασθαι αὐτῷ".[3] It is the favourable decision of God as the Judge for which Paul and the Romans
are to strive in prayer. "Wer von einem 'gemeinsamen Ringen mit
Gott' spricht, verkennt das Bild. Der Agonist ringt nicht mit dem,
vor dem er den Agon vollbringt; er bemüht sich um seinen Beifall
und legt deshalb in seine Kunst seine ganze Kraft hinein." Schlatter's remarks are the most ingenious of all, based as they are on the
correct observation of the legal use of the Agon image. But it is
questionable whether his explanation of this use is correct, since it
is hardly only the thought of the judge and his decision which lay
behind the judicial Agon. It was rather the thought of the opponent
which lead to the description of a legal issue as an Agon.[4] In any
case Schlatter errs in the assumption that Paul's Agon is *only* the
Agon of prayer. The phrase συναγωνίσασθαί μοι finds more than a
formal parallel in συναναπαύσωμαι ὑμῖν in v.32.[5] Paul hopes that,
after the successful issue of his ensuing conflict in Jerusalem in

---

[1] Ibid, p. 41.

[2] Ibid, pp. 55f.—similarly E. Stauffer, TWNT I, p. 139: "Im Gebet verwirklicht sich die Einheit zwischen Gotteswille und Menschenwollen, die
Einung menschlichen Ringens und Tuns mit göttlicher Machtwirkung".

[3] A. Schlatter, Gottes Gerechtigkeit, Ein Kommentar zum Römerbrief,
Stuttgart [3]1959, p. 392.

[4] Cf. Cicero ad Att. XIV 7.1.16: est studium contentionis, quod in oratione
adhibetur, unde ipsae orationes in causis veris, et quidam in primis in forensibus, ἀγῶνες dicuntur, et declamationibus umbraticis opponuntur.

[5] Cf. also ἀναπαύειν in I Cor 16:18, II Cor 7:13 and Philem 7 and 20.
Ignatius frequently uses the same verb in his letters, always in the phrase
κατὰ πάντα ἀναπαύειν —Eph 2:1, Magn 15:1, Trall 12:1, Rom 10:2, Smyrn
9:2, 10:1 and 12:1.

which the Romans are also to take part in prayer, they may together be granted rest from their toil in Rome—taking ὑμῖν in more than a purely locative sense. They will share his rest as they have shared his labour.

The above discussion has already indicated the way in which *Col 4.12f.* is to be interpreted. Paul reports that Epaphras is always "ἀγωνιζόμενος ὑπὲρ ὑμῶν ἐν ταῖς προσευχαῖς that you may stand mature and fully assured in all the will of God". It is further said of him that he has "πολὺν πόνον ὑπὲρ ὑμῶν and on behalf of those on Laodicea and Hierapolis". Once again the text gives clear indication that the use of ἀγωνίζεσθαι is to be understood on the background of the picture of Paul's own missionary Agon. The proof of this point presupposes the findings on Col 1:28-2:2. That Epaphras' activity also in prayer, is seen in connection with Paul's own work is suggested in the first place by the term συνεργόι in v.11, and is further underlined with the designation of Epaphras as δοῦλος Χριστοῦ Ἰησοῦ in v.12, a title which Paul otherwise only assigns to himself and once to Timothy (Phil 1:1). Secondly, the purpose of his Agon on behalf of[1] his fellowbelievers is phrased in almost the same terms as the goal of Paul's own Agon in 1:28 and 2:2 (cp. 1:28, ἵνα παραστήσωμεν πάντα ἄνθρωπον τέλειον ἐν Χριστῷ with 4:12, ἵνα σταθῆτε τέλειοι καὶ πεπληροφορημένοι [cf. πληροφορία τῆς συνέσεως in 2:2] θελήματι τοῦ θεοῦ).[2] Through prayer Epaphras contends for his own countrymen the same Agon which Paul has contended for all men. Thirdly, his πόνος also places him closely at Paul's side. This toil certainly includes more than the thought of prayer in v.12. However T. K. Abbott rightly observes that the term belongs together with ἀγωνίζεσθαι, and refers to the well known phrase in Plato Phaedrus 247 B as an example.[3] As Paul's συναιχμάλωτος (Philem 23) Epaphras has also shared the conflicts which have led

---

[1] The choice of the preposition ὑπέρ over περί is conditioned by the thought of prayer, as in Rom 15:30 and I Clem 2:4: ἀγὼν ... ὑπὲρ πάσης τῆς ἀδελφότητος.

[2] P. Ewald, Epheser, Philemon, Kolosserbrief (KNT), Leipzig ²1910, p. 441: "Die Worte besagen nur dasselbe als Ziel des Gebets des Epaphras, was Paulus 2:1f. als Gegenstand seines ἀγωνίζεσθαι allen gegenüber ... bezeichnete und worauf nach 1:28 sein und seiner Gehilfen Bestreben ging". Cf. also Lohmeyer, An die Kolosser (KEK), p. 168, who draws the same parallel.

[3] T. K. Abbott, Ephesians and Colossians (ICC), ad loc., and supra pp. 26f. For further examples of this connection see the studies in the first section of this work. The close connection between ἀγωνίζεσθαι and πόνος does not, however, imply a clear reference to the athletic image.

up to Paul's and his imprisonment, and these toils together with the captivity itself are in both cases evaluated in the same way, as a toiling on behalf of the addressees. Thus we find a further parallelism—Paul: ἡλίκον ἀγῶνα ἔχω ὑπὲρ ὑμῶν (2:1); Epaphras: ἔχει πολὺν πόνον ὑπὲρ ὑμῶν (4:13).

Attention has frequently been drawn to the interesting textual variants for πόνον in v.13. Even though the accepted reading is by far the best attested (א ABCP 436 and probably lat. and vulg.) the other readings are significant. In the first place the amendment ἀγῶνα underlines the correctness of connecting this verse with the preceding, as we have done. The very fact that κόπον, πόθον, ζῆλον and ἀγῶνα have replaced πόνον in some MSS suggests, in addition, that offence was taken at the last word. Thus the best witnessed emendation has κόπον, a word common in Paul and characteristic of his language. Nevertheless, if κόπον stood in the original text it is difficult to explain the appearance of the other variants. The best solution to the problem is to be found in the otherwise careful avoidance of the term by Paul and the other early Christian writers.[1] The reason for this avoidance[2] is not hard to explain. It was this term's usual connection with the popular picture of the toils of the hero, especially of Hercules, and of the moral toils of the sage, which gave it an offensive ring.[3] This connotation clearly lies behind the use of the word in connection with the toils of Peter and Paul in I Clem 5, a passage which clearly reflects the language of the diatribe.[4] Justin also knows of this popular use (Apol. I 21, of Hercules 'toils'). Thus it is relatively easy to explain the rise of various emendations to the Pauline text. But it would be wrong to conclude that it was impossible for Paul to use the term even once; its use in v.14 betrays a neutral meaning, as also in Diogn XI 8 and Herm Mand XI 20.

A few *summary remarks* may serve to indicate the main con-

---

[1] Only here in Paul, and in Rev 16:10f. and 21:4.

[2] It is not sufficient simply to state that the reason for the variants lies in the rarity of πόνος (Abbott and Lohmeyer). This fact itself requires explanation.

[3] Thus correctly A. von Harnack, "κόπος (κοπιᾶν, οἱ κοπιῶντες) im frühchristlichen Sprachgebrauch", ZNW, 27 (1928), p. 4, and F. Hauck, TWNT III, p. 827 note 6.

[4] Cf. the final chapter. Clem otherwise only uses the word in OT citations —16:3f. and 12. In Diogn XI 8 and Herm Mand XI 20 the word only means as much as pain.

clusions of this section. If the athletic termini in these six passages have been so carefully examined this has been dictated by the realisation that it is here, as well as in I Cor 9:24ff., Gal 2:2 and Phil 2:16, that the weight of the study must lie in order to correct the usual misunderstandings of Pauline Agon imagery.

1. With regard to the metaphorical strength of the terms concerned little more can be added to the conclusions of E. Eidem in his thorough study.[1] In every instance the presence of a *conscious reference to a specific athletic image* must be regarded as *unlikely*, and a warning must be issued against the—especially English, in this case—error of over-interpretation. But Eidem is on uncertain ground in maintaining that their original connection with the sphere of the games was not at all present in Paul's consciousness. It is far safer to emphasise his other statement, that these termini could at any moment come to life. Space does not allow this to be demonstrated from the exegesis of the Church Fathers.[2] It is questionable whether Paul's language is completely colourless at this point, especially since the respective termini contribute to a unified picture of the Agon for the Gospel. The fact that this thought could on one occasion give rise to a clearly conscious metaphor (I Cor 9:24ff.; cf. also Phil 3:12ff. below) must include the possibility of at least a slight metaphorical colouring even in the use of isolated athletic termini. Paul is here not so far removed from the language of the diatribe. There also the writer can simply refer to the sage's Agon without developing the image, whereas on other occasions the image is explicitly developed. To what extent Paul's readers perceived an image behind his words cannot be conclusively determined by our non-Greek ears. Nor is this in the final analysis the major problem.

2. Of vital and prime significance is the observation that all passages contribute to the conclusion that the Apostle conceived of his apostolic mission as an Agon for the Gospel or for the faith. The recurring connection of ἀγών / ἀγωνίζεσθαι with κόπος / κοπιᾶν indi-

---

[1] Eidem, pp. 138f.

[2] Note the one example from Euseb. H.E. III 4.9, supra p. 120. The language in IV 11.8 (of Justin τοῖς ὑπὲρ τῆς πίστεως ἐναγωνιζόμενος συγγράμμασιν) and IV 7.5 (ἐκκλησιαστικῶν ἀνδρῶν ... τῆς ἀληθείας ὑπεραγωνιζομένων) is interesting but hardly reveals a point of contact with Paul's Agon for the Gospel. The Fathers often read too much imagery into the Pauline text; see the final chapter.

cates the manner in which this Agon is to be understood. In the first place it is untiring *toil and labour, an intense wrestling* and struggle for the spread, growth and strengthening of the faith as the goal of his mission. Although the term ἀγών is not nearly as frequent as κόπος, both may be regarded as precise characterisations of Paul's missionary work. Secondly, the thought of the *continual struggle against opposition* is never far removed when speaking of his Agon. The athletic termini express with particular force the intensity and earnestness of his struggle against all barriers to the free course of the Gospel and its proclamation, whether in the form of resistance from Jews or Gentiles. The parallel with κόπος allows a third conclusion. Both terms indicate not only an active struggle for the Gospel in the above two senses, but also a passive *suffering* for the same;[1] here the Agon termini are the more expressive. This suffering 'for' the Gospel is viewed as the necessary concomitant of the Apostle's proclamation. Without developing a Pauline theology of suffering at this point, it can be said that the study has further shown the necessity of viewing Paul's afflictions within the framework of his apostolic commission.[2] Even they contribute towards the attainment of the goal of his apostleship—the glory of God the Father through His crucified and risen Son. His own sufferings, no less than this preaching, have the same 'ὑπέρ—character' for his congregations.

3. All three motifs appear in the four passages which reveal an extension of the Agon to include the activity of his coworkers, and also of the members of an entire congregation under special duress (Phil 1:27ff.). It is further indicative that this broadening in application can be detected above all during the imprisonment of Paul, at that moment when he sees the possibility of his own contest for the faith drawing to a close—a feature which, as we shall see, clearly underlies the use of the athletic image in the Pastoral Epistles.

These remarks may seem to state the obvious. It is thus all the more astonishing that scholars have been content to speak of a general religio-ethical concept of the Agon in Paul, or even, which is worse, of the conception of life itself as a moral Agon, parallel to

---

[1] For these two aspects or sides in κόπος see F. Hauck, TWNT III, p. 828.
[2] For this connection see also K. H. Rengstorf, Apostolat und Predigtamt, Stuttgart ²1954, pp. 22ff., and the discussion of Phil 3:12ff. infra.

diatribal thought. Admittedly the passages treated so far do not present all the Pauline material, but it must again be stressed that it is in these texts, together with I Cor 9:24ff., Gal 2:2 and Phil 2:16, that the most unified concept of the Agon is to be found in Paul. To complete the picture, however, we must turn to the passages which point to a picture of the Christian 'race of faith'.

THE Ἀγωνία OF JESUS IN GETHSEMANE, LK 22:44

The development of a traditional picture of prayer itself as an Agon has been rejected for Rom 15:30 and Col 4:12.[1] No exception is provided by the picture of Jesus' 'agony' in Gethsemane in Lk 22:44 which has been referred to as illustrating the Agon of prayer.[2] The reference is in place only in so far as ἀγωνία (καὶ γενόμενος ἐν ἀγωνίᾳ ἐκτενέστερον προσηύχετο) indicates a real struggle and not simply fear. It is true that ἀγωνία and ἀγωνιᾶν frequently occur, especially in later Greek, in juxtaposition with φόβος (and δέος) and φοβεῖσθαι.[3] But enough references are at our disposal to show that even at Paul's time and later, these first two terms still often carried a hint of their original agonal colouring. This comes to light in the use of ἀγωνία to express fear of the imminent and uncertain future (e.g. Diog. Laert. VII 112: ὁ δὲ φόβος ἐστί προσδοκία κακοῦ ... ἀγωνία δὲ φόβος ἀδήλου πράγματος; cf. Diod. Sic. XIX 26: περὶ τοῦ μέλλοντος ἀγωνιᾶν), especially of defeat and catastrophe (Stob. ecl. II 92W: ἀγωνία δὲ φόβος διαπτώσεως καὶ ἑτέρως φόβος ἥττης), and therefore for "die letzte Spannung der Kräfte vor hereinbrechenden Entscheidungen und Katastrophen".[4] Even at a late time the verb could be used in an active sense similar to ἀγωνίζεσθαι.[5] The active

---

[1] As well as these two Pauline passages, I Clem 2:4 and Eusebius H.E. III 23:19, already cited, note also Justin Apol. II 13: καὶ εὐχόμενος καὶ παμμάχως ἀγωνιζόμενος.

[2] Cf. Sanday and Headlam on Rom 15:30 and Lightfoot on Col 4:12. — Vv.43f. are not found in many of the Gospel collections of the early Church, but can be found in others from the second century. Schlatter (Erläuterungen zum Neuen Testament I, p. 585) concludes that they possibly form a "Zusatz eines anderen Christen, der der Kirche eindringlich vorhalten wollte, wie schwer der Kampf war, den Jesus damals bestand". E. Klostermann, Das Lukasevangelium (HNT), ²1929, p. 215, speaks of a "lukanische Sprachfarbe tragender Einschub". But it is just this Lukan colouring, especially the characteristic appearance of the angel, which allows us to retain these verses in the original text, cf. B. H. Streeter, The Four Gospels, London ³1927, pp. 61 and esp. 137.

[3] Cf. F. Field, Notes on the Translation of the NT, p. 77, and Moffatt, in "The Expositor" VIII, vii, pp. 91ff.

[4] E. Stauffer, TWNT I, p. 140. For the element of the decisive in ἀγωνία see supra, p. 54.

[5] Cf. also Or Sib III 710.

meaning of decisive struggle must also be given to ἀγωνία in Lk 22 : 44. It does not suggest that the wrestling of Jesus emphasises a struggle for peace of soul, for inner composure in view of the cruel irrevocable fate which awaited him, but rather an intense and decisive struggle for victory.[1] "Jesus gerät in ἀγωνία, was eine letzte Anspannung seine Kräfte vor der Entscheidung, einen Angst-Kampf um den Sieg andeuten will".[2] L. Brun who has given detailed attention to vv. 43f. is probably right in noting as the background of this struggle the attacks and temptations of Satan who plays a major role in Luke's account of the life and passion of Jesus (4:13, 22:3.31.53, 22:28,40,46; cf. John 12:27-31). We here see the beginning of the climax to the struggle between Jesus and his archenemy who wishes to destroy his work and rob him of the victory by tempting him in the hour of his betrayal. In this struggle it is the appearance of the angel which provides strength for the battle proper which follows.[3]

A passage from Clement of Alexandria which is possibly based on Lk 22:44 offers a second interpretation which is equally as good. In Quis Dives Salv. 23 Christ says: "On your behalf I wrestled (διαγωνίζεσθαι) with death and paid your penalty of death ... Let it be Christ who conquers in you, since it is on your behalf that he struggles (ἀγωνίζεσθαι)". Jesus ἀγωνία, if Lk 22:44 is meant, here appears as the active struggle with death, clearly not fear of death.

It is just possible that later Christian writers had the same scene in mind—though not necessarily in its Lucan form—when they spoke of Christ as the great athlete who had suffered first and now stood by those who suffered martyrdom for him.[4] The martyrdom of Blandina (cf. Euseb. H.E. V 1.36ff.) is summed up in the following lines full of imagery: ἡ μικρὰ καὶ ἀσθενὴς καὶ εὐκαταφρόνητος μέγαν καὶ ἀκαταγώνιστον ἀθλητὴν Χριστὸν ἐνδεδυμένη, διὰ πολλῶν

---

[1] Cf. K. H. Rengstorf, Das Evangelium nach Lukas (NTD), ad loc., and Stauffer, op.cit., p. 140, lines 36f.: "Das ist nicht die Angst vor dem Tode, sondern die Angst um den Sieg —angesichts des nahenden Entscheidungskampfes, von dem das Schicksal der Welt abhängt". So also Cremer-Kögel, p. 75f.: ἀγωνία "hier nicht die sich zurückziehende, fliehende, sondern die um den Ausgang zitternde, bis zum Äussersten spornende Furcht", quoting also Arist. Rhet. 1 :9 for the distinction between ἀγωνιᾶν and φοβεῖσθαι.

[2] L. Brun, "Engel und Blutschweiss —Luk 22.43-44", ZNW, 32 (1933), pp. 265ff. (p. 272).

[3] Ibid.

[4] This thought is not behind the picture of Christ as the πρόδρομος in Hebr 6:20.—In addition to the passages here cited note Acta Philippi 144 (Bonn.-

κλήρων ἐκβιάσασα τὸν ἀντικείμενον καὶ δι' ἀγῶνος τὸν τῆς ἀφθαρσίας στεψαμένη στέφανον. A similar thought lies behind the long address to Christ in the apocryphal Acts of Thomas (39; Bonn.-Lip. II 2, p. 157): ὁ ἐπαμύντωρ καὶ βοηθὸς ἐν ἀγῶνι τῶν ἰδίων δούλων, ὁ τὸν ἐχθρὸν ἀποστρέφων καὶ ἀποσοβῶν ἀφ' ἡμῶν, ὁ εἰς πολλοὺς ἀγῶνας ὑπὲρ ἡμῶν ἀγωνιζόμενος καὶ νικᾶν ποιῶν ἡμᾶς ἐν πᾶσι· ὁ ἀληθὴς ἀθλητὴς ἡμῶν καὶ ἀήττητος· ὁ στρατηλάτης ἡμῶν ἅγιος καὶ νικηφόρος (cf. II Tim 2:3-6). Points of resemblance between Lk 22:43f. and the early Christian Martyrdom-accounts can be detected. Martyrdom was frequently pictured as an Agon against Satan,[1] the best example for this being found in the Passio Perpetua. Secondly, a feature which also recurs often, the sufferers were granted a glance of the heavenly glory in the moment before the agony of death, or were momentarily transferred into the heavenly world and conversed with heavenly beings.[2] But it is not necessary to follow M. Dibelius[3] and conclude from similar features in Luke's account—including the sweat falling as drops of blood—that "Jesus hier nach der Schablone des Märtyrers gezeichnet wurde".[4] Luke, or even a later writer, is not concerned with presenting an ideal picture of the death agonies of Jesus, the perfect martyr. His scene rather portrays Jesus wrestling for a positive victory. Here already he is fighting on behalf of mankind, not only for his peace of mind.

This digression takes us some distance from the discussion of Paul. It is nevertheless necessary to correct not only a false psychologising of Jesus 'agony' in Gethsemane, but also the misunderstanding that any of the first Christian writers reflect a picture of

Lip. II 2, p. 85) where Christ is addressed as the καλὸς ἀγωνοθέτης, he who crowns the victors over the opponent (ὁ ἀθλῶν σὺν ἡμῖν in the variant text); similarly 146 (p. 88), also Tertullian ad Mart. 3 and Nilus of Ancyra, de Monastica Exercit. 344: ὁ ἀγωνοθέτης Χριστός (in: Antike Berichte über die Essener, Berlin 1961, p. 58 —LKIT 182).

[1] Cf. the final chapter.

[2] Cf. Brun, op.cit., p. 271, who cites Acts 6:15, 7:56 and Mart Pol 2:2, 9:1, 12:1, 15:1f.

[3] M. Dibelius, "Gethsemane", in BuG I, pp. 26off., and his Formgeschichte des Evangeliums, Tübingen [4]1961, pp. 202f.

[4] Op.cit., p. 267; cf. also p. 266: "Jesus ist der Märtyrer, der menschliches Leiden auf seinem bitteren Todesweg erfahren hat, es aber überwand durch seine Unterwerfung unter Gottes Willen. Dieses Märtyrerbild hat die kirchliche Vorstellung über Gethsemane geformt". There are certainly martyrological features in all of the synoptic passion accounts, but the above characterisation applies to none of them.

prayer itself, and even Jesus' own wrestling with God in prayer, as an Agon. As in the two Pauline passages discussed, Jesus wrestling in prayer is to be seen within the framework of a wider conflict, here the messianic struggle for victory over against Satan and death.

CHAPTER SIX

THE CHARACTERISATION
OF THE CHRISTIAN CALLING AS A RACE

1. THE RIGHT CHRISTIAN Δρόμος

Up to this point the prime application in Paul's use of the athletic image has been certainly to his own mission for the Gospel, and not to a general concept of the Christian life as a contest, parallel to diatribal thought. This has been seen to apply even where the Agon for the Gospel, including the Agon of suffering, is extended to include fellow-workers and fellow-believers, for this application is to be understood on the background of, and in connection with, Paul's own contest.

Paul nevertheless still paints the life of every believer as a foot race, without reference to his own mission or office. The most obvious reference, that to I Cor 9:24f., requires careful treatment, as has been already shown. It may here suffice to repeat two main points. 1. Verse 24b, with its application of the image in τρέχειν to the addressees presents not the paraenetic climax or scopus of the section, but belongs rather to the introduction of the image preparatory to the elaboration of the Apostle's own Agon. 2. The entire reference to the athletic image, including the opening picture of the foot race, has as its tertium the necessity of 'enkrateia' and not only of maximum exertion. Again, the immediate point of reference is Paul's own self-restriction in the interests of the Gospel. Nevertheless, the paraenetic implications for his readers and the relevance of the principle of 'enkrateia' to the discussion of the eating of meats offered to idols is apparent. Bearing in mind these two observations it is clear that we can say little more about the Christian 'race', on the basis of this passage, than the following: The life of faith is a forward movement, a progression towards a final goal (βραβεῖον v.24, στέφανος v.25). The effort of an athlete and his intentness are necessary to reach this goal. But to its attainment belong also self-restriction and renunciation. An 'ethic of activism' finds no basis here.

Nor is an ethic based on exertion to be found in the three other passages which must here be mentioned. The use of τρέχειν in *Rom* 9:16 is in this respect very significant: ἄρα οὖν οὐ τοῦ θέλοντος οὐδὲ τοῦ τρέχοντος, ἀλλὰ τοῦ ἐλεῶντος θεοῦ. Beardslee remarks that Paul's "athletic metaphors usually emphasise the strenuous moral exertion which is necessary for victory, though once the metaphor is used to state precisely the reverse"—referring to the verse under consideration.[1] But this statement is misleading, expressing at the most a half truth. The first half of the sentence is manifestly false, if we bear in mind the results of the previous chapter, while the second half requires modification, since Rom 9:16 cannot be taken as expressing a negation of all earnest striving after righteousness—as little as Phil 2:12 can be taken as establishing human endeavour as the basis of salvation. Bengel has already given the best answer in his usually precise and pointed manner.[2] It is only the desiring and striving of the self-sufficient man which possesses no validity before God. Over against the free but gracious will of God is placed the proud, self-confident will and striving of man looking to his own recourses.

Commentators correctly note a quiet reference to the popular picture of the foot race in the verb τρέχειν. Michel directs attention to the hellenistic ring of the verbs θέλειν and τρέχειν as characteristic for human effort and endeavour.[3] This point largely counters Schlatter's query as to the presence of an expressly athletic image,[4] and is not invalidated by the Old Testament quotation (Ex 33:19) in the preceding verse. References to septuagintal language do not help to illuminate v.16 despite the striking formal resemblance to Eccles 9:11: ὅτι οὐ τοῖς κούφοις ὁ δρόμος καὶ οὐ τοῖς δυνατοῖς ὁ πόλεμος.

---

[1] W. A. Beardslee, Human Achievement and Divine Vocation in the Message of Paul, p. 68.

[2] Cf. Gnomon, ad loc., and G. Bornkamm, Studien zu Antike und Christentum, Gesammelte Aufsätze II, München 1959, p. 91.

[3] O. Michel, Römerbrief, p. 239. Th. Zahn, Römerbrief, p. 450 note 5, also agrees that the athletic image underlies the use of τρέχειν even where the image is not developed; so also Sanday and Headlam, Romans, p. 254. Michel (op.cit., p. 250) thinks that the picture of the foot race is again taken up in vv.30ff. While these verses are certainly to be interpreted on the background of the principle in v.16, it is not so certain that διώκειν has the same metaphorical weight as τρέχειν.

[4] A. Schlatter, Gottes Gerechtigkeit, p. 300: "Ob eine Erinnerung an das Stadion mitwirkt und Paulus den Frommen ... mit dem Wettläufer vergleicht, ist nicht gewiss. Der rennende Mensch kann auch ohne diese Vergleichung den Eifer veranschaulichen, mit dem der Mensch seinen Willen ausführt und erfolgreich zu machen sucht".

Whereas Paul points to the supreme freedom of God's grace which cannot be obligated by man's effort, the OT poet concludes his pessimistic observations on the futility of human exertion with the maxim: "Time and chance meets them all". The negative character of Paul's words also suggests as highly improbable a reference to the use of רוץ / τρέχειν in such passages as Ps 58(59):4, 118(119):32, Prov 1:16 and Is 59:7.[1] The image of the runner in these passages is intended to illustrate not effort, but the intentness on a course of behaviour, whether according to, or against, God's commandments.

Granted the hellenistic character or tone of the verbs in v.16, as well as the possibility of the metaphor having been borrowed from the Stoic diatribe,[2] it would be tempting to regard Paul's maxim-like words as a direct refutation of the Stoic or hellenistic ethic. Taking the verse by itself it is, in effect, just this, as is also Paul's argument in Rom 6 and 7.[3] Whereas the Christian thankfully looks to God's free grace as determining and giving new direction to his own will and effort, the Stoic sage regards "als das eigentliche Sittliche das Moment der Anspannung, der Kraftleistung".[4] However, a direct polemic against Stoic thought hardly underlies Paul's words at this point since he has in mind specifically the manifestation of divine grace in the election and guidance of Israel in its history. Here, as in all Paul's words on the mystery of election and predestination, the emphasis lies on the unfathomable and inexplicable grace of God which is determined by nothing which man is or does.

A clearer picture of the Christian life of faith as a foot race appears in Gal 5:7 and Phil 3:12-14. In *Gal* 5:7 we have the pained rhetorical question of the Apostle: Ἐτρέχετε καλῶς · τίς ὑμᾶς ἐνέκοψεν ἀληθείᾳ μὴ πείθεσθαι. A reference to the progress of the runner on the race course is enhanced by the probability of a continuation of the metaphor in ἐγκόπτειν, suggesting a breaking into or obstruction of the Galatian Christians in their course of following the 'truth'.[5] The

---

[1] See supra pp. 50ff.
[2] Thus H. Lietzmann, An die Römer, p. 92.
[3] For a brief but excellent comparison between the Pauline and Stoic ethic with these chapters in mind, cf. R. Bultmann, "Das religiöse Moment in der ethischen Unterweisung des Epiktet und das Neue Testament", ZNW 13 (1912), pp. 97ff., esp. pp. 184ff.
[4] Bultmann, op.cit., p. 100.
[5] Thus G. Stählin, TWNT III, p. 855, lines 16ff., and—though with reser-

picture is not that of a lagging runner who has fallen back in the race,[1] but of the runner who has allowed his progress to be blocked, or who is still running, but on the wrong course. The subjects of the verb remain unnamed, but are certainly to be identified with the heretics who have led the Galatians astray by their insistence on the necessity of still observing certain points of the Mosaic Law. It is also likely that behind the activity of these Judaizers Paul also saw the hand of Satan who in I Thess 2:18 is responsible for impeding the course of the Apostle himself, and who here appears as the counterpart of ὁ καλῶν ὑμᾶς (v.8).[2]

The verb καλεῖν (cf. IV Macc 11:20, 16:16) could also belong to the present metaphor, but this conclusion is not necessarily supported by the appearance of κλῆσις in the metaphor in Phil 3:14, and καλεῖσθαι at I Tim 6:12—in the latter case the verb immediately refers to 'eternal life', rather than to the καλὸς ἀγὼν τῆς πίστεως in v.11. If the imagery is continued the thought is that the Galatians have not entered the course of their own will and choice. It is God who has called them to run the race of faith, and it is He Whom they have deserted in turning to 'another Gospel' (1:6).

The pictorial character of τρέχειν is better enhanced by the expressive καλῶς. It has already been noted as a characteristic feature of the use of ἀγωνίζεσθαι, that the verb is most frequently qualified by an adverb.[3] The present connection with τρέχειν may equally suggest a standard phrase for the successful running of an athlete, and an interesting counterpart to the frequent designation of a contest as a καλὸς ἀγών (cf. also II Clem 7:1).

Nevertheless, while insisting on the presence of an athletic metaphor in Gal 5:7, the possibility of an influence from septuagintal thought must be kept open, as also in the case of IV Macc 14:5, even though surrounded by numerous references to the distinctly athletic picture of the runner.[4] The designation of behaviour as a running 'without lawlessness' (Ps 58[59]:4) or 'in the way of God's

---

vations—Burton, Galatians, p. 282. But the metaphor is hardly found also in Rom 15:22 and I Thess 2:18, as Stählin thinks. Nor is the image necessarily better preserved in the less well attested variant ἀνακόπτειν, as Lightfoot, Galatians, ad loc., thinks, applying it to the ῥαβδοῦχαι (Thuc. 5.50) who kept the course.

[1] Against Beardslee, op.cit., 68.
[2] Stählin, op.cit., pp. 855f.
[3] Cf. supra pp. 71.—The most frequent adverb is γενναίως.
[4] Cf. supra p. 61.

commandments' (Ps 118[119]:32), or 'to do evil' (Prov. 1:16 and Is 59:7) could well lie behind Paul's phrase. Even more striking is the resemblance between the Apostle's complaint and that in LXX Jer 8:6: διέλιπεν ὁ τρέχων ἀπὸ τοῦ δρόμου αὐτοῦ, and 23:10: καὶ ἐγένετο ὁ δρόμος αὐτῶν πονηρός, even though an athletic image is obviously missing in both passages. The likelihood of a mixture of hellenistic imagery and septuagintal thought is to be conceded at Gal 5:7 more than in any other Agon passage in Paul.

These references counter the view that τρέχειν here, as in Rom 9:16, "is used as a figure for effort looking to the achievement of a result".[1] Just as the OT writer can speak of a man's life or actions as a running, with stress on intentness rather than on exertion, so also Paul can designate the Christian life of faith as a running in a race, without so much as suggesting the idea of extreme effort. Schlier thus correctly writes: "Das τρέχειν ist hier auf das Glaubens-leben des einzelnen Gemeindegliedes bezogen. Das Moment des An-strengenden des Christenlaufes ist im Wort selbst nicht betont... Dieser Wahrheit" (that is, the 'truth of the Gospel', 2:5 and 14) "und damit der Wahrheit gehorchen heisst im guten Lauf des Lebens eilen".[2]

There is no trace of any interest on the part of Paul to picture the life of the Christian—and certainly not his moral life—as a contest or struggle. If the athletic image is consciously chosen it is only to illustrate the character of the life of faith as a forward advance, a set course which must be kept in order to reach the goal.[3] Over against the προκοπή of the life of righteousness through faith stands the ἐγκοπή of this life through the righteousness sought by means of the observance of the Law. The bridge between Gal 2:2 and 5:7 is thus not difficult to find. In the last analysis it is the advance of the Gospel which is at stake through this reversion to 'another Gospel', thereby also challenging the effectiveness of Paul's own missionary ἀγών or δρόμος. The cessation of the 'good race' on the part of the Galatians means, at the same time, that the Apostle has, at least as far as they are concerned, 'run in vain'.

---

[1] Against Burton, op.cit., p. 282, and L. Schmid, p. 31.
[2] H. Schlier, Galaterbrief, p. 236.
[3] Cf. R. Bring, Galatians, p. 239: "The fact that righteousness must be received and that faith is waiting for the consummation of salvation, implies ... a constant advance. The Galatians' advance and growth in faith has been hindered, broken through Judaizers".

2. THE STRIVING FOR PERFECTION IN CHRIST

PHIL 3-12:14

The times are past when an organic process of development towards moral perfection could be read into Phil 3:12-14. Nevertheless, Paul's words have also been misunderstood in more recent times when they have been taken only as an injunction to persistent self-development and moral endeavour, or understood as outlining a general picture of the Christian life as an athletic contest in which advance and progress are to be gained only by the continual struggle against the flesh.[1]

Before entering into a closer examination of the significance of the image in these verses, two points must be established as preliminary but basic observations. (1) Paul's words do not serve to outline a general concept of the Christian calling as a contest in the sense that it requires maximum moral endeavour to reach the goal of perfection. As in I Cor 9:24ff. the immediate purpose of his words is not paraenetic, as has often been supposed. The verses stand within an apologetic-autobiographical context (3:4ff.), containing also a decidedly polemical tone (vv.12f.). (2) The τελειότης which is the goal of the Apostle's striving dare not be reduced to moral perfection, but must rather be understood as the culminating point of his apostolic ministry and his life 'in Christ'. Those scholars are therefore correct who attempt to understand this passage on the basis of Paul's apostolic self-consciousness on the one hand, and his 'Christ-mysticism' on the other. However, since the paraenetic weight of the passage is stronger than in I Cor 9:24ff. it is necessary to discuss these verses in this chapter.

Turning first to the metaphor itself, it is surprising to note that a concrete reference to the athletic image is only contained in v.14: κατὰ σκοπὸν διώκω εἰς τὸ βραβεῖον κτλ. Here again, only the word βραβεῖον (Luther destroys the image with his translation "Kleinod") is taken directly from the language of the games, although σκοπός in this instance clearly refers to the winning post of the race on which the runner intently fixes his gaze. The use of this word in an athletic sequence is quite natural and certainly not unique, appear-

---

[1] For the sake of brevity reference is made to the list of misrepresentations of Paul's use of the athletic image, above, pp. 78ff.

ing in the diatribe, in Philo[1] and again in I Clem 19:2 and 63:1 in this transferred sense.[2]

That the verb διώκειν in v.14 belongs closely to the athletic image does not justify the conclusion that the metaphor begins already in v.12 with the appearance of the same verb, as Barth would believe.[3] This metaphorical character is not to be found in I Thess 5:15 (διώκειν τὸ ἀγαθόν) to which Barth refers, since the 'religious' use of the verb clearly belongs to the frequent septuagintal (MT רדף) and NT occurrences of διώκειν which suggest a zealous striving after a blessing or virtue, whether righteousness, justice, peace, or the knowledge of God etc.[4] Nor does the juxtaposition of διώκειν and καταλαμβάνειν necessarily suggest the presence of the image already in v.12; they appear together in Ex 15:9, Sir 11:10 and Lam 1:6 in the more original sense of pursuit and capture in war. It is further unnatural to supply βραβεῖον from v.14 as the missing object in v.12; the two verses stand far too far apart for this.

If it is at all possible to fix the beginning of the conscious metaphor, we should look to the verb ἐπεκτεινόμενος in v.13b[5] which vividly pictures the runner straining towards the goal with outstretched empty hands. If this is correct the image must already at least be suggested in the first half of the sentence, τὰ μὲν ὀπίσω ἐπιλαν-

---

[1] E. Fuchs, TWNT VII, p. 415, also refers Paul's present use of this metaphor to diatribal usage. The Greek philosophers frequently use the word figuratively for the moral and intellectual aim and goal of life, e.g. Plato, Georg. 507D, Theaet. 194A, Arist., Eth. Nich. II 6, 1106b, 32 and VI 1,1138b, 21 (σκοπός = τὸ μέσον) and III 12,1119b,13 (= τὸ καλόν); cf. also Epict. Encheir. 27 and Marc. Aur. II 16, VIII 1 and 17, X 37. An interesting linguistic parallel is found in Epict. IV 12,15 with its exhoration τετάσθαι τὴν ψυχὴν ἐπὶ τοῦτον τὸν σκοπόν, μηδὲν τῶν ἔξω διώκειν. Philo also uses the word in his picture of the moral Agon, Vit Mos I 48, also Sacr. AC 116.

[2] In 19:2 the metaphor is clear with ἐπανατρέχειν, but is also suggested by the technical expression προκεῖσθαι in 63:1 (cf. Hebr. 12:1).

[3] K. Barth, Erklärung des Philipperbriefs, p. 106. Nor does the verb λαμβάνειν suggest the tert. comp. of the runner, as Barth thinks (p. 107); the use of λαμβάνειν and καταλαμβάνειν in I Cor 9:24 cannot be adduced for support.

[4] LXX: Deut 16:20, Ps 33(34):14, Prov 12:11, 15:9, Sir 27:8, Is 51:1, Hos 6:4(3); NT: Rom 9:30f., I Tim 6:11, II Tim 2:22. Rom 12:13, 14:19, Hebr 12:14, I Cor 14:1; also II Clem 10:1, 18:2 and 20:4.

[5] In agreement with Eidem, p. 116, who rightly sees in the colourless διώκειν, strengthened through its connection with καταλαμβάνειν, the psychological transition to the use of the metaphor in the mind of the writer. But this transition is not suggested by τέλειος which, as Eidem points out (p. 183 note 1), is also used of athletes. The thought underlying τετελείωμαι in v.12 refers to that which precedes, not to the following image.

θανόμενος, even though it is rather the task of the runner, correctly speaking, not to look back, but to keep his eyes fixed on the goal before him. The context, though not necessarily the verb ἐπεκτεί-νειν, indicates that Paul thinks of himself as being in the last and decisive stages of the race, but it is idle to seek any more concrete features in the image.[1] What the Apostle wishes to stress is not how far he has already run, or how far he still has to go, but rather the fact that he has *not yet* reached the goal of his endeavour.—The suggestion that the entire image is borrowed from the chariot races in the circus, a familiar picture in Rome where the letter was sup-posedly written, hardly deserves serious consideration—the 'proof' is all too tenuous.[2] In any case, Rome was hardly the origin of the letter.

Far more important than the formal analysis of the image is the question: what thought or point does the Apostle wish to illustrate by its use? Beardslee's characterisation of the image as suggesting "the incompleteness of the present situation, either as to its actual results, or as to the inner character of the contestant",[3] as well as the customary references to this passage as the prime and most expressive witness in the Pauline letters to the "already—but not yet" dialectical tension of the life of faith,[4] are correct but generalise Paul's thought in these verses. The Apostle's interest is not centred

---

[1] E.g. E. Lohmeyer, Philipperbrief (KEK), p. 146: "Er (der Läufer) ist an dem Punkt angelangt, da die Rundung der Bahn wieder in die Gerade einbiegt und das Ziel sichtbar wird".

[2] Cf. Bröse, Theologische Studien und Kritiken, 1920/21, p. 70, and R. H. Lightfoot, Philippians, p. 152f., who refers to Soph. Elec. 738 for διώκειν used of charioteers, but agrees that the athletic image is more natural. Κλῆσις hardly completes the image as in IV Macc 11:20 and 16:16 (καλεῖσθαι). Chrysostom's picture of the king calling the victor from the arena up to the royal seats to receive his prize is too daring (Eidem, p. 118). Nor need we see in Paul's words a picture of God standing at the end of the course holding out the prize (Heinzelmann [NTD 8], ⁶1953, p. 102). Κλῆσις is best taken as a 'nomen actionis' signifying God's act of calling in Christ, not that to which the believer is called.

[3] Beardslee, op.cit., p. 68.

[4] Bultmann, who refers to this passage almost as frequently as to the ὡς μή in I Cor 7:29-31, speaks rather of the 'Nicht mehr' and 'Noch nicht' character of existence in faith (cf. Urchristentum, p. 204f., ET: p. 184; GuV II, pp. 56 and 132, and his Theologie des NTs., passim). But it is questionable whether Bultmann has the right to read the existential principle of 'Offenheit für die Zukunft' into Paul's words. Paul *knows* his goal and *strives* toward it, even though, and because, he knows of his continual dependence on the grace of God.

on enunciating a general principle of Christian life and ethics—
whether the accent lie on the 'not yet', or on the necessity of
striving for the goal of perfection—but on providing a pointed
answer to a specific problem in hand.

As in the equally difficult passage I Cor 9:24-27 the problem is
to be read out of the immediately preceding context. These two
passages have more in common than the use of the popular athletic
image. Paul begins in 3:2ff. with a sharp word (κύνες!) against his
opponents who also in Philippi threaten to destroy his work. The
autobiographical verses (vv.4bff.) which describe his progress from
the past in which he trusted in the flesh or in the Law, to the present
when he has counted all his past boasting as refuse in order to gain
Christ and be found in him, presuppose an attack on Paul's claims
to apostolicity at the hands of opponents who rose up against him
with their own claims of authority. Paul can counter and match
every boast and sign of authority which they produce: circumcision,
an unimpeachable Jewish background and upbringing, and strict
adherence to the Law (vv.5f.). But all these claims, on which they
seek to base their authority, Paul for his part now considers loss
having gained Christ and his righteousness (v.9). They may claim
perfection in the Law, he himself only claims Christ; they pursue
the exact enactment of the requirements of the Law as their goal,
Paul strives only to become more Christ-like, to "know him and the
power of his resurrection, to share in his sufferings, becoming like
him in his death" (v.10). Herein lies the final 'proof' of his apostolic
authority; for Paul, suffering and death in the faithful fulfilment of
his commission is the final ratification of his office,[1] for in them is
revealed the power of the cross—this is also always presupposed in
every mention of the resurrection—and resurrection of Christ.

It is with this front still in mind that Paul continues his defence in
vv.12-14 with a decided apologetic overtone—witness the strong οὐχ
ἤδη and οὔπω, and the emphatic ἐγώ (vv.12f.). This defence is itself a
paradox, for over against the claims to perfection of his opponents,
Paul himselfs claims or asserts his imperfection; the final seal, suffering and dying for his Lord, has not yet been set on his work.

If this front against which the Apostle defends himself has been

---

[1] For this sequence of thought see K. H. Rengstorf, Apostolat und Predigtamt, Stuttgart ²1954, p. 24 together with note 64, and B. Weiss, Das Neue
Testament II, Leipzig 1902, p. 438, who also sees in v.2 a reply against the
evil-workers of v.2 who claim this superiority over Paul.

correctly sketched, the interpretation of v.12 with its perpetual problem of ascertaining the unmentioned object of λαμβάνειν and καταλαμβάνειν, as well as the meaning of τετελείωμαι, must follow a different course than that usually taken by the commentaries. Even where δικαιοσύνη has not been supplied from v.9 as the unnamed object in v.12, it has repeatedly been supposed that it is this concept which still underlies Paul's words in this and the following verses. That this interpretation is, in fact, very old, can be seen from the addition into the Western Text[1] of the interpretive phrase ἢ ἤδη δεδικαίωμαι. It is very doubtful whether the words were introduced under the influence of I Cor 4:4 since the sense is here different. Verse 9 probably directly suggested the addition. But the meaning which results is problematical. Especially in his letters to the Romans and to the Galatians Paul does not tire in emphasising that the believer is justified (Rom 5:9 δικαιωθέντες νῦν, 3:24ff., 5:1, 6:7)—the attributed righteousness of Christ is a present reality, even though the final verdict of God, the righteous Judge, is still awaited in the future. Verse 9 also agrees with this emphasis—'the righteousness of Christ through faith', for which he has counted all else refuse, is already his and not conceived as still awaited. True, Paul speaks in Gal 5:5 of waiting for the hope (that is, the object of hope) of justification, but even if it be agreed with Oepke, that these words reflect "die ursprüngliche eschatologische Fassung der Rechtfertigung",[2] it is certain that this eschatological view is not to be found in the late letter to the Philippians. The other possibility would be, assuming that Paul still has the concept of righteousness in mind in vv.12ff., that he is here thinking of the growth and progress of sanctification. The perfection for which Paul strives is then thought of as "moral and spiritual perfection".[3] Older commentaries reflect this understanding of the text and interpret Paul's polemical tone accordingly. Thus Heinzelmann finds a polemic against a moral laziness which is content to rest on the righteousness of faith,[4] and sees in Paul's concept of Christian perfection, perfec-

---

[1] E.g. D, Irenaeus, Ambrosiaster.

[2] A. Oepke, Galaterbrief (ThHK), p. 119.

[3] Vincent, Philippians (ICC), pp. 107f. —Paul "is stimulated by the past to renewed energy in Christian self development".

[4] Heinzelmann, op.cit., p. 102.; similarly Dibelius, An die Philipper (HNT), pp. 90f. —Christian perfection exists paradoxically in imperfection, in continually running for the goal, in obedience to the heavenly calling.

tion in striving, in running for the goal faithfully following the knowledge of Christ already gained. Similarly, Lightfoot[1] thinks that he can detect a protest "against the false security of antinomian recklessness, which others deduced from the doctrine of faith". Paul points to his own "spiritual insecurity, his earnest strivings, his own onward progress". Finally Barth, while rejecting 'righteousness' as the missing object in v.12, nevertheless bases his exegesis on this concept, stating that Paul's love for the athletic image is most closely connected with his struggle for the righteousness of God. He who possesses the gift of the righteousness of God knows only a life lived "in höchster...aufgeregtester Aktivität".[2] Barth sees in Paul's polemical tone a rejoinder to those who object that he, the Apostle, has no need of such striving. But where does the text suggest such an objection on the part of the Philippians? If Paul's words are so interpreted the vital force of vv.10f., as a reply to those who have attacked his authority, is lost.

Paul's words in these verses are far too concrete to allow the following image to be interpreted merely as a general picture of the necessity for striving after moral growth and spiritual progress. For the same reason the missing object in v.12 must necessarily be supplied. Earlier commentators have frequently pointed out that an object has been deliberately omitted in order to place more emphasis on the verbs in their absolute use to stress the incompleteness of Paul's situation as one continually striving for the goal.[3] This observation, correct in itself, does not release the exegete from the obligation of determining from the context the object of the Apostle's striving.

The goal must obviously be found in vv.9-11.[4] The easiest solution is to take Χριστός from v.9 as the missing object. Certainly, the thought of ultimately gaining Christ, of being found in him at the

---

[1] Lightfoot, Philippians, pp. 151f. Ewald and Wohlenberg, Der Brief an die Philipper (KNT), p. 184, find a correction of the view that Paul himself has no need of progress or deepening of the life of faith, but correctly reject the idea that vv.12ff. have anything to do with moral perfection. Paul speaks against the conception of moral perfection amongst the Judaizers.

[2] K. Barth, Philipperbrief, p. 106; similarly Schmid, p. 71: "Durch die Tatsache, dass uns das neue von der δικαιοσύνη θεοῦ erzeugte Wollen geschenkt ist, wird die δικαιοσύνη zugleich Besitz und Ziel. Sie ist uns dazu gegeben, damit wir sie erstreben mit der ganzen Intensität unseres Wollens".

[3] Cf. Eidem, p. 116, B. Weiss, op.cit., p. 438, and Barth, op.cit., p. 107.

[4] Vincent, op.cit., p. 107 includes all that is said in vv.8-11.

last day, is also contained in vv.12ff., but this goal and the path to it is again more closely defined in vv.10f.: τοῦ γνῶναι αὐτὸν καὶ τὴν δύναμιν τῆς ἀναστάσεως αὐτοῦ καὶ κοινωνίαν παθημάτων αὐτοῦ, συμμορφιζόμενος τῷ θανάτῳ αὐτοῦ. These words bring us very close to that realm of thought in Paul which is usually called his Christ mysticism. Dibelius has repeatedly emphasised this aspect of the present passage.[1] The parallelism between v.12c and d suggests 'Christ' as the missing object. Because he has been gained by Christ, the goal of Paul's endeavour is to gain Christ himself. But the path to union with Christ is expressed more exactly with the term γιγνώσκειν. Dibelius sees behind the use of this term and of τελειοῦσθαι in v.12 the language of the hellenistic mysteries in which that man is τέλειος who has been granted the gift of γνῶσις through the vision of the deity.[2] The attractiveness of this thesis is increased when it is remembered that Philo also speaks of the mystic vision of the deity in the term of an Agon. In Mut Nom 81ff. he writes, "the task of him who has the vision of God (τοῦ τὸν θεὸν ὁρῶντος) is not to leave the holy contest (ἱερὸς ἀγών) uncrowned, but to bear away the victor's crown". Even more interesting is the passage in the Corpus Hermeticum to which attention has been drawn earlier in this work (X 19, supra pp.35ff.). Here τὸ γνῶναι τὸ θεῖον is included as the object of the ἀγὼν εὐσέβειας.

However, it is just the vital words in vv.10f. which show how little Paul's mysticism has to do with the hellenistic Mysteries at this point. Dibelius himself draws the decisive line of distinction: "Nicht Weihen, sondern Arbeit, Kampf und Leiden machen Christus ähnlich".[3] For Paul in his specific situation as an Apostle, to know Christ, to become more Christ-like, means to share in his sufferings and to become like him in his death in the enactment of his apostolic commission. His mysticism here goes beyond the familiar schema otherwise found in his letters where union with Christ and the state of being 'in Christ' is gained by dying with him in his

---

[1] For the following see esp. Dibelius, An die Philipper (HNT), ad loc., and "'Ἐπίγνωσις ἀληθείας", Neutestamentliche Studien G. Heinrici zum 70. Geburtstag, Leipzig, 1914 (= BuG II, pp. 8f.).

[2] Cf. R. Reitzenstein, Die hellenistischen Mysterienreligionen, pp. 338f., Dibelius, BuG II, p. 8, and BAG, s. τέλειος and τελειοῦσθαι.

[3] An die Philipper, p. 91. W. Michaelis, An die Philipper (ThKH), p. 59, takes τοῦ γνῶναι αὐτόν as the missing object, but finds here not the gnosis of the mystic, but "die Vertiefung der Gemeinschaft mit Christus als stete Erneuerung des inneren Menschen, die sich im Wandel bewähren muss".

death and being raised with him in his resurrection (cf. esp. Rom 6:3ff.).[1] This thought is also indicated here when Paul speaks of the 'power of his resurrection'. But for Paul this δύναμις which flows from the union with Christ is also already at work where one would perhaps least expect it—in the κοινωνία τῶν παθημάτων of Christ, in becoming like him in his death. That which this power effects is not lordship over suffering in the Stoic sense, but the manifestation of the power of God in them—"in order that the life of Jesus may be made manifest in our mortal flesh" (II Cor 4:11). It is for this reason that the Apostle can take the, in itself, daring step of placing his own sufferings at the side of Christ's, despite the qualitative difference which separates them. In the cross of His Son who took on the μορφή of the servant and in the sufferings of his servant, the Apostle, God reveals His strength. Thus these very sufferings are again an assurance for Paul that he will also share in the future resurrection of the dead (v.11b), the final work of 'power'.

On the basis of what has already been observed it must be granted that Lohmeyer's thesis—martyrdom as the entire theme of the letter—finds its firmest support in the verses under discussion. But Lohmeyer goes the further step of relating them not only to the martyrdom of Paul, but also to the sufferings of the Philippians themselves. Accordingly, Paul's words are understood as an attempt to check and correct a false evaluation or over-estimation of the role of martyrdom in the Christian life as it was apparently held by certain members of the Philippian congregation. Those few who have had to suffer for the faith seem to consider themselves the 'perfect', and thus, martyr-proud, place themselves on a level above those who have not been immediately affected by the persecution. To counter this view Paul emphasises the necessary striving and running, from the starting point given in Christ to the goal set by God.[2] Lohmeyer's observations are helpful at this point since it is recognised that the obviously pointed use of τελειοῦσθαι is immediately related to vv.10f., and not to v.9 with its mention of δικαιοσύνη. He correctly notes that already in Judaism the thought of death is attended with the idea of perfection, and cites the following two

---

[1] Rom 6:5: σύμφυτοι γεγόναμεν τῷ ὁμοιώματι τοῦ θανάτου αὐτοῦ, with its 'sacramental mysticism' does not provide a direct parallel to v.10c which speaks of a concrete fellowship of suffering. The same applies to the use of the related adjective in Rom 8:29: σύμμορφοι τῆς εἰκόνος τοῦ υἱοῦ.

[2] Der Brief an die Philipper (KEK), p. 143.

passages for support—Sap 4:7,13: δίκαιος δὲ ἐὰν φθάσῃ τελευτῆσαι ἐν ἀναπαύσει ἔσται ... τελειωθεὶς ἐν ὀλίγῳ ἐπλήρωσεν χρόνους μακρούς (cf. also v.16), and Philo Leg All III 74: πότε οὖν, ὦ ψυχή, μάλιστα νεκροφορεῖν σαυτὴν ὑπολήψῃ; ἆρά γε οὐχ ὅταν τελειωθῇς καὶ βραβείων καὶ στεφάνων ἀξιωθῇς; ἔσῃ γὰρ τότε φιλόθεος, οὐ φιλοσώματος.¹ This same connection appears again in the New Testament, apart from the present passage, in the Epistle to the Hebrews (2:10, 5:9, 7:28, 10:14, 12:2 and 23).² But even more instructive than the above references is IV Macc 7:15, where the connection with martyrdom becomes quite apparent. It is related that the βίος νόμιμος of the martyr Eleazar was perfected by the Seal of death (ὃν πιστὴ θανάτου σφραγὶς ἐτελείωσεν). Further evidence from the early Christian martyrdom accounts also points to the development towards an almost technical use of τελειοῦσθαι. The following examples may suffice—Martyrium Andreae Alterum (Bonn.-Lip. II 1, p.64): Ἐτελειώθη δὲ ὁ ἅγιος καὶ ἀπόστολος τοῦ Χριστοῦ Ἀνδρέας μαρτυρήσας ὑπὲρ τοῦ ὀνόματος τοῦ κυρίου, Martyrium Matthaei 31 (Bonn.-Lip. II 1, p. 261): Ἐτελειώθη δὲ ὁ ἅγιος τοῦ θεοῦ ἀπόστολος καὶ εὐαγγελιστὴς Ματθαῖος,³ and also the phrase μαρτυρίῳ τελειοῦσθαι in Eusebius H. E. VI 2,12 (similarly VII 11,26 and 15,5). This use of τελειοῦσθαι in connection with the theme of martyrdom obviously goes beyond the normal use of the related verb τελευτᾶν to designate death.

Even though his choice of terms is different, Ignatius of Antioch also offers an explanatory parallel to Paul's words in Phil 3:10ff. when he writes to the Ephesians: "For though I am a prisoner for the Name, οὔπω ἀπήρτισμαι ἐν Ἰησοῦ Χριστῷ · νῦν γὰρ ἀρχὴν ἔχω τοῦ μαθητεύεσθαι (Eph 3:1; cf. ἔτι ὢν ἀναπάρτιστος in Philad 5:1).⁴ The perfect, ἀπήρτισμαι, should here be translated in the same way as τετελείωμαι in Phil 3:12: "I have not yet been perfected". Already in his present sufferings Ignatius is becoming more and more a disciple of the Lord (also Rom 5:1,3), but only in death, in martyr-

---

¹ Op.cit., p. 144 note 1.

² For delaited studies on τέλειος/τελειοῦν in Hebrews see M. Dibelius, "Der himmlische Kultus nach dem Hebräerbrief", in: Theologische Blätter 21/1942, pp. 1ff., (BuG II, pp. 16off.) and Kögel, "Der Begriff τελειοῦν im Hebräerbrief" (Theol. Studien M. Kähler dargebracht, pp. 35-68).

³ Cf. also the heading Ἡ τελείωσις Θωμᾶ τοῦ ἀποστόλου (Bonn.-Lip. II 2, p. 289). Acta Petri et Pauli (Bonn.-Lip. I, p. 221): Ἐτελειώθη δὲ ὁ δρόμος τῶν ἁγίων ἀποστόλων καὶ μαρτύρων is probably a recollection of Acts 20:24 or/and II Tim 4:7, but is also relevant here.

⁴ For the following see R. Bultmann, "Ignatius und Paulus", in: Studia Paulina, in honorem J. de Zwaan septuagenarii, Haarlem 1953, pp. 50f.

dom, does he expect to be granted the status of a true disciple (Rom 4:2f., Eph 1:2, Pol 7:1). He, like Paul, also knows of a fellowship of Christ's sufferings, of suffering with him: εἰς τὸ συμπαθεῖν αὐτῷ πάντα ὑπομένω, αὐτοῦ με ἐνδυναμοῦντος (Smyrn 4:2; cf. also Magn 5:2 and Rom 6:1). But that which separates Ignatius from Paul at this point becomes already apparent when he regards the martyr's death itself as the highest goal of the Christian life and can consequently call himself a μιμητὴς τοῦ πάθους τοῦ θεοῦ μου (Rom 6:3). Bultmann points to the decisive point of distinction: "Wirkt sich der Tod Jesu für Paulus in seinem gegenwärtigen apostolischen Leben und Wirken aus (2. Kor 4,7ff.), so ist er für Ign. ein Vorbild, das es nachzuahmen gilt".[1] Of course Ignatius also knows that martyrdom is not the only necessary climax to the Christian life, but there are nevertheless tendencies in his thought which point to a later exaggerated evaluation of martyrdom.

For Paul only those who are in possession of the Spirit can already be called the τέλειοι (I Cor 2:6, 3:1). But this 'perfection' is not 'ausweisbar', cannot be certified like the righteousness of the Law of the Judaizers. The righteousness of Christ, though in itself a perfect gift of God, awaits the final eschatological completion at the resurrection when the believer will stand before the Judge "perfect in Christ" (Col 1:28)—Thus Paul's longing and striving for the ultimate goal, unimpeded and complete union with Christ.[2] It is just in the paradoxical path to this final goal that the Apostle nevertheless sees the confirmation of his apostleship. Just as God revealed His righteousness and His strength in the ignominious cross of His Son and in raising him from the grave, so Paul also can see in his sufferings and possible death in office the strong hand of God at work. To his opponents' claims of certifiable perfection Paul answers with the claim to the uncertifiable righteousness by faith and to the hidden strength of God working through his weakness and imperfection. Even the goal of becoming more Christlike in suffering and in death serves the glory of God. "For we have this treasure in earthen vessels, to show that the surpassing power comes from God and not from us" (II Cor 4:7).

Returning to the athletic image in vv.12ff., it is apparent that these verses serve to illustrate what Paul means by his present state

---

[1] Ibid. Cf. the final chapter for the development of the Agon of martyrdom.
[2] Cf. Phil 1:23, II Cor 5:8 and I Cor 13:12 (cp. Phil 3:10).

of imperfection. The stress is on the 'not yet' character of the present, and the thought of running and striving for the goal also serves this point. Not so much the effort of the runner but the goal for which he strives is central, a goal which is given in Christ.[1]

With this same central emphasis in mind it is easier to decide several other questions raised by these verses. For example, two possibilities of interpreting the phrase "forgetting that which lies behind me" (v.13) have always been weighed over against each other. Either Paul wishes to indicate with τὰ ὀπίσω his life as a faithful Pharisee which was broken off when he was "grasped by Christ" (v.12), or he pictures his entire life as a believer as a foot race in which τὰ ὀπίσω means the progress he has made as a Christian.[2] Does ἐπιλανθανόμενος refer to forgetting his Jewish past in which he can no longer pride, or to putting behind him the past blessings and progress he has experienced in his Christian life, lest self-satisfaction creep in? The second alternative is certainly the more probable,[3] but it is far more likely that any periodisation of his life was far from Paul's mind when he penned these words. They simply serve to elaborate the image, and are thus best taken as "nur anschauliche Schilderung des διώκειν".[4]

The same emphasis on the fact that Paul's goal is never realized in the present, but always lies in the future lies behind the phrase ἡ ἄνω κλῆσις. Not the heavenly origin of this 'calling' is meant (as in Hebr 3:1), but rather the direction in which this calling leads, that is, the 'heavenward' calling.[5] One is justified in detecting a

---

[1] "Die Hauptsache ... ist weniger der Einsatz des Christen ... als vielmehr die Tatsache, dass dem Christenlauf ein Ziel vorgesteckt ist" (E. Fuchs, TWNT VII, p. 415f.). —ἐφ' ᾧ (v.12) = because (cf. Blass-Debr. §235,2) — For the other view, see E. Stauffer, TWNT II, p. 637, lines 12ff.

[2] Cf. Eidem, p. 118.

[3] Against Ewald-Wohlenberg, op.cit., pp. 189f., who themselves draw attention to the use of the present participle ἐπιλανθανόμενος instead of ἐπιλαθόμενος —the act is not confined to the past being rather a continual process.

[4] Cf. W. Michaelis, An die Philipper (ThHK), p. 59, who rightly objects to Barth's and Lohmeyer's "das schon Geleistete".

[5] Ewald-Wohlenberg, op.cit., p. 190, "die nach oben weisende Berufung". For the reason stated above Lohmeyer's reference (op.cit., p. 147 note 4) to the Jewish concept of the 'Bath-Qol', as well as to the voice from heaven at the moment of death in the martyr reports, is not applicable. The reference to Greek Apoc Bar 4: ἐν αὐτῷ μέλλουσιν τὴν ἄνω κλῆσιν προσλαβεῖν καὶ τὴν εἰς παράδεισον εἴσοδον (cf. also BAG s. ἄνω) rather supports our interpretation. Barth, op.cit., p. 110, is hardly right in taking κλῆσις and βραβεῖον as one and the same thing —"die droben in Kraft stehende Berufung".

polemical tone in these words also. Verse 19 characterises the opponents as τὰ ἐπίγεια φρονοῦντες. Over against the claim that legalism
is the precondition to perfection, the earthly βραβεῖον of the Judaizers, Paul points to another prize which can never be earned or
claimed as a full possession in this life. Perfection lies alone in the
hands of God Who will bring to completion that which He has begun
in calling men 'in Christ Jesus'.[1]

The exegesis of Phil 3:12ff. within 3:2-16 has revealed for us a
different situation to that which Lohmeyer detects behind these
verses. It is now necessary to return briefly to his contention that
the Apostle here wishes to correct a false estimation of the role of
martyrdom held by certain members of the congregation in Philippi.
The truth in his argument lies in the recognition that for Paul the
path to perfection leads through suffering and death. But it is incorrect to take the situation of the Apostle as an exact paradigma for
every believer. This is certainly not the meaning of the words
συμμιμηταί μοῦ γίνεσθε in 3:17. This verse which again begins a more
direct attack on his enemies rather supports the exegesis of 3:12ff.
presented above. These verses do not offer a general treatment on
the value of martyrdom as such. Paul draws his sufferings and death
into the argument in answer to the attacks of his opponents. They
cannot be seen on the same level as those of any other member of
the Philippian congregation since for Paul they have the character
of the seal and ratification of his apostolic commission from God.
Phil 3:12ff. certainly contains a precise summary of the Christian
ethic, but it is first and foremost the apostolic ethos which is sketched.[2]

Nevertheless, it is quite apparent that this autobiographical
section also offers a parallel to I Cor 9:24-27 in so far as a *decided
paraenetic emphasis* is again present. We here meet with a consistent
feature of the autobiographical-apologetical sections in Paul's
letters, a feature also to be noted repeatedly in the most vehement

---

[1] On βραβεῖον as reward, cf. G. Bornkamm, "Der Lohngedanke im Neuen
Testament", Studien zu Antike und Urchristentum, Gesammelte Aufsätze
II, p. 91: "Dieser Lohn heisst praemium, nicht pretium, eine unberechenbare,
unvorstellbare Belohnung, nicht ein berechenbarer, dem menschlichen An-
spruch verfügbarer Preis für seine Werke".

[2] Correctly seen by W. Michaelis, op.cit., p. 59: "Nicht sehnsüchtiges
Ausschauhalten, auch nicht warten auf das Martyrium, sondern ange-
strengte Arbeit an sich selbst in der Bewährung im apostolischen Beruf und
Leiden".

defence of his apostleship in II Cor 10-13. From his own specific situation the Apostle draws parallel consequences for his readers in their own situation. The movement is from his own person, from the specific to the general.[1] In the case of the present passage this takes place in v.15,[2] where Paul joins himself together with his readers in the ὅσοι. The use of the adjective τέλειος is pointed and obviously takes up the catchword of the opposition who link perfection with the zeal for the Law. It is difficult to determine whether ὅσοι is meant to refer to Paul and the Philippian congregation over against the Judaizers, or to parties or factions within the congregation itself, those who 'think otherwise' then being those who have allowed themselves to be influenced by the Judaizers in their attitude to the legal and cultic requirements of the life of faith. The first of these two alternatives is, however, to be preferred, since the epistle does not hint at a split in the congregation itself. It is at least certain that the word is not to be interpreted on the background of the language of the mysteries,[3] nor is it necessary to see in the term the catchword of the Philippian Christian super-martyrs'.[4]

The intention of vv.15f. is perfectly clear. Perfection, which is always *spiritual perfection in Christ* (cf. vv. 9, 12 and 14) is never a present possession, but rather *always a goal*. That which God has begun in calling men in Christ He Himself will perfect at the last day. In this sense only can one speak of Christian perfection. It exists, paradoxically, in Christian imperfection, in the earnest longing for the fulfilment, in running for the final goal.[5]

It is this eschatological character—eschatological in its foundation and fulfilment—which here distinguishes the Christian ethic from the legalistic ethic.[6] This same factor contributes to the absesen

---

[1] We can agree with Barth (op.cit., p. 110): "Selbstbiographie ist bei Paulus hier ... gerade nicht Selbstzweck, gewiss auch nicht blosses Parergon, wohl aber vollwertiges Paradigma der paulinischen Darlegung. An den Bedingungen, unter denen er existiert, sollen die Leser die Bedingungen erkennen, unter denen sie selbst existieren".

[2] Verse 17 begins a new paraenetic section, though with the same opponents still in mind. The term ἀδελφοί becomes an almost technical form of address characteristic of the paraenetic style of Paul (over 50 times) and of the Epistle of James.

[3] Against Lietzmann, An die Philipper (HNT) and also BAG s.v. 2b.

[4] Against Lohmeyer, op.cit., p. 148.

[5] Barth, op.cit., p. 111.

[6] For the connection between Pauline ethics and eschatology, see most recently W. Schrage, Die konkreten Einzelgebote in der paulinischen Paränese, pp. 13ff.

of the concept of progress (προκοπή) as it is found in the Stoic picture of the moral Agon. Here advance is essentially connected with the acquisition of individual virtues to be gained or developed from man's own natural disposition (φύσις).[1] Because Paul rejects a 'Tugendethik', this concept of progress and growth is also impossible. When he does use the term προκοπή it is to express the advance of the Gospel (Phil 1:12) or the collective spiritual growth of a congregation (Phil 1:15),[2] 'spiritual' here denoting that which is given through the gift of the Spirit. It is entirely in keeping with this last emphasis that Paul speaks of Christians as τέλειοι only in so far as they are πνευματικοί, that is, endowed with the gifts of the Spirit (I Cor 2:6 and 3:1). If there is progress it is above all growth in maturity and steadfastness of faith within the life 'in Christ'.[3] This again comes to expression in Pauline paraenesis. The Apostle can demand growth or progress in the concrete life of his readers (cf. the use of περισσεύειν in I Cor 14:12, 15:58, II Cor 9:8, I Thess 4:1-10, and Phil 4:17), but what is meant is always progress on a course which has already begun with the acceptance of the Gospel. This progress includes of course, growth in sanctification. But the process of sanctification always follows God's act of justification.

The same line of thought is present here in Philippians where spiritual perfection, perfection in Christ, stands in opposition to a moral, outward perfection. The final word in v.16 is of major significance. The warning is: Let us not swerve from the course in which we are running, lest we surrender, by returning to the Law, that which we have already gained in Christ. With these words the Christian ethic outlined by means of the picture of the Agon, and

---

[1] Cf. G. Stählin, TWNT VI, pp. 706f.

[2] Only in I Tim 4:15 is the term used individually, and even here the word expresses the progress to be made in the faithful enactment of Timothy's office, to growth in the χάρισμα granted him at his ordination (v.14).

[3] Cf. Beardslee, op.cit., esp. ch. IV, Progress, Growth, and Perfection. "The 'perfect' man in Paul's thought is best understood as the 'mature' man, the responsible adult who has experienced and is experiencing what it is to be in Christ". But the same author completely misrepresents Phil 3:12ff. when stating that "Paul here speaks of maturity as the result of moral struggle and discipline" (p. 73). That perfection is an eschatological category is clear from I Cor 13:8-13, Col 1:28 and 4:12. "Perfection belongs to the coming age, but this age is already present in faith in Christ. What is perfect can already invade this age as a sign that in Christ the old has been pervaded by the new" (J. N. Sevenster, Paul and Seneca, Leiden/Brill 1961, p. 144).

applied to the situation of every believer, is characterised as an ethic of steadfastness, endurance and perseverance. The task of the believer is to persevere in, and live according to, that which he has received in Christ. In this sense Paul's ethic and the ethic which is expressed by means of the athletic image, is above all a 'Bewährungsethik',[1] not merely an 'ethic of maximum exertion'.

3. The Crown or Prize of the Race

It must at first sight seem strange that the prize or crown plays such a subordinate role in Paul's use of the athletic metaphor. The occurrence of βραβεῖον[2] with στέφανος again in I Cor 9:24f. has been found to represent a 'topos' or commonplace of the diatribe with the usual motivation for exertion, the prospect of a crown which is greater than any which can be won at the games. Both words have in this instance little more purpose than to complete the metaphor which Paul is developing, a judgment which also applies to στεφανοῦσθαι in II Tim 3:5. It would therefore be false to see in v.25 the motive for the Agon. In the case of Paul's own apostolic Agon this is to be found in vv.19-23—all his endeavour is directed to the goal that the Gospel may prove as effective as possible, "in order that I may by any means save some." Even where the picture of the race is transferred to the Christian calling it is the divine initiative and God's own goal for man which provides the motive for striving towards the prize (Phil 3:12b), not the tempting offer of the prize itself.

Apart from the above two passages στέφανος only again appears in Phil 4:1 and I Thess 2:19 where the crown may, as we have seen, just as well represent a symbol of joy and honour without recalling the athletic image. Even if the image is taken from the games, the reference remains fleeting and undeveloped. Apart from the more precise characterisation of the crown as a 'crown of righteousness' in II Tim 4:8 we only have the vague and traditional description, ἄφθαρτος, in I Cor 9:25. The reason for this lack of interest in developing the image of the Christian crown or prize is not hard to

---

[1] Cf. the centrality of ὑπομονή in Pauline paraenesis. E. Stauffer (TWNT I, p. 637) unfortunately emphasises only the one side, the element of exertion.

[2] Vincent, Philippians (ICC), p. 110, wrongly claims that βραβεῖον is not a term. tech. of the games. The Greek use of the term and its occurrence as a Latin and Coptic loanword denies this.

imagine. In the first place the entire weight of the athletic metaphor lies on the characterisation of the present situation of the Apostle and the athlete of the Gospel, or of the Christian on the course towards the fulfilment of his calling. In the second place Paul has no need to describe what he means by the βραβεῖον, nor is there any danger that his words will be misunderstood to mean that the prize is still dependent on man's exertion. Within the context of Phil 3:12ff. the prize can be nothing else than the perfection, by God, of that which He has begun in calling men in Christ Jesus. It thus becomes clear that the prize is certainly a reward in the sense that God will crown faithfulness and constancy in this calling, but not in the sense that it is dependent on the exertion of the 'runner' or can be calculated by him.[1] Both beginning and end of the course lie alone in the hands of God, the initiator and perfector.

The apparent small interest in developing the picture of the Christian crown or prize might seem to be augmented by two passages in Colossians, 2:18 μηδεὶς ὑμᾶς καταβραβευέτω, and 3:15 ἡ εἰρήνη τοῦ Χριστοῦ βραβευέτω ἐν ταῖς καρδίαις ὑμῶν. Ewald and Wohlenberg, for example, relate Phil 3:14 to the first passage, finding a similar polemic against the Judaïzers who know of and strive after another βραβεῖον than the Apostle.[2] Straub also retains the metaphor when he translates the phrase with "den Kampfpreis aberkennen".[3] Some of the Fathers also saw in both cases a conscious reference to the athletic image. Two quotations from the Biblical Homilies of John Chrysostom may suffice to illustrate this point. On Col 2:18 he writes: "Let no one adjudge away from you (κατα-βραβευέτω) the Body of Christ, that is, thwart you of it (ὑπηρεαζέτω). The word καταβραβευθῆναι is employed when the victory is with one party and the prize (βραβεῖον) with another: when though a victor you are thwarted. You stand above the devil and sin; why do you again subject yourself to sin?" And again on Col 3:15: "If two thoughts are fighting together, set not anger, set not spitefulness to hold the prize (βραβεῖον), but peace.... If the peace of God stands

---

[1] Paul speaks of the crown which awaits him at the last day (II Tim 4:8), but there is a wide gap between this certainty and the demanding tone of the Manichaean psalmist: "Give me my garland for which I have toiled", or "Pay unto me the reward of my many contests" (A Manichaean Psalm-Book, Part II, ed. C. R. C. Allberry, Stuttgart 1938, 88.9 and 101.30f.; cf. also 91.14 and 94.13).

[2] An die Philipper (KNT), p. 191.

[3] Straub, Die Bildersprache des Apostels Paulus, p. 28.

forward as umpire it bestows the prize on that which bids endure and puts the other to shame .... He (Paul) has represented an arena (στάδιον) within, in the thoughts, and a contest and a wrestling and an umpire (ἀγῶνα καὶ ἄθλησιν καὶ βραβευτήν) ..."[1]

If we bear in mind the lavishness with which the athletic image is used in the writings of Chrysostom, often going beyond Paul in revealing distinct Stoic features, we are entitled to see in both citations a decided overinterpretation of Paul, as far as the metaphorical character of the two verbs in question is concerned. Past philological studies[2] have confirmed the view that both verbs have here lost their original point of reference to the games. The simple form βραβεύειν originally refers to the function of the βραβευτής who presided over, and presented the prizes at the contests. LXX Wis 10:12 still retains this connotation: Wisdom appears as the 'umpire' in the Agon between Jacob and the angel (Gen 32:24ff.). However there is a wealth of evidence to show that the verb was mostly used in the more general applied sense to rule, control, judge or arbitrate, and it is with this meaning that it appears in Col 3:15—"Let the peace of Christ be the ruling principle in your hearts; let it decide the issue in all inner and outer conflicts". In this connection one observation is still of interest. Striking is the number of instances in Jewish literature in which God appears as the βραβευτής. LXX Wis 10:12 may again be mentioned, bearing in mind the divine origin of σοφία, but the picture is most clear in Philo[3] and especially in Josephus: God 'controls' the fortunes of warfare (Bell 1.215 = Ant 14.183), He 'administers' to all a fit retribution (Bell 7.271), 'directs' everything to its goal according to His will (Ant 4.47), and 'administers' harmony and peace (Ant 4.50).[4] It is possibly this picture which lies behind the parallel verse in Phil 4:7, although the verb φρουρεῖν is used instead of βραβεύειν. This verse with ἡ εἰρήνη

---

[1] Hom. 62.343.44, 62.354.48, and 357.32 (transl. acc. to Sawhill, The Use of Athletic Metaphors in the Biblical Homilies of St. John Chrysostom, pp. 32ff.). Cf. also Lightfoot, Philippians, p. 221.

[2] For the following see above all Field, pp. 196f., also Liddell-Scott, s.vs., BAG, s.vs., and summaries of the philological evidence in Eidem, pp. 119-124 and Stauffer, TWNT I, p. 636.

[3] Philo Vit Mos I 16: παρ' ἑκόντων ἔλαβε τὴν ἀρχήν, βραβεύοντος καὶ ἐπινεύοντος θεοῦ.

[4] Cf. also Plutarch Vit. Brut. XL: θεοῦ καλῶς τὰ παρόντα μὴ βραβεύσαντος. The verb is also used of deciding the issue in battle in Josephus Ant. 6.173, Bell. 6.143 (φόβος as subject), 4.229 (χρόνος), and 7.194 (καιρός). In Ant. 5.232, 6.31, 7.195, and 9.3 the verb simply means to rule or administer.

τοῦ θεοῦ as its subject may also account for the variant θεοῦ for Χριστοῦ in Col 3:15.

A metaphorical use of the compound καταβραβεύειν must likewise be rejected in Col 2:18.[1] The evidence, presented and discussed by Field[2] suggests that the translation 'condemn' is here best in place. The verb in v.18 thus repeats with more force that which has already been said in v.16 with the verb κρίνειν. "If any by-sense was in the Apostle's mind in choosing this word in preference to κατακρίνειν, it may, possibly, have been that of 'assumption' or 'officialism', as it follows εἰκῇ φυσιούμενος."[3] The conclusion must be that neither Col 2:18 nor 3:15 contribute towards a picture of the Christian Agon and its prize.

---

[1] The same has already been established for I Esdr 9:14: συνεβράβευσαν αὐτοῖς = joined/assisted them in ruling.

[2] Op.cit., pp. 196f. In addition to Eustathius Hom. in Iliad 402ff. and Demosthenes contra Midian 544 discussed by Field, note also the second cent. A.D. text in F. Preisigke, Sammelbuch griechischer Urkunden aus Ägypten I, Berlin 1915, No. 4512,57.

[3] Field, ibid.

CHAPTER SEVEN

THE AGON MOTIF
AND THE MILITARY IMAGE IN PAUL

Throughout the first part of this study reference has continually been made to the military image which often accompanies and complements the athletic image. In many cases the parallelism of application goes so far as to lead to a mingling of the two metaphors. In the diatribe, Philo, IV Maccabees, and, to a lesser degree, Josephus, they almost appear interchangeable, despite the difference in emphasis which each image bears. A similar relationship appears to present itself in the Corpus Paulinum,[1] one which necessitates a brief examination of this relationship in so far as it helps to throw added light on the role of the Agon motif in Paul.

That which Sevenster says in characterising the use of the military image in Seneca also applies to the entire diatribe. "The image of the soldier is used in connection with the man who bears all the vicissitudes of fate in a manly fashion, who wages war with his passion resolutely, who even rejoices in misfortune like a soldier in war, who accepts all ordeals as orders, who bears all setbacks as a soldier does his wounds, and who is capable of such conduct because he has made his inner life an impregnable fortress."[2] Although Philo's use of the image is more complex, the situation is similar in his thought, especially where it reflects distinct influence from the

---

[1] For a more thorough examination of the possible origins and the use of the military image in Paul, see Eidem, ch. IV, pp. 188ff., H. Edmonds, "Geistlicher Kriegsdienst. Der Topos der militia spiritualis in der antiken Philosophie", in: Heilige Überlieferung, Festgabe J. Herwegen 1938, pp. 21-50, O. Bauernfeind, TWNT VII, pp. 701ff., G. Kittel, TWNT I, pp. 195ff., A. Oepke-K.G. Kuhn, TWNT V, pp. 292ff., and for the later Christian use, A. von Harnack, Militia Christi, and H. von Soden", ΜΥΣΤΗΡΙΟΝ und sacramentum in den ersten 2 Jahrhunderten der Kirche", ZNW 12, 1911, pp. 206-224.

[2] J. Sevenster, Paul and Seneca, p. 162; cf. supra p. 42 with note 4, also Maximus Tyrius (4.9, 13.3f, and esp. 10.9): "God stands over the world as a general; the watchword is 'heimarmene', man is the soldier, life itself the campaign"; also Vettius Valens (V 9) who proudly calls himself the στρατιώ-της τῆς εἱμαρμένης and all men the slaves of 'heimarmene'.

Stoa. IV Macc also shows a close relationship between the two metaphors; in 9:23f. the struggle of martyrdom appears as a "holy and
noble campaign for piety" (cf. also 11:20f.). In each case the one
image complements the other.

Can the same phenomenon be detected in Paul? The difference
between his use of the two images is usually characterised as follows:
In the picture of the Agon Paul emphasises the motif of the goal for
which the 'athlete' strives; in the military picture, on the other
hand, it is the thought of the enemy and the need to stand fast
against his onslaughts which predominates. In the second case the
stress is on defence, not on attack.[1] This may suffice as a general
distinction between the two metaphors, but this study of Paul has
shown that the situation is in fact more complex.

In the first place the thought of the goal certainly is uppermost
where the image is that of the runner (Phil 3:12-14, Gal 5:7, Phil
2:16 and I Cor 9:24f.), but the thought of the opponent is also
present where the image is that of the wrestler or pancratiast (I
Cor 9:26f.).

In the second place it has been found that the isolated occurrences
of athletic termini also show an affinity to the military image in so
far as here also the Agon is a struggle against opposition. This is
most clear in Phil 4:3, Col 1:28-2:2, and especially in I Thess 2:1-2
and Phil 1:27-30 where the ἀντικείμενοι are specifically mentioned,
and where the Agon against opposition includes suffering. Bearing
in mind the frequent use of athletic termini in a pale sense, often in
military contexts, one is entitled to question whether a conscious
athletic image is at all present in the mind of reader or writer. By
the same token, however, it is quite certain that an express military
image is also absent. The conclusion of L. Schmid is no doubt
correct at this point: If the above passages carry any metaphor it
must be that of the athlete, "weil der Blick des Paulus bei seiner
Abwehr des Gegners ganz und gar nicht an diesem hängen bleibt,
sondern das Interesse auf der Ausrichtung des Werkes und des da-
durch zu erlangenden Zieles liegt".[2]

Within the commonly recognized confines of the Corpus Paulinum
we find no passage with an express mixture of the two metaphors.
Only Eph 6:10-20 and II Tim 2:3-5[3] come into question. Even in

---

[1] Schmid, pp. 22ff., and Sevenster, op.cit., p. 164.
[2] Schmid, p. 34.
[3] Cf. the following chapter.

Eph 6:12 it is more than doubtful whether there is a genuine mingling of images with the fleeting introduction of πάλη to describe the battle against Satan and the powers of darkness, and the panoply of God to be worn in this struggle. The picture of a wrestler wearing this complete list of armour is rather incongruous, to say the least! Two alternatives, which may even be combined, remain to explain the meaning of πάλη in this passage. 1. The word could be used with the colourless meaning of 'struggle'.[1] This usage is well attested in Greek literature[2] and also in Philo who otherwise carefully remains within the picture of the wrestler when using the term. In Abr 243 where he describes the panoply of the Logos in its πάλη against the πάθη the word can mean little more than 'struggle'. 2. If any metaphorical content is to be retained in the word this must be conditioned by the use of αἷμα and σάρξ in the same verse. Its sense will then be: "Our battle against the powers of darkness is not like the contest of the wrestler, for he can easily come to grips with his opponent." This second interpretation is all the more probable bearing in mind the injunction in the previous verse to stand fast against the wiles (μεθοδείαι) of the devil (v.11). The enemy is all the more dangerous because he remains unseen!

The real affinity between the athletic and military image in Paul immediately comes to light when we note his use of στρατεύεσθαι and related words in II Cor 10:3-5. Paul never explicitly calls himself a soldier of God or of Christ but this passage clearly pictures Paul as such. Earlier at the beginning of his defence of his right both to accept or reject the support of the Corinthian congregation (I Cor 9), Paul adduces three examples from everday life[3] to illustrate the right of every worker to reward for his labour. The first illustration, that of the soldier (τίς στρατεύεται ἰδίοις ὀψωνίοις ποτέ, v.7) is followed by that of the winegrower and the shepherd. It is unlikely that we should here see express metaphors for the work of the preacher of the Gospel. Nevertheless the illustrations are not idly chosen, since Paul's apostolic activity clearly appears as a military campaign in

---

[1] The colourless use of παλαίειν and related compounds has already been noted above; cf. LXX Gen 32:24, Jud 20:33, Esther 1:1 and Aqu Job 35:8; also Herm Mand XII 5,2, and Sim VIII 3,6 (ἀντιπαλαίειν and καταπαλαίειν).

[2] Cf. Eidem, p. 143, and H. Greeven, TWNT V, pp. 717f.

[3] J. Weiss, Der erste Korintherbrief (KEK), ad loc., calls this a "diatribenartiges Argument aus der Natur der Dinge —für den populären Stil des Paulus bezeichnend".

II Cor 10:3-5: "For though we are subject to all human limitations we do not war (στρατευόμεθα) according to these limitations; for the weapons of our warfare (ὅπλα τῆς στρατείας ἡμῶν) are not human and weak, but have power through God to destroy[1] strongholds, demolishing arguments and every proud obstacle to the knowledge of God, and taking captive (αἰχμαλωτίζοντες) every thought to obey Christ."

It is important to note that these words appear in the same context in which Paul always pictures himself as an athlete of the Gospel, that is, in an apologetical context. Paul finds himself in a 'Kampfsituation' in which he is forced to defend his apostleship (chapters 10-13). The battle pictured by means of the metaphor is, however, anything but a matter of defence. It is rather an all-out attack on all human reasoning and sophistry which stands in hostility to the simple proclamation of the Gospel. It is the Gospel itself, the mighty preaching of the knowledge of God in Christ which is the Apostle's weapon. The goal of this campaign is not merely the destruction of all fleshly wisdom that stands against God; the victory is only won when the Gospel has captured and turned the strongholds of reason into obedience to Christ, that is, to faith. *The image of the* στρατεία *pictures the life and work of the Apostle in its totality, together with his present struggle against the Corinthian opponents. It thus* takes its place alongside the picture of the Agon as a characterisation of Paul's entire apostolic work.

One could come to the conclusion, on the basis of the one passage alone, that the military image is relatively unimportant as a picture of Paul's missionary work and the battles connected with it.[2] Several other passages help to complete the picture and correct this impression. In II Cor 6:7, once again in defence of his διακονία (v.3), Paul defends his apostleship by referring to his sufferings, but above

---

[1] Philo, Conf Ling 129-131, offers a striking parallel to this passage, speaking of the καθαίρεσις of the ὀχύρωμα of speech which turns away and misdirects thought from the honour of God. There is no better boast than this, τὸ βεβαιοῦσθαι καθαιρήσειν πάντα λόγον ἀποστρέφειν διάνοιαν ὁσιότητος ἀναπείθοντα ...

[2] O. Bauernfeind, TWNT VII, p. 711, concludes: "Man gewinnt den Eindruck, dass unsere Wortgruppe in der Diktion der paulinischen Gemeindebriefe nicht eigentlich heimisch ist". But his attempt to explain its use from Paul's pre-Christian period as a hellenistic zealot for the Jewish tradition is not convincing. The origin of Paul's use of the image is here unimportant; clear is, that he considered himself a miles Christi in the same way as he could think of himself as an 'athleta Christi'.

all to the gifts of faith and the Spirit and the ὅπλα τῆς δικαιοσύνης with which he is armed "to the right and to the left",[1] meaning thereby the powerful proclamation of God's gift of righteousness in Christ.

Two terms further complete the picture. In Phil 2:25 and Philem 2, Epaphroditus and Archippus are singled out and honoured with the title "fellow soldier" (συστρατιώτης). They, like Paul's συναθληταί (Phil 4:3) are those who have taken a leading part in assisting the Apostle in his missionary labours and who now hold a leading position in the congregation.[2] But it is unlikely that the word is to be understood as a technical expression for the leader of a congregation.[3] A further application of the image appears in Rom 16:7, Col 4:10 and Philem 23 where Paul calls individual companions and fellow workers his συναιχμάλωτοι. The argument of G. Kittel is here convincing.[4] If Paul had simply meant to emphasise a literal captivity of these coworkers we would expect either συνδέσμιος or συνδεσμώτης, since the Apostle otherwise only uses the term δέσμιος of himself. The use of this specific word is no doubt meant to recall the familiar military metaphor. They who have taken an active part in all his struggles for the Gospel as his "fellow soldiers" have also faithfully stood at his side through persecution, trial, and imprisonment as "fellow captives" of Christ and the Gospel.[5] The 'higher' battle which they wage is accompanied by a 'higher' captivity. Once again the στρατεία of Paul himself stands in the background.

Harnack correctly notes that Paul does not speak of Christians generally as 'soldiers', but rather reserves the term for himself and his coworkers.[6] The standing picture is that of the Apostle or

---

[1] For the sense of this phrase see Eidem, p. 212, and Straub, Die Bildersprache des Apostels Paulus, pp. 38, 155.

[2] There is no cause to limit the word's meaning to followship in suffering as does Lohmeyer, An die Philipper (KEK), ad. loc., although this aspect is also present.

[3] Cf. Lohmeyer, An Philemon (KEK), ad loc., and Bauernfeind, op.cit., p. 711.

[4] G. Kittel, TWNT I, pp. 196f.

[5] The meaning of the word should not be reduced to 'fellow Christians' as in Dibelius, An die Kolosser (HNT), ad. loc.; cf. also Lohmeyer, An die Kolosser (KEK), p. 166 note 5.

[6] Harnack, Militia Christi, p. 14. But he is certainly wrong in finding the central motif for the use of the image in the proof by analogy that the missionary has the right to be supported by the congregation (ibid., pp. 15 and 17; cf. also Harnack, Die Mission und Ausbreitung des Christentums, Leipzig ⁴1924, pp. 428ff.; ET: The Mission and Expansion of Christianity, transl. by

missionary as a soldier of God.[1] His campaign lies between the
initial triumph of God in Christ (Col 2:15; cf. also Eph 4:8) and
the final celebration of this victory at the Parousia (I Cor 15:24-28).
The central thought—God's victory in Christ in which the apostle
is granted a share—appears under a slightly changed military image
in the difficult passage II Cor 2:14: τῷ δὲ θεῷ χάρις τῷ πάντοτε
θριαμβεύοντι ἡμᾶς ἐν τῷ Χριστῷ. Here the normal meaning 'to lead
in triumphal procession' must be retained over against the seemingly
easier sense 'to cause to triumph'.[2] Paul pictures the triumphant
procession of God making its way through the world, and himself
as one of the captive slaves in this train. It is just through his δοῦλος,
Paul, that God's victory in Christ is manifested and celebrated. This
thought, at first strange, is not restricted to this one passage in Paul.
It again occurs, once more under a different image, in I Cor 4:9
where the apostles are pictured as a spectacle (θέατρον) for the world
of angels and men.[3] In these passages the familiar Pauline paradox
receives pointed expression: It is through His frail servants, through
'earthen vessels' (II Cor 4:7), that God manifests His power and
His victory over the world in Christ. They alone can share in His
triumph who have first allowed themselves to be taken captive by
Him.

Up to this point the use of the two images runs parallel. The
second use of the military metaphor in the Corpus Paulinum is
nevertheless also of interest in the present connection, since it is
this image, and not the picture of the Agon, which provides the
closest parallel in Paul to the concept of the moral Agon in hellenistic popular philosophy. But one point must be established at the
outset. If we have been unable to ascertain any 'Auseinandersetzung' with hellenistic moral philosophy in Paul's use of the athletic
image, the same must be noted as applying to his application of the
military image to the life of every believer.

Rom 7:23f. with its powerful description of the situation of the
man who is still caught in the power of sin under the law is strictly
addressed "to those who know the law" (7:1): "But I see in my

---

J. Moffat, New York 1961, pp. 414ff.). The point is not so much the rights
of the missionary as his duty to fight for the Gospel, and even to suffer for
it if necessary.

[1] It is worth observing that the phrase 'miles Christi' only occurs in II Tim
2:3. Otherwise Paul rather appears as a 'miles Dei'.

[2] Cf. Field, pp. 181f., BAG, s.v., and G. Delling, TWNT III, p. 160.

[3] Cf. infra, Conclusion.

members another law at war (ἀντιστρατευόμενον) with the law of my
mind and making me captive (αἰχμαλωτίζοντα) to the law of sin
which dwells in my members. Wretched man that I am! Who will
deliver me from this body of death?" However it is clear that these
words of desperation also provide a cutting answer to the Stoic
sage's self-satisfaction and confidence in victory in the battle between the law of his mind (λογισμός) and his πάθη. Both Jew and
Greek stand under the same condemnation through trusting in their
own recourses.

It is just at this point that Paul's picture of the Christian warfare
differs; its first characteristic feature is the stress on the recources,
the armoury, which comes from outside of man, from God.[1] The
moral athlete trusts in his own prowess and strength, the soldier of
God relies only on the strength and the weapons which he receives
from God.[2] In this distinction lies the chief motive for the preference
for the military image over against the athletic as an illustration of
the Christian's struggle against sin and the powers of sin.

The second characteristic of the Christian's warfare, its eschatological setting,[3] distinguishes it even more from the moral battle of
the hellenistic moral philosopher. The internal conflict of the believer against sin (Rom 6:12-14) is part of the great cosmic struggle
against Satan and the powers of darkness (Eph 6:12). In this
conflict the 'sons of light' (I Thess 5:4-8 and Rom 13:11-14) are
joined with the powers of the old aeon in the last great eschatological
struggle until God "has put all his enemies under his (i.e. Christ's)
feet" (I Cor 15:25). It is the ἐκκλησία, God's military summons in
the world, which is at war, not merely the individual believer.

The fact that the believer wages his warfare on the basis of a
victory which has already been won by Christ rules out two concepts
of man's task as a battle. The victory is not to be gained by the
isolated struggle of the individual against his fate and passions, nor
is it to be won by an earthly Armageddon.[4] The victory already

---

[1] The same emphasis is also present in the picture of the Apostle's warfare
in II Cor 6:7 and 10:3ff.

[2] The panoply of God receives most detailed description in Eph 6:1off. and
I Thess 5:8, but note also Rom 13:13f. and 6:13f.

[3] Emphasised correctly by Beardslee, Human Achievement and Divine
Vocation, pp. 69f.

[4] Cf. the 'Sons of Light' of the Dead Sea Community who regarded themselves as the militia of God which, aided by the celestial hosts, would triumph
over Belial and his hosts in a campaign lasting forty years.

belongs to God, so that the watch-word of the Christian 'warrior' is "watch, stand fast". Parallel to Phil 3:12ff., the Christian's task is essentially the preservation of that which he has already been granted through Christ, awaiting the eschatological victory and perfection.

CHAPTER EIGHT

THE AGON MOTIF IN THE PASTORAL EPISTLES

1. The Athlete and Soldier of Christ

The Pastoral Epistles present themselves as Paul's personal letters of encouragement and exhortation to his disciples and co-workers who now assume greater responsibility with the end of Paul himself in view. If we presuppose the correctness of this situation as suggested by the letters themselves the picture of the Agon which they present offers no great problems. Nor can there be any talk of a wide rift at this point between Paul himself and the 'Deutero-Paulines'. On the contrary, the three characteristic features of the use of the athletic—as well as the military—image in the Pastorals reveal a natural development from Paul's use in his earlier letters.

The three characteristics of the twin metaphors in the Pastorals are the following: 1. Both are exclusively applied to him who is to walk in the Apostle's footsteps as an athlete and soldier of the Gospel. Instead of apostolic apology we find pastoral paraenesis and, right at the end, a retrospective 'apostolic confession'. 2. Both images appear in a more established or stereotyped form. Gone are the rhetorical questions, present instead is only direct exhortation. 3. Once more it is the 'Kampfsituation' of the preacher and teacher, brought about by the fight against heresy, which forms the background to both images.

It is significant that the athletic termini play an increasingly important role in the later letters of Paul.[1] This development reaches its most pointed form in the Pastorals so that one may conclude, keeping in mind the specific situation of the addressee, that the five passages which come into consideration in I and II Tim contain genuinely Pauline thought.

The picture of the Agon in the Pastorals has often suffered from

---

[1] T. Nägeli, Der Wortschatz des Apostels Paulus, Göttingen 1905, pp. 83f., rightly suspects that "das eine oder andere solcher Wörter (sc. ἀγών etc.) erst in den Gefangenschaftsjahren des Paulus ein Bestandteil seines produktiven Wortschatzes wurde".

the same distortion in interpretation as the Pauline passages studied up to this point. In place of the 'good fight' of him who has been entrusted with the Gospel there has appeared a generalised picture of the moral-religious struggle of the Christian. That which the writer of I Tim 6:12 meant when exhorting his reader to 'fight the good fight' has often been turned (in many a confirmation address!) into a piece of general paraenesis far removed from its original context and purpose.

A glance at the two occurrences of the military image, by itself in I Tim 1:18f. and together with the athletic image in II Tim 2:3-5, is again necessary in order to gain a correct picture of the scope of the Agon in the two epistles to Timothy. The parallelism between the two metaphors is emphasised by two distinct features. 1. Apart from the doubtful case in Eph 6:12, only II Tim 2:3-5 reveals a genuine mixture of the two images in the NT. 2. In the second place there is also a striking correspondence in phraseology between ἡ καλὴ στρατεία in I Tim 1:18 (also καλὸς στρατιώτης in II Tim 2:3) and ὁ καλὸς ἀγών in I Tim 6:12 and II 4:7.

It is above all in these phrases and in the use of the definite article that we are entitled to detect the traditional character of these images. Dibelius remarks that the contrast between physical and spiritual γυμνασία in I Tim 4:8 reflects an original polemic against athletics as we have also noted it in tracing the history of the philosophical use of the athletic image.[1] We have also found this original polemic in the frequent designation of the sage's Agon as καλός. Philo's exhortation in Leg All II 108 illustrates this point most clearly, in reference both to the contest itself and to the incomparable crown which is to be won: κάλλιστον ἀγῶνα τοῦτον διάθλησον καὶ σπούδασον στεφανωθῆναι κατὰ τῆς ... ἡδονῆς καλὸν καὶ εὐκλεᾶ στέφανον, ὃν οὐδεμία πανήγυρις ἀνθρώπων ἐχορήγησεν.[2] The original polemic contained in the adjective 'good' is completely lost in I Tim 6:12 and II 4:7, and an attack against the games and against athletics as such is certainly not contained or intended in the comparison between the two kinds of exercise in I Tim 4:8. Nor

---

[1] M. Dibelius, BuG II, p. 195 note 1.

[2] Cf. also Mut Nom 82: καλὸν ἆθλον, Leg All III 48: καλὸς δρόμος καὶ πάντων ἄριστον ἀγώνισμα, and Vit Mos II 136: ἀγώνισμα καλόν. W. Grundmann (TWNT III, p. 552) also concludes that the use of καλός in the Pastorals, apart from the Jewish phrase καλὰ ἔργα, has been taken from "der durch die Gedanken stoischer Ethik geformten Vulgärsprache".

is a polemical tone present in the military image in I Tim 1:18[1] or in II Tim 2:3 where we again find a pointed use of καλός. The positive reference to the example of the soldier rules out this possibility. Perhaps the phrase ἡ καλὴ στρατεία was formed by analogy (possibly by the author of the epistle himself) with the phrase ὁ καλὸς ἀγών.

In adopting this traditional phrase the writer makes it quite clear what he means by calling the contest or fight 'good'. The old hellenistic connotations of the adjective have disappeared. It is even probable that the phrase had already become established as a stereotyped metaphor in the Pauline communities; the use of the definite article would also seem to point in this direction.[2]

Only at this point, in the adoption of a popular image together with traditional terminology, can any influence of the hellenistic picture of the moral Agon on the picture of the Agon in the Pastoral Epistles be detected. The situation is thus exactly the same as in the recognised letters of Paul. The usual references to the common concept of man's moral and religious task on earth as an Agon or military campaign, whether in the diatribe or in the Mysteries, do not suffice the explain or illustrate the picture of the Agon in the Pastorals. This also applies to *I Tim* 1:18f. where the paraenetic use of the military image (ταύτην τὴν παραγγελίαν παρατίθεμαί σοι ... ἵνα στρατεύῃ ... τὴν καλὴν στρατείαν) obviously presupposes its familiarity to the reader. Any word of explanation as to why, or in how far, Timothy's actions are a 'campaign' is lacking. Those who make this point see in the general concept of life as a στρατεία, the 'formaler Ausgangspunkt' for the present stereotyped use of the image.[3]

---

[1] W. Lock, The Pastoral Epistles (ICC), Edinburgh 1924, p. 19, points to v.17 (τῷ βασιλεῖ τῶν αἰώνων) to show that the contrast is with service to earthly kings. But even this comparison is artificial. Cf. also Grundmann (TWNT VII, p. 712): "Völlige Unbefangenheit ist es, die neben dem allgemeineren Partizip στρατευόμενος (II Tim 2:4) die handgreiflichere Berufsbezeichnung στρατιώτης (v.3) zulässt. So kommt es dahin, dass der Vollstrecker des Auftrages Jesu im übertragenen Sinn die gleiche Bezeichnung trägt, die die Vollstrecker seiner Kreuzigung im eigentlichen Sinne tragen".

[2] W. Straub, Die Bildersprache des Apostels Paulus, pp. 64 and 102. The language of the Pastorals seems to stand behind καλὸς ἀγωνιστής in Acta Petri et Andreae 2 (Bonn.-Lip. II 1,117) and καλὸς ἀγωνοθέτης in Acta Philippi 144 (Bonn.-Lip. II 2,85).

[3] W. Grundmann, op.cit., pp. 711f. Cf. also M. Dibelius, Die Pastoralbriefe (HNT), Tübingen ³1955, p. 27: "Der Kriegsdienst des Frommen", and W. Lock, op.cit., p. 19.

But the point of the image in this passage is only fully understood on the background of Paul's own campaign against the falsification of the Gospel (II Cor 10:3-5). The context of the first chapter of I Tim clearly defines the scope of Timothy's warfare; it is a struggle against heresy and false teaching. The παραγγελία of v.18 is, then, the charge to carry on the very same struggle which Paul himself has already fought at Corinth and in the other centres of his missionary activity, with the only difference that Timothy is now faced not only with the problem of the Jewish front, but above all with the danger of the hellenisation of the Gospel and its consequent distortion (vv.3-7). Timothy is to look for strength in the fight against those who have attacked his authority and right to leadership in the προφητεῖαι spoken over him at his ordination (cf. Acts 13:1-3). The conditions[1] for his warfare are a firm faith and a good conscience. To enter into the fray against error with a tottering faith and a flecked conscience spells defeat from the start. However it is not Timothy's behaviour or inner attitude which makes this fight for the truth of the Gospel 'good'. The battle which he is to wage is in itself good since it is given to him from above, from the Lord who has appointed him, like Paul (v.12), to his service.

It is this same thought, the conditions for the effective fight, which underlies the mixed use of images in *II Tim* 2:3-6. Here, even more clearly than in the former passage, one may direct attention to the diatribe-like manner of argumentation which, as in I Cor 9:7, draws three examples from everyday life, that of the soldier, athlete and farmer.[2] Again it is perfectly clear that the words apply to the specific position of Timothy as a leader in the congregation (cf. v.2).[3] In I Cor 9:7 the examples of the soldier, winegrower and shepherd serve to illustrate the rights of the evangelist. The metaphor contained in the designation of Timothy as a καλὸς στρατιώτης here in v.3 gives the verbs στρατεύεσθαι, ἀθλεῖν and

---

[1] It is unlikely that faith and a good conscience are meant to represent the weapons for this warfare.

[2] The three images are sharply demarcated. Harnack wrongly doubts the change in image and connects v.5 with the military image in v.4 (Militia Christi, pp. 16f.).

[3] Grundmann notes the specific point of application in this second passage but generalises I Tim 1:18f. in saying of Timothy's Agon: "In ihrer Durchführung soll Timotheus den zu betreuenden Christen Vorbild sein" (op.cit., p. 712).

κοπιᾶν an even stronger metaphorical character in respect to the actual activity of the evangelist.[1]

In each case the relevant image is clear, but not so clear the intention behind its use. The immediate point of the military image must be determined by συγκακοπαθεῖν, a thought taken up from 1:8 and continued in 2:9f. The tertium comparationis is not the reward or wage of the soldier, as in I Cor 9:7, but rather wholehearted devotion and "entsagungsvolle Konzentration"[2] as the chief condition for his service, especially in view of the necessity to face suffering. This injunction gains emphasis through the thought of Timothy's subordination under him who has enlisted him (στρατολογήσας).

It is above all in this respect that Timothy's military service differs decisively from that of the Stoic sage. The latter also knows of the necessity to keep himself free from entanglement in the everyday affairs of life (Epict. III 22), but is, in the final analysis, responsible to himself alone. The Christian 'soldier' has only one goal and purpose —whole-hearted devotion to the given task in the effort to please his Lord.[3]

---

[1] The metaphor is even stronger in the reading of G lat. and Ambrosiaster who add τῷ θεῷ after στρατευόμενος in v.4. The addition suggests that all three images were understood as metaphors for the work of the evangelist, and not merely as parallel illustrations as in I Cor 9:7.

[2] Grundmann, op.cit., p. 712. Lock, op.cit., p. 93, rightly observes that v.4 in connection with I Cor 9:7 does not imply that Paul demands of the minister of the Gospel that he completely abstain from any secular trade. He himself did not! Harnack incorrectly sees in this verse a command to refrain from any and every trade. "Er hat den Stand des Klerus im Unterschied von dem der Laien zwar nicht geschaffen, aber ihm den festen Halt gegeben" (Militia Christi, p. 16). By applying νομίμως in v.5 to the military image he finds two rules for the Christian 'soldier': a) he receives his wages from others and b) does not entangle himself in the occupations of everyday life. However, not the command to refrain completely from an occupation or trade is the point, but the demand not to become involved in such and in the affairs of this life. In the foreground stands not "die Soldfrage, sondern die radikale Abwendung von allen freudigen und traurigen Anforderungen des Lebens und die Hinwendung zur vollen Bereitschaft gegenüber Christi" (C. Maurer, TWNT VI, p. 641; for the other view see also Schlatter, Die Kirche der Griechen im Urteil des Paulus, Stuttgart ²1958, p. 232).

[3] Cf. Ign Pol 6: ἀρέσκετε ᾧ στρατεύεσθε, I Cor 7:32-34: πῶς ἀρέσῃ τῷ κυρίῳ, Rom 8:8: θεῷ ἀρέσαι, and 15:3: οὐχ ἑαυτῷ (sc. Christ) ἤρεσεν. The necessity of subordination and obedience in the 'Christian army' is elaborately developed in I Clem 37. —The position of Timothy as a miles Christi finds an analogy in the title 'miles' for the third grade in the hierarchy of the Mithras cult. But any relationship exists only in the common use of military termini (cf. Grundmann, ibid., note 39).

The tertium comparationis in the following two pictures is parallelly not the crown of the athlete or the firstfruits of the farmer, but rather the conditions under which they are to contest and work in order to gain the reward of their toil. Deut 20:6 and Prov 27:18 already speak of the farmer's right to the produce of his labours. The image receives an entirely opposite application in v.6 since all the stress lies on κοπιῶντα. Not the natural claim of the farmer but the necessity of hard toil before he can reap the benefits of his labours is the important thing.[1]

It is now clear how the athletic image in v.5 is to be interpreted: ἐὰν δὲ καὶ ἀθλῇ τις, οὐ στεφανοῦται ἐὰν μὴ νομίμως ἀθλήσῃ. If the parallel to the other two images is to be retained the emphasis must here lie in νομίμως ἀθλεῖν; the feature of the crown has no independent significance but serves to motivate the athlete's adherence to the laws of the contest.[2] The question is, how is this adverb to be understood? The need to comply with the rules, both in training and in the contest itself,[3] is also a recurrent feature of the moral-philosophical use of the athletic image, as can be seen to advantage in Epict. III 10: ὁ θεός σοι λέγει 'δός μοι ἀπόδειξιν εἰ νομίμως ἤθλησας, εἰ ἔφαγες ὅσα δεῖ, εἰ ἐγυμνάσθης, εἰ τοῦ ἀλείπτου (i.e. ruling reason) ἤκουσας. Within the present context the adverb most probably refers to συγκακοπαθεῖν. The athlete or wrestler is not allowed to lighten his struggle by bypassing the rules. When applied to Timothy this means that he as an athlete of Christ must also be prepared to suffer; this also belongs to the conditions of his Agon. This is as much as can safely be read from the immediate context.[4] Since

---

[1] Dibelius, op.cit., p. 81. Straub, op.cit., p. 69 misses the point when he finds the lesson in the rule: make use of your right to live by the Gospel.

[2] A similar sentence but with the stress on the crown in Plutarch Non Posse Suav. Viv. 1105.1: ἀθληταὶ στέφανον οὐκ ἀγωνιζόμενοι λαμβάνουσι, ἀλλὰ ἀγωνισάμενοι καὶ νικήσαντες.

[3] For these rules see already Wettstein, Novum Testamentum II, p. 357 and J. H. Krause, Gymnastik und Agonistik der Hellenen I, Leipzig 1841, pp. 362ff. The adverb in the present context must refer to the rules of the contest itself rather than to the training and encratistic exercises which precede it. A competitor who did not abide by the rules could be disqualified from the prize by the judges.

[4] Cf. Eidem, p. 109. For a less satisfactory attempt to explain νομίμως, see Wohlenberg, Die Pastoralbriefe (KNT XIII), Leipzig ³1923, p. 291: preach the Word in agreement with its own essence without weakening it through human considerations! The interpretation of L. Schmid (pp. 103f.) and Schlatter (op.cit., p. 233) is a little too imaginative: The concrete situation is Paul's summons to Timothy to join him in Rome. In the clash of obligations

these rules are dictated by the Lord who has assigned him this contest, the thought of obedient subordination is again present as in the military metaphor. A second concurrent meaning may be detected behind these words since it remains probable that νομίμως contains a rejection of the heretics who do not 'contend lawfully', seeking their own ends and not the goal of the divine ἀθλοθέτης.

The difficulty in determining the application of the three images arises from the fact that they receive no explicit application, nor are they further developed in the text itself. He who contests the genuineness of the Pastorals could grasp at this point to support his argument. The author has taken up familiar images—probably from Paul himself in I Cor 9:7 and 24ff.—and given them a different accent without giving them a clear ad hoc application. This he could not do because the background of the epistles, being fictional, remains vague.[1] But this argument can be reversed to support just the opposite view. Because Paul can presuppose the immediate recognition of the point of application, namely to the work of the minister of the Gospel, he has no need to explain further what he means. This must be clear to him who has long stood at his side as a coworker. The Apostle leaves it to Timothy to apply the images to himself in his present specific situation (cf. II Tim 2:7), a situation characterised by the struggle against heresy and the threat of suffering, as in Paul's own Agon.

2. TIMOTHY'S γυμνασία IN GODLINESS

Up to this point there can hardly be any objection to the thesis that the athletic image in the Pastorals also applies to the role of the minister of the Gospel as a successor of the Apostle himself. The situation appears to be different in the three remaining passages (I Tim 4:7-10, 6:11-12 and II Tim 4:6-8) where the scope of the image seems to be widened to include a reference to the task of every believer. It is thus not surprising that *I Tim* 4:7-10 has been taken as the basis for a general discussion on the evaluation and position of training and exercise in the theology of Paul.[2] Is this generalisation even here legitimate?

---

between Ephesus and Rome the greater claim is made by his fellowship with Paul, this being also the will of God.

[1] Cf. Lietzmann, op.cit., p. 81.

[2] Cf. Schmid, ch. IV "Die Übung und ihre Stellung in der paulinischen Theologie", pp. 93ff.

The answer to this question depends on the solution of three problems which arise immediately from the text. In v.7f. Timothy is exhorted: γύμναζε δὲ σεαυτὸν πρὸς εὐσέβειαν. ἡ γὰρ σωματικὴ γυμνασία πρὸς ὀλίγον ἐστὶν ὠφέλιμος · ἡ δὲ εὐσέβεια πρὸς πάντα ὠφέλιμός ἐστιν. 1. What is this 'bodily exercise' to which Paul contrasts a 'spiritual exercise', and 2. what is the nature of this 'exercise in piety'? 3. What is the relationship of v.10, with the phrase εἰς τοῦτο γὰρ κοπιῶμεν καὶ ἀγωνιζόμεθα, to the first metaphor? Do γυμνάζειν and ἀγωνίζεσθαι refer to the same Agon which Timothy has to contest?

Before examining each question it must be noted from the start that this passage appears within the same context as the two passages already treated in this chapter. Once again it is Timothy's fight against heresy which forms the back-drop to these verses. This is clear from the opening verses of the chapter with their warning against 'deceitful spirits and doctrines of demons' (v.1), against those who demand abstinence from marriage and foods (v.3) and who propound godless myths and old-wives fables (v.7). Verse 11 continues with practical advice for Timothy's behaviour in countering these errors. This framework already indicates the two motives behind the picture of Timothy's γυμνασία. These verses contain 1. a rejection of a certain training or exercise propounded by the opponents and 2. suggest at the same time the legitimate and necessary training which Timothy must follow in order to oppose and defeat them. Thus we are again compelled to relate the image to Timothy in his specific office as a καλὸς διάκονος of Christ Jesus (v.6).

Dibelius correctly notes that v.8 bears the ring of a "feste Sentenz". In fact this sentence, together with I Cor 9:25, provides the chief evidence for the assumption that Paul's use of the athletic image stands within a definite tradition. Here, for the second time, occurs a reflection of the standard polemic against the contests of the athletes and their exercising of the body alone, contrasting these with the noble Agon of the philosopher and his training of the soul. But Dibelius is equally correct in noting that this is only the original scope of the traditional language of this sentence.[1] In the present instance it has received a completely different point. It is thus idle to seek behind the writer's words his attitude to Greek sports and gymnastic training. Such a judgment is as far removed

---

[1] Dibelius, op.cit., p. 55.

from his mind as it is in I Cor 9:24ff. E. Eidem and C. Spicq prefer to restrict σωματική γυμνασία to the exercises and training of the athlete but fail to give a convincing explanation of the connection between the verses immediately preceding and the image itself. According to Eidem Timothy shall exercise himself in piety and holiness in opposition to the laziness of those who merely dabble in myths. The thought of his 'spiritual exercise' leads to the *contrast* with the training of the Greek athlete.[1] In the interpretation of Spicq we rather find a *comparison* between the two types of training. The 'spiritual exercise' of Timothy is consequently—and falsely—interpreted by analogy with the ideals which were represented by the Greek institutions, the gymnasium and the palaestra.[2]

The only way in which a connection between vv.7bff. and the preceding verses can convincingly be established is to see already in σωματική γυμνασία a metaphor which refers back (cf. γάρ in v.8) to the errors of the heretics against which the author has been warning. Despite the strong protests of Eidem it is best to see in this phrase not the hellenistic culture of the body but an external dualistic asceticism as propounded by the heretics and reflected in the warnings contained in v.3 and probably also in v.7a.[3] The objection that the errors of vv.1-5 still lie in the future[4] is unfounded; the author clearly views the prophecies of the Spirit (4:1ff.) as fulfilled in the present aberrations which threaten the congregation under Timothy's charge.

Since Paul's words present a warning against the encroachment of hellenistic influences into the church we here obtain for the first time a direct judgment on that which most closely corresponds to

---

[1] Eidem, pp. 146f. similarly M-M., under γυμνασία.

[2] C. Spicq, "Gymnastique et Morale d'apres I Tim 4:7-8", RB 54, 1947, pp. 229ff. See further infra. According to Spicq πρὸς ὀλίγον reflects the evaluation of an old man who has become less sensible to the beauties and glories of athletics (p. 239)!

[3] Thus A. Oepke, TWNT I, p. 775; also B. Weiss, Die Briefe Paulus an Timotheus und Titus (KEK), Göttingen ⁷1902, p. 172, Schmid, p. 99, J. Jeremias, Die Briefe an Timotheus und Titus (NTD), ad loc., Dibelius, op. cit., p. 55, and Schlatter, op.cit., pp. 123f. Lock, op.cit., leaves the question open.

[4] Cf. W. Hendriksen, Commentary on I and II Timothy and Titus, London 1959, p. 152, and Wohlenberg, op.cit., p. 160. The further objection of Hendriksen that γυμνασία is an inappropriate word for fasting is valueless considering the wide transferred use of this term. Wohlenberg's understanding of 'bodily exercise' is fantastic: "Pflege der Gesundheit, Ausbildung körper-

the hellenistic moral Agon. In its Christianised form it appeared as the attempt to reach moral and religous perfection through ascetic exercises, through artificial and self-constructed ways to salvation. In the command to keep the soul pure through abstention from sexual intercourse and food there appears the same dualistic view of man which underlies hellenistic popular moral philosophy. The pre-Gnostic myths of the heretics probably supported this dualism with speculations about the origin of the soul and its destiny after death.[1]

What is the answer to this false 'gymnasia'? The verdict that it has little value[2] does not amount to a complete negation of the necessity for self-denial and control over the body. I Cor 9:25ff. pictures Paul himself as practising self-control in all things by keeping his body continually under subjection. But the scope of his 'enkrateia' is, as we have seen, not the narrow negative dualism between the eternal soul and the transitory body with its passions. The Apostle checks his σῶμα, his own physical desires and inclinations, as a necessary condition for total devotion and application to the missionary task assigned to him.

The γυμνασία πρὸς εὐσέβειαν which is contrasted with 'bodily exercise' has a similar goal.[3] It is not the self-centred ascetic struggle of the individual for his own moral and religious perfection, but the training necessary for the unhindered pursuit of God's purposes.[4] One can imagine that Timothy's enemies have accused him of moral laxity since he refuses to follow their demands for abstention. But he too is to practise a γυμνασία, a vigorous development and appli-

---

licher Kraft ... als Tüchtigmachung des Leibes für irdische Berufsarbeit, zwecks Gewinnung irdischer Subsistenzmittel".

[1] Schlatter, op.cit., p. 123.

[2] The contrast provided by πρὸς πάντα supports this translation for πρὸς ὀλίγον, despite the temporal meaning in Jam 4:14.

[3] If v.8 represents a standing aphorism its origin is probably to be located in Hellenistic Judaism; cf. IV Macc 11:20 where the martyrs are called διὰ τὴν εὐσέβειαν εἰς γυμνασίαν πόνων, and Philo where the γυμνασία and ἄσκησις of the soul has εὐσέβεια as its ultimate goal (also II Clem 20:3 ἀσκεῖν θεοσέβειαν). The term εὐσέβεια does not appear as a foreign element in the Pastorals. It serves as a central concept, beside πίστις, to describe the total life of the believer over against God.

[4] According to Wohlenberg, op.cit., p. 160, Timothy is to pursue a "gottgefällige, wirklich heilige und darum heilsame Askese" with ζωή (v.8b) as his goal. But the point is not his own goal but the glory of God (πρὸς suggests the goal of action as in Rom 3:26, I Cor 7:35, 10:11, 14:26 etc.). Wohlenberg artificially takes 'piety' as the norm for Timothy's training.

cation of all his strength and ability that he might serve the glory of God with every thought and action. Such exercise is not restricted to a negative physical asceticism, nor even to the self-disciplinary 'enkrateia' of I Cor 9:25ff., but rather implies a positive developing of his strength nourished[1] above all "by the words of faith" (v.6).

The explanation of πρὸς πάντα in the phrase "having the promise of life which now is and is to come"[2] certainly extends the scope of Timothy's training beyond the confines of his churchly office. The necessity to deepen and intensify the life of faith is the task of every believer, just as the same promise of life applies to every believer. And yet the present command concerns Timothy precisely in his present situation over against the heretics. His own exercise of piety is the prerequisite for a successful struggle against the opponents' insistence on a false physical exercise. This conclusion gains support not only from vv.11ff. with their advice as to how Timothy shall conduct himself in his position of authority, but also from v.10.

The entire missionary activity of Paul and Timothy has been a demonstration of the complete trustworthiness of this promise of life and of their implicit trust in the living God to fulfil His promise —εἰς τοῦτον γὰρ κοπιῶμεν καὶ ἀγωνιζόμεθα.[3] In this familiar phrase (cf. Col 1:29 and Phil 2:16) Timothy is included in the κόπος and ἀγών of Paul's missionary work, with all its attendant toil, its tireless exertion, and its struggles against all manner of setbacks and opposition. Their Agon has had, and still has, as its goal the honour and glory of God, the proclamation and demonstration of His faithfulness to this promise of life. In so far the γυμνασία of v.8 and the ἀγών of v.10 are united. Both are not directed towards the

---

[1] The word ἐντρεφόμενος may well provide a contrast to the fasting of the heretics in v.3 and thus also belong to Timothy's training in piety. A further rejection of their error may also stand behind νῦν in v.8. He who takes the physical body as his enemy flees from the present life to gain a future! But piety knows of the full gift of life already here in the flesh.

[2] Any thought of meriting this life is excluded; it is a gift to him who has sought the honour of God. Cf. Schlatter, op.cit., p. 125.

[3] B. Weiss and Wohlenberg prefer to read ὀνειδιζόμεθα (Rom 15:3) instead of the equally well attested ἀγωνιζόμεθα. Even though the second reading can more easily be explained as an insertion from Col 1:29 (εἰς ὃ καὶ κοπιῶ ἀγωνιζόμενος cf. also Phil 2:16), it is just the Pauline phrase which speaks for the reading adopted here and in the latest commentaries.

winning of this life only for the ministers of the Gospel themselves; nor do they serve their own perfection or salvation.[1] The promise of life to all men (v.10b) is the *basis* and the *motive* for their life's task, that which gives their Agon its earnestness and urgency.

The above understanding of the nature and purpose of Timothy's 'training in piety' can be further clarified in a discussion of the essay of C. Spicq mentioned above.[2] The author correctly notes that the writer's injunction concerns the addressee in his specific office as leader of the Ephesian congregation. He who has been 'trained' as a close pupil by the Apostle (p. 229) now receives the command to carry on the spiritual exercise demanded by his responsible position (p. 233). Spicq offers a thorough study of the role of gymnastic training in the education of the Greek youth, emphasising the moral and intellectual ideals connected with such exercises. They aimed at developing not only physical health, strength and beauty, but also a certain ἕξις, a sound condition of the mind and soul as well as of the body (p. 234). Even in the transferred use of γυμνάζειν,[3] with the standard polemic against the degeneration of the games and of athletics (pp. 239ff.), the central emphasis of the picture remains the same: It stands for the maximum development and increase of innate strength of the soul and of inplanted virtues until the ideal of εὐεξία is reached.

It is just at this point that Spicq begins to turn Timothy into something that approaches a Christianised version of the Stoic moral athlete! By means of a false process of analogy εὐσέβεια becomes a virtue which is to be developed to perfection like any Stoic virtue. A few statements will illustrate this point. Timothy's office demands of him that he realise the ideal of Christian virtue in order that he, like the trainer, may show others how this ideal is to be realised. His first duty is to advance to the attainment of positive virtues, to strive for perfection, perhaps even to reach it (p. 236). The development of his good natural disposition ("bonnes dispositions initiales"),

---

[1] Εἰς τοῦτον refers not to the τέλος of Christian γυμνασία in v.8 but clearly to the words in v.9. This must be stressed against Dibelius who sees in v.10 a reflection of Col 1:29, but with a different tone. There κοπιᾶν and ἀγωνίζεσ-θαι refer to the nature of Paul's mission, here to the exercise in godliness in which he and Timothy are engaged!

[2] Cf. supra p. 173, and the Introduction, p. 13.

[3] In the NT γυμνάζειν only appears again in Hebr 5:14 and 12:11 (A. Oepke, TWNT I, p. 775, here detects a soft ring of Greek perfectionism), and in II Pet 2:14 where the use is quite pale and non-metaphorical.

his natural resources and inborn talents ("ressources natives") through assiduous exercise and perseverance shall contribute to the perfection of his ἕξις as the intermediary between his natural talent and the sacred acts of his ministry. Spicq counters the obvious objection to this point by drawing attention to the divine power and the "grace of his ordination" on which Timothy is dependent in his struggle (p. 237). Nevertheless his training in godliness receives a self-centred emphasis; to excel in his acts is the aim and motive for his effort. Where is the text's stress on the honour of God as his chief goal? Verse 10 is completely misrepresented as stating that salvation is given by preference to those who practise γυμνασία. That these words speak not of Paul and his pupil's striving for their own salvation but for the actualisation of God's promise of life to all men, is overlooked.

At the bottom of this false exegesis lies a misunderstanding of the term εὐσέβεια. Piety or godliness—in the Pastorals the term is always directed against the heretics—is as little a virtue as is πίστις, describing, as it does, the entire life of the believer over against God. It is not founded on man's natural disposition which is far more ἀσέβεια (Rom 1:18, II Tim 2:16, Titus 2:12), but on the "new creation" which is brought about by the gifts of the Spirit. It is the gifts of the Spirit, faith, love, righteousness and hope, which are to be deepened and intensified, and this alone is the Christian γυμνασία.

In this same point lies the reason for the absence of the diatribe's concept of γυμνασία in the ethics of Paul. The 'Tugendethik' of the Stoic necessarily has something of a patch-work or mosaic quality, since it aims at developing to the full the latent innate virtues in their individuality. In Paul, on the other hand, the new life is a unity which arises from one factor or one source, the justifying act of God through Christ and the gift of His Spirit.

3. THE "GOOD CONTEST OF FAITH"

In I Tim 4:7ff. we note a feature which also stands behind the use of the athletic images in I Cor 9:24ff. and Phil 3:12ff. No distinction is made between the behaviour of Paul and Timothy as believers and their duty as ministers of the Gospel. The striving to appear 'approved' at the last day (I Cor 9:27), to win the 'prize of the high calling' (Phil 3:14) or to gain 'life' (I Tim 4:8) is intrinsically bound up with their obligation to fight the Agon committed to them with their office.

I Tim 6:11-12, with its apparently stereotyped metaphor (ἀγω-νίζου τὸν καλὸν ἀγῶνα τῆς πίστεως) and seemingly general meaning, provides no exception to the above pattern. In a short but important study on vv.11-16, "Das Formular einer neutestamentlichen Ordinationsparänese",[1] E. Käsemann has succeeded in pointing out the exact scope of this paraenetic and doxological section. Already the address ἄνθρωπε θεοῦ draws attention to the addressee in his specific office (similarly II Tim 3:17) as one who, like "men of God" in the Old Testament (I Sam 2:27, I Kings 12:22 and 13:1, Deut 33:1, Ps 90:1), has been summoned by God as an instrument for His service. Käsemann may be correct when he goes beyond this point in claiming that the hellenistic Jewish use of this phrase suggests that "man of God" came to be a variant for πνευματικός.[2] Its use to designate him who has been ordained, and who as such is the bearer of the Spirit in a special sense, is then quite understandable. The paraenetic use of the verb διώκειν also reflects the language of the LXX.[3] The command itself is conditioned by vv.5ff. In opposition to those who crave material riches Timothy is to strive after righteousness, godliness, faith, love, patience and meekness.[4] These words are in effect a concise commentary on the training in godliness in I Tim 4:7f. (cp. 4:8 "godliness is of value in every way" with 6:6 "there is great gain in godliness with contentment"). Gal 5:22, where similar Christian virtues are called the "fruit of the Spirit", shows how little they are to be thought of as parallels to the hellenistic ἀρεταί (cf. II Tim 1:7 and 14).

The command to carry on the good contest of faith follows on

---

[1] First published in: Neutestamentliche Studien für Rudolf Bultmann, Berlin 1954, pp. 261-268, now in: Exegetische Versuche und Besinnungen I, Göttingen 1960, pp. 101ff.

[2] Op.cit., p. 108, following Dibelius, op.cit., p. 67, with reference to Philo Gig 61, Ep Arist 140 and Corpus Herm. I 32 and XIII 20; cf. also J. Jeremias, TWNT I, pp. 365ff. Weiss and Schlatter only see a stress on the thought of Timothy as God's possession.

[3] Cf. A. Oepke, TWNT II, p. 233. This use of διώκειν and φεύγειν is exclusive to Paul and the Pastorals: II Tim 2:22 "flee from youthful passions and pursue righteousness", I Cor 6:18 "flee from adultery", 10:14 "flee from idolatry"; for διώκειν also Rom 9:30, 12:13, 14:19, I Cor 14:1, Phil 3:12 and 14, I Thess 5:15.

[4] Hendriksen, op.cit., p. 204, rather sees a contrast to the word-battles and disputes of the opponents in 6:4. Timothy must carry on the fight which springs from and is inspired by his faith.

smoothly from v.11, the metaphor itself being easily suggested by the verb διώκειν.[1] It here becomes clear how little πίστις can be regarded as one virtue amongst others; but it is at the same time very difficult to determine the exact significance of the genitive τῆς πίστεως. Three suggestions can be excluded from the outset. 'Faith' is hardly the orthodox faith, the 'fides quae' which Timothy is to defend.[2] The wider context of vv.11-16 is certainly once again the errors of the heretics, but the concept πίστις can hardly have the meaning of the 'right faith', especially following on from v.11. Nor is faith itself here pictured in the personified form of an agonist striving after the goal, the perfection of salvation.[3] Equally impossible is the attempt to take the genitive as a genitivus objectivus, picturing faith as the goal of Timothy's striving.

The only satisfactory solution is to interpret the genitive as a genitivus appositivus. Faith, by its very nature, demands a struggle on the part of the believer. It is the field, or, to retain the image, the arena in which the Agon is to be contested. The entire life of faith demands the complete application of the strength and will of the believer to preserve this faith under all circumstances, in temptation, in doubt, and when under attack from without. That which is demanded of the spiritual athlete can best be summed up as "Bewährung des Glaubens".[4] The same emphasis lies in the command to Timothy to grasp, to hold and retain as his own, the gift of "eternal life"; this does not appear as a future prize lying at the

---

[1] There is no need to contest the presence of an athletic metaphor here or in II Tim 4:7, as do Moulton and Milligan (cf. M-M., s.v. ἀγών, and G. Milligan, "Lexical notes from the papyri", ExT VII Vol. 6, 1908, p. 33). These authors prefer the military picture behind this pale use of athletic termini and refer for support to the Athenian inscription of the third century B.C. (Ditt.Syll. 214,10) which speaks of the battles of the Athenians and Spartans: πολλοὺς καὶ καλοὺς ἀγῶνας ἠγωνίσαντο μετ' ἀλλήλων. However 1. διώκειν in v.11 suggests the athletic image here in 6:12, while the phrase τὸν δρόμον τετέλεκα assures the same for II Tim 4:7. 2. In any case we have also repeatedly seen that the pale use of athletic termini did not lead to a complete loss of their metaphorical content. This applies also to their 'military' use; cf. e.g. Herod. 8,102.

[2] Cf. Phil 1:27: συναθλοῦντες τῇ πίστει τοῦ εὐαγγελίου, but esp. Jude 3: ἐπαγωνίζεσθαι τῇ ἅπαξ παραδοθείσῃ τοῖς ἁγίοις πίστει (cf. H. Windisch-H. Preisker, Die katholischen Briefe [HNT], Tübingen ³1951, p. 39).

[3] Thus B. Weiss, op.cit., p. 224.

[4] Similarly Cremer-Kögel, p. 76, Schmid, p. 62, Schlatter, op.cit., p. 167, and Wohlenberg, op.cit., p. 210; cf. I Clem 6:2 where those who have run τὸν τῆς πίστεως βέβαιον δρόμον have steadfastly kept the faith in persecution and suffering. Possibly this last thought is also contained here (as held by Schmid, p. 54, with reference to the confession of Jesus during his Passion).

end of the Agon,[1] but as that which is to be grasped and retained in the present Agon of faith.[2]

Up to this point there seems to be nothing in these two verses, apart from the opening address, to distinguish them from general Christian paraenesis. Earlier commentators, by referring Timothy's καλὴ ὁμολογία to his baptismal confession, have thus stressed that the context speaks "nur von der Beweisung des Christenstandes, aber nicht von der Berufsarbeit des Timotheus".[3] But is this the only possible understanding of the "good confession"?

Here we must return to Käsemann's article which attempts to show that vv.11-16 reflect the formula of an ordination-paraenesis. His conclusions are the following: "Hier (wird) nicht eine allgemeine und jederzeit mögliche Paränese vorgelegt. Der Verfasser greift vielmehr vorgeformtes paränetisches Gut auf, das sich auf ein ganz bestimmtes kirchliches Handeln bezieht und für den durch Timotheus repräsentierten Gemeindeleiter[4] und nur für ihn von grundlegender Bedeutung ist. In diesem gottesdienstlichen Handeln hatte er ein Bekenntnis abzulegen und einen Auftrag[5] entgegenzunehmen". That is, Timothy is now reminded of his ordination confession and the commission then entrusted to him with the same words of exhortation used on that occasion. The present verses thus treat of the obligation of him who has been ordained into the office of leader of the congregation.[6]

---

[1] It is improbable that the image is continued in ἐπιλαβοῦ, to picture the action of the runner straining to reach the prize (the picture itself is incongruous!), or in ἐκλήθης to signify the summons or invitation to compete. The calling is to life, not to the Agon (cf. Phil 3:14).

[2] Wohlenberg, op.cit., p. 210, refers the verb to the final moment at the end of the Agon. But the aorist can just as well signify the decisive grasping of life in the present (cf. I Tim 4:8 supra).

[3] Weiss, op.cit., p. 225: also Wohlenberg, op.cit., p. 210f. For further authors of this view see E. Käsemann, op.cit., p. 103 note 13, and ibid. for the view that the reference is to a confession before heathen authorities. Eidem's attempt to explain this confession on the background of the games is ingenious but impossible. He points to Pausanias Geogr. V 24,9 where we hear of the ceremony which brought the examination of the competitors to an end. The contestants made their oath before an image of Ζεὺς ὅρκιος, surrounded by relatives, friends and trainers as witnesses. Eidem himself questions whether this oath can legitimately be called a confession.

[4] Käsemann naturally presupposes the non-Pauline origin of the Pastorals.

[5] The ἐντολή of v.14 is understood as the "Amtsauftrag" given at ordination (op.cit., p. 106).

[6] Op.cit., p. 103; cf. also J. Jeremias (NTD), ad loc., and O. Michel, TWNT V, p. 216 together with note 49.

It is here unnecessary to repeat Käsemann's whole argument or to discuss the correctness of his insistance on the presence of an original piece of ordination-paraenesis. In the present context it will suffice to develop further the first point raised in support of his thesis.[1] We have already noted two passages in which advice to Timothy in his specific office is strengthened with a reference to his ordination. The striking point is that in both cases his duty is illustrated by means of the athletic and military image. This applies to II Tim 2:2ff. where the command to suffer as a good soldier of Christ and to "contest lawfully" is preceded by a reference to the apostolic tradition which was once entrusted to Timothy, and which he is faithfully to commit to others. The reference to his ordination is even clearer in I Tim 1:18f. where he is reminded of the prophecies spoken over him to equip him for, and bind him to, the good στρατεία. Since we have also related Timothy's "exercise in godliness" to his office (I Tim 4:7f.), and since, as we shall see, II Tim 4:7f. also speaks of Paul's own Agon as an Apostle including his entire missionary work with its sufferings which are now at an end, we may conclude that both the "good confession" and the "good Agon" refer to Timothy's position in the congregation as a commissioned leader. The fact that his ordination (cf. also II Tim 1:6) appears three times in connection with a characterisation of his duty as a "campaign" or Agon clearly indicates the accepted use of these images to describe the work of the minister of the Gospel.

Despite the similarity of vv.11-12a with general baptismal paraenesis it is not difficult to see the relevance of these commands for the ordained leader of the congregation. The attributes which he is to pursue (v.11) are easily understood as those which are particularly demanded of him in his office and in his present struggle against heresy and suffering. The command to carry on the good contest (v.12a) has reference to the necessity to prove and preserve his faith in this same situation. The author obviously lays stress on the parallel situation behind Timothy's confession and that of Jesus made to the wordly authorities during his Passion. This parallel is hardly meaningful unless Timothy's confession is also viewed as made over against a hostile world. His Agon thus includes the "Bewährung des Glaubens" in suffering as a continued witness to the world.[2]

---

[1] Käsemann, op.cit., pp. 104f.
[2] Cf. Käsemann, op.cit., pp. 103 and 104.

It is fitting that the last Agon passage to be examined, also the last in the Pastorals, provides the perfect summary and final note to the picture of the Agon which we have been able to gain from Paul's writings. The 'apostolic confession' of *II Tim 4:6ff.* contains a double perspective. Looking back on his life's task, and looking forward to its approaching end with his death, Paul can say: "For I am already about to be offered up; the time of my departure has come. τὸν καλὸν ἀγῶνα ἠγώνισμαι, τὸν δρόμον τετέλεκα, τὴν πίστιν τετήρηκα. Henceforth there is laid up for me the crown of righteousness, which the Lord, the righteous judge, will award to me on that day, and not only to me but also to all who have loved his appearing".

To understand these words fully the first five verses of the chapter must also be taken into consideration. Here we have a final precise summary of the duty of Timothy—the reference to the divine Judge to whom he is responsible (v.1) lends special weight to the following exhortation—to conduct himself as a "man of God" (3:17), as an evangelist and minister of the Gospel (4:5). Again we have the twofold emphasis on the need to be faithful in his preaching and teaching in order to oppose the heretics (vv.2-4) and the necessity to remain steadfast in suffering (v.5).[1] This is the Agon of Timothy which still lies before him. Its earnestness is heightened not only by the growing threat of heresy within the church, but also by the departure of the master in whose footsteps he is now to follow. It is thus surprising that Wohlenberg can conclude: Paul speaks generally of his life as a believer and not of his apostolic missionary activity with its strenuous exertion and suffering.[2] Can Paul himself so easily separate between the two, we ask!

Already v.6 points out the onesidedness of this view. Paul's departure,[3] the spilling of his blood in martyrdom, is pictured as a

---

[1] Text A adds (from 2:3) "as a good soldier of Christ Jesus".

[2] Wohlenberg, op.cit., p. 335. To reach this conclusion he has to reject the relevance of Col 1:29, 2:1 and Acts 20:24 for the present passage. But he fails to see that even I Tim 6:12 goes beyond a general picture of the contest of faith. Even less applicable is Hebr 12:1 where the scope of the image goes beyond its point of application in Paul and the Pastorals. Wohlenberg redeems the situation somewhat by adding: "Allerdings, für den Apostel, war dem Christenstand und -berufe, welchen er mit allen Jüngern teilte, durch die Besonderheit seiner Lebensführung das Sondergepräge seines apostolischen Amts aufgedrückt" (ibid). Even Eidem (p. 113) prefers to think only of Paul's life as a Christian, instead of including and emphasising his work as a preacher of the Gospel.

[3] Lock, op.cit., p. 114 unnecessarily suggests that the picture is that of a soldier striking his tent; cf. Phil 1:23.

libation (cf. Phil 2:17) offered to the glory of God. His suffering till death is not only the end of his life, but also the final act of his office.

The scope of the athletic metaphor in v.7, following Paul's earlier use of the image, must also include his apostolic life of service. The three clauses express much the same thing (Bengel: res bis per metaphoram expressa nunc tertio loco exprimitur), the first in the general picture of the Agon (Phil 1:30, Col 2:1, I Thess 2:2),[1] the second in the more explicit picture of the runner (I Cor 9:24, Gal 2:2, Phil 2:16, 3:14),[2] the third in a non-metaphorical explanation of the significance of the first two images. Those who wish to see in this verse only a general characterisation of Paul's life of faith here translate "I have kept/preserved the faith", and point to I Tim 6:12 for an exact parallel to Paul's Agon and 'race'. However, quite apart from the fact that Timothy's Agon must also be seen within the framework of his ministry of the Gospel, another objection must be raised. Evidence[3] can be adduced to show that τὴν πίστιν τηρεῖν is a standing expression with the meaning "to remain faithful or true". The phrase thus offers a parallel to τὴν ἐντολὴν τημεῖν ("to remain faithful to one's commission") in I Tim 6:14. In other words: Neither the Agon nor the 'course' have been of his own choosing. They have been committed to him by the Lord before whom he is soon to appear, and to whom he is prepared joyfully to render account of his faithfulness to the task committed to him.

The triumphant retrospective glance gives way to the look of faith and hope into the future. He who has remained faithful to the end (cf. Matt 10:22) also trusts in the faithfulness of him who has not only commissioned him, but who, as the righteous Judge,[4] will also

---

[1] Weiss correctly concludes: "Der bestimmte Artikel zeigt, dass es auf den ihm speziell verordneten Kampf, d.h. auf sein apostolisches Amtsleben geht" (op.cit., p. 315).—For the suggestion that the reference is to the military image (also Lock, op.cit., p. 114), cf. supra p. 179 note 1. Deissmann exaggerates the agreement between this phrase and a 2. cent. inscription from the theatre at Ephesus (Inscr. Brit. Mus III 604,7f.: ἠγωνίσατο ἀγῶνας τρεῖς, ἐστέφθη δύω); cf. supra p. 4.

[2] In Acts 20:24 Paul's δρόμος is specifically equated with his διακονία (cf. the reference to the 'course' of John the Baptist in 13:25). References such as to Vergil Aen. IV 653 (Dido): "vixi et quem dederat cursum Fortuna peregi", and to the concept of life as a 'race' in the diatribe, illustrate the familiarity and frequency of this image but are far removed from the picture of Paul's δρόμος.

[3] Cf. the examples given by Dibelius-Conzelmann, op.cit., p. 91.

[4] In this instance κρίτης would have suggested to Greek ears the picture of the βραβεύς or ἀγωνοθέτης. But it is doubtful whether we have any more

give him on the last day the crown of righteousness which has been laid up in store (ἀποχεῖσθαι) for him. This is not the certainty of the man who, trusting and priding himself in the strength of his own achievement,[1] now looks forward to the reward which he has merited. It is rather the certainty of faith and hope. He who has remained faithful to the end—and this of course includes the retention of his 'fides'—has fitted himself into God's plan of salvation, has given God the honour. His being crowned on the last day is God's own last crowning act on that which He has created and perfected.

Any vestige of the "Verdienstgedanke" is excluded in the description of the crown as a στέφανος τῆς δικαιοσύνης.[2] It is not a crown which rewards "das Gott wohlgefällige Verhalten" or the "Stand der Gerechtigkeit",[3] but one which consists of the gift of righteousness, which only the Judge, as He Who alone is δίκαιος, can give (cr. Rom 3:21-26 but esp. Gal 5:5). The descriptive genitive complies with the other NT pictures of the heavenly crown ("of life" Jam 1:12, Rev 2:10; "of glory" I Pet 5:4; "incorruptible" I Cor 9:25; also "of immortality" Mart Pol 17:1, 19:2); in each case the nature of the crown is described, not that which it rewards.

The last words of v.8 seem to be an afterthought with the specific purpose of avoiding the impression that he, Paul, will gain this crown on the basis of special achievement. He knows that this promise applies not only to himself but also to all who have longingly looked forward to his second Epiphany, his Parousia.[4] It is not

---

allusions to the games in v.8. Eidem (p. 112f.) points out that the crowning of the victorious athletes took place after all the contests were over and not after every event. But it is not necessary to see such a concrete reference in the statement that the crown of righteousness is laid up until the last day, until the final celebration of the victory.

[1] Dibelius-Conzelmann, op.cit., p. 91, take offence at the tone of Paul's words and ask whether Paul himself in such a situation would have spoken only of his success and not also of his weakness, whether he would have praised his own instead of God's acts! Such a statement robs the passage of its joyful certainty not in the achievement of Paul himself, but in the righteous Judge.

[2] Cf. Ep Arist 280, Test Levi 8:2; also Test Benj 4:1.

[3] Weiss, op.cit., p. 316, and Wohlenberg, op.cit., p. 335.

[4] Deissmann (Licht vom Osten, p. 315; ET; p. 372f.) wrongly draws a connection between στέφανος and ἐπιφάνεια, and points to the oriental practice of presenting crowns to the king at his παρουσία, his arrival or visit.—Schmid (p. 120f.) strangely finds in this last sentence a reference to the "Rivalitätsgedanke" suggested by the athletic image. The sight of the fellow-believer's effort is to act as an incentive!

special achievement or merit which distinguishes the Apostle from other believers, but a specific task and its faithful enactment.

We are now able to see more clearly why Paul should twice speak of his and Timothy's ministry as a καλὸς ἀγών. The phrase is certainly traditional, but references to the typically hellenistic tone of καλός (containing the idea of the good and the beautiful) are beside the mark. That which the adjective emphasises is not only the way in which the Agon is to be fought, but also the objective character of the contest as it has been committed to them. It is Good and Noble because it stands within the purpose of God's plan, because it seeks His glory, and because it brings to light His strength and power, even when it demands endurance in suffering. This amounts to a total absense of the agonistic thinking usually connected with the picture of the athlete. *Not the honour and glory of the 'spiritual athlete', but the honour of God Who has set the contest, is that which is sought in the good contest of faith for the faith.*

One last observation: Even though Paul's Agon does not include his final martyrdom it is not difficult to see also in this passage the beginnings of the martyr-terminology of the early Church. In I Clem 5 and 6, and in Acta Petri et Pauli 88 (Bonn.-Lip. I, p.221), martyrdom is again the completion and perfection of the ἀγών and δρόμος of the faithful, in particular of the two great Apostles. The central emphasis in this last testimony of Paul, "I have remained faithful to the end", appears again twice in the NT, perhaps with hints at the same image: in Jam 1:12, "Blessed is the man who endures trial, for when he has stood the test he will receive the crown of life which God has promised to those who love Him", and in Rev 2:10, "Be faithful unto death, and I will give you the crown of life". It is doubtless such passages as these (cf. also Matt 10:22) which were combined with the already familiar picture of the Agon of steadfastness in suffering (e.g. IV Macc) to form the language and conception of Christian martyrdom, from the Martyrdom of Polycarp onwards.

The inclusion of this chapter has been based on the premise that the five passages examined at least contain or reflect genuinely Pauline thought, even if not written by the Apostle himself.[1] The

---

[1] The question of the authenticity of the Pastorals cannot be decided on the basis of one problem such as that examined here. Nor need the results of this chapter be taken as added proof for the so-called "Teilungshypothese".

results of the study have established the correctness of this working-hypothesis, for at this point, in the conception of the Agon, there is no distinct break with Paul in his earlier recognised letters. E. Eidem[1] speaks, with reference to the Pastorals, of a narrowing down in the application of the image to the leader of the congregation. The nature and aim of the letters, and the situation of the addressee, makes such an application likely from the start. But it is wrong to point to I Cor 9:24ff. and Phil 3:12ff. to show that we can detect a movement from a more general to a more specific use of the athletic metaphor. Already in these passages it is first and foremost the Agon of the Apostle himself which is illustrated, even though the paraenetic implications of the image are clear.

Those who insist on the non-Pauline origin of these letters can easily object that a later author understood Paul's concern in using the image and carefully transposed it into a later situation. This chapter does, nevertheless, underline an important methodological consideration. The attempt to clarify the theological thought of the Pastorals should first be made on the basis of the thought contained in the recognised Corpus Paulinum. Once a different origin has been posited it is relatively easy to find further points of disagreement.

[1] Eidem, p. 163.

CONCLUSION

PAUL'S PLACE IN THE AGON TRADITION

In summarising our findings we return to the questions which were raised in the introduction to this study. Where are we to locate the source(s) for Paul's use of the athletic metaphor? What is the relationship between his use of the image and that of its prototypes? What is his concern in using this imagery and what place does that which it illustrates take in his thought?

The search for *the origins of the Apostle's use of the Agon metaphor* must lead to a complete rejection of the thesis that he was at this point solely dependent on his own observations and experience. Older, in particular, English works elaborate on the Apostle's keen powers of perception, on his human feeling for the glories of the games, and on his familiarity with the rules and conventions which attended them. In so doing they paint not only an idealised picture of the Paul as a thorough-going hellenist, but also of the games of his time.[1] The picture of the great Greek Agones at their prime is taken to illustrate the various images in Paul without at the same time attempting to prove that the individual features to which he is thought to allude were still alive in the games as they were celebrated in the first century A.D.[2] In actual fact the Pauline metaphors from the sphere of the games are so general in their lack of concrete details that it is not hard to imagine that any hellenistic Jew could have either written or understood them without himself having gained a first hand knowledge of the games from a bench in the stadium. His use of this imagery certainly shows Paul as a

---

[1] Cf. supra p. 3 with note 3, and the references in Eidem, p. 164. For a typical exaggeration of Paul's familiarity with the games see F. W. Farrar, The Life and Work of St. Paul, London 1896, p. 166, and esp. E. Curtius, "Paulus in Athen", SAB, 1893, p. 931, who claims that no other author in hellenistic times had the picture of the athletic sports so clearly in his mind as did Paul!

[2] Even though the first century A.D. saw the attempt to revive the splendour of the games, E. N. Gardiner (Greek Athletic Sports and Festivals, London 1910, p. 219) is still correct when he observes: "Few perhaps realise how corrupt and degraded were Greek athletics during St. Paul's life time". But Paul is only concerned with the intention of the Games.

hellenistic Jew. However his contact with Palestinian Judaism remained a feature of his life, from the days of his Pharisaic training
in Jerusalem onward. Considering the deep-lying abhorrence of
Palestinian Judaism for Greek athletics and gymnastics as typical
phenomena of heathendom, one must question Paul's so-called love
for, and familiarity with Greek sports!

The obvious answer to these objections to the derivation of Paul's
use of the Agon image from personal experience and observation is
to be found in the long-recognised fact that we can trace the development towards a popular metaphorical use of athletic terminology. That Paul himself stands in this tradition is a natural conclusion after a study of the language of the *popular moral philosophy*
of Paul's day as it is reflected in the writings of the Stoic diatribists.
Especially the pale metaphors in Paul receive their natural explanation if it is assumed that the image was long in use. But do the
many linguistic parallels in the diatribe allow us to agree with the
categorical statement of E. Norden: "Das Bild des Paulus vom
Wettkampf ... stammt, wie jeder in der griechischen Literatur Be-
wanderte zugeben muss, aus der popularisierten stoischen Moral-
philosophie"?[1]

We may accept this verdict if it is limited to the adoption of an
image and terminology which had become popularised in Paul's day,
but not if it also extends to the adoption of its content and application as well. Five points of contact can be established. (1) Paul's
preference for the picture of the runner, with isolated references to
the boxer, wrestler and pancratiast, all have *formal parallels* in the
diatribe. (2) Furthermore, there recurs a familiar feature of the
popular philosophical use of the image in the contrast between the
vain contests of the athletes and the noble Agon of the sage—in
Paul the contrast between the two crowns and the two types of
training (I Cor 9:25; also I Tim 4:8). (3) Thirdly, we have found
in Paul a terminology which can be paralleled with the diction of
the diatribe, for example ἐγκρατεύεσθαι in I Cor 9:25 and the phrase
καλὸς ἀγών in I Tim 6:12 and II Tim 4:8. (4) Attention may also be
drawn to the close connection between the athletic and military
image in the Pauline letters as in the diatribe—without thereby
suggesting that the diatribe was the only source of Paul's use of the

---

[1] E. Norden, Die antike Kunstprosa II, p. 467; a similar verdict by P.
Wendland, Die urchristlichen Literaturformen (HNT), p. 467.

military metaphor. (5) A further argument for the dependence of Paul, or his indebtedness to, the language of popular moral philosophy probably lies in the picture suggested by θέατρον in I Cor 4:9, one which is a variant or companion of the Agon image in the diatribe.

The sage in his heroic battle for equanimity against the blows of fate and fortune considers himself a spectacle to gladden the hearts of the gods and of men.[1] From a purely formal point of view Paul's image is the same: "For I think that God has exhibited us apostles last of all like men condemned to death,[2] ὅτι θέατρον (Vulgate 'spectaculum') ἐγενήθημεν τῷ κόσμῳ καὶ ἀγγέλοις καὶ ἀνθρώποις" (cf. also I Cor 15:32).[3] But its application is entirely different. Seneca and Epictetus wish to glorify the sage with this picture. His heroic self-confidence and autonomy is a source of wonderment and admiration. Paul, on the other hand, uses the picture to illustrate the humility and indignity to which the apostles, as the servants of God, are subjected.[4] G. Kittel draws attention to two more points of difference.[5] Behind Paul's use of the picture is a reminiscence of the sufferings of Job viewed by angels and men. In the second place God is not one of the spectators but He Who has set up this spectacle. Those who view it see only the ignominy of the Apostles, and overlook that which it realy represents: God uses the weakness of His servants in order to demonstrate His power and strength (as in II Cor 11:30, 12:5.9f. and 2:14). The picture thus offers a parallel to that of the Agon in Paul.

The necessary *distinction between picture and content* in I Cor 4:9 must also be applied to the athletic imagery in Paul's letters. In both cases one can admit the likelihood that Paul adopted these

---

[1] Cf. esp. Seneca De Prov. 2,7-12, and Epictet. Diss. II 19,25, III 22,59.

[2] Ἐπιθανάτιοι = criminals sentenced to death in the arena. Schlatter, Paulus der Bote Jesu, ad loc., takes the picture from the theatre where criminals were tortured and executed on the stage. But θέατρον is here best taken as θέαμα/'spectaculum'.

[3] The picture already appears in the accounts of Jewish martyrdoms; cf. Philo Flacc 72 and Leg Gai 368, but esp. IV Macc 17:14. It continues in the Christian martyr acts; cf. already Hebr 10:33 and Euseb. Palest. Martyrs I, IV, VIII, IXf.

[4] Cf. A. Bonhöffer, Epiktet und das Neue Testament, Giessen 1911, p. 170, Eidem, p. 173, G. Kittel, TWNT III, p. 43, J. Sevenster, Paul and Seneca, Leiden 1961, p. 115, and J. Hering, The first Epistle of Paul to the Corinthians, p. 29 note 4.

[5] G. Kittel, ibid.

images from the popularised language of Stoic moral philosophy.[1] But, and this is decisive, it is impossible to maintain that Paul's indebtedness went beyond this point. The frequent references in commentaries and other literature to the Stoic sage wrestling against his passions and against fate illustrate the popularity of an image and no more. The analogy has, in fact, been misleading since it has suggested that the scope of the Agon in Paul is the same as that in the diatribe. His concept of the Agon is not different in so far as it reveals only new nuances, new emphases in keeping with his theology. One must go further since *the entire scope of the Agon has been altered.*[2] It has been *transferred from individualistic 'moral ethics'* to 1. an *'apostolic ethos'*, to an illustration of the nature, conditions and rules which apply to the office of the Apostle and the minister of the Gospel, and 2. to a *description and characterisation of the life of faith* and its conditions.

The oft-noted Stoic influence on the language of the Pauline and Pastoral Epistles does not immediately imply also a Stoic colouring in their thought. Nor does it suggest a thorough aquaintance on the part of Paul with the details of Stoic teaching acquired in the school of Tarsus! If he knew anything of Stoic philosophy his knowledge was acquired through contact with the many wandering philosophers who roamed the Mediterranean world.

The second channel through which Paul received the image was certainly *Hellenistic Judaism.* But it must be emphasised that much of that which has been said concerning Paul and the diatribe also concerns the Hellenistic Jewish use of the athletic metaphor. Our three main sources all show distinct signs of Stoic influence, that is, the works of Philo, Wisdom of Solomon and IV Maccabees. Two factors nevertheless speak for the probability that Paul received the popular image via the Greek speaking synagogue. 1. In the first place the Stoic Agon of virtue is here interpreted as the *"Agon of piety"*, that is, the struggle of the pious to maintain and preserve the right relationship to God. The Agon has here received a decided-

---

[1] In the case of I Cor 4:9 P. Wendland exaggerates the agreement over against A. Bonhöffer who rejects any relationship. Bonhöffer (op. cit., pp. 54f.) does not distinguish sufficiently between image and content. The insistance on a difference of application in Paul does not force the conclusion that the popular image was unusable for Paul because of its popular connotations. His letters clearly show his ability to fill the image with a new content.

[2] The failure of Eidem, and esp. Schmid, to observe this central point constitutes the main weakness of their respective works.

ly 'theological' tone. And it is in keeping with this emphasis that 2. the *Agon of suffering* appears in IV Macc. The contest of the martyrs is not only against persecution and suffering, but also the struggle for the preservation of godliness *in* suffering. Here we have a far more direct parallel to the Agon *of* faith *for* the faith in Paul.

Eidem has furthermore correctly pointed out that the Hellenistic Jew probably saw athletic metaphors in his Greek OT, even where they are not suggested by the original text. This applies above all to the passages which speak of man's behaviour as a 'running' in godliness or ungodliness. Eidem suspects that we here have the reason why Paul preferred the picture taken from the foot-race to all others.[1]

A central problem remains, one which has not yet been answered by the reference to an Agon tradition. *How did Paul come to connect the athletic image with his own and his coworkers missionary work?* Can we point to a connection between the two in a pre-Pauline form. The Cynic or Stoic certainly considers himself to be divinely 'called' to a special task. His mission is to demonstrate the might of reason, to proclaim peace of mind and happiness in the pursuit of virtue, in the simple life in accordance with nature. His duty is to remain true to his κλῆσις, and to trust the deity who has called him.[2] Like Hercules, the prototype of the moral athlete, the Cynic and Stoic sage travels the world suffering hunger, thirst and privation in carrying out this mission.[3] He considers himself a messenger sent and commissioned by Zeus (ἄγγελος ἀπὸ τοῦ Διὸς ἀπέσταλται, Epict. III 22,23), a messenger, scout and herald of the gods (ἄγγελος καὶ κατάσκοπος καὶ κῆρυξ τῶν θεῶν, III 22,69).[4] Paul speaks of himself in similar terms as "a servant of Jesus Christ, κλητὸς ἀπόστολος, set apart for the Gospel of God" (Rom 1:1, I Cor 1:1).

Against these surprising similarities there arise certain objections.

---

[1] Eidem, pp. 179f.

[2] Epict. Diss I 29,46f. and 49 (ὡς μάρτυς ἀπὸ τοῦ θεοῦ κεκλημένος), and II 1,38f.

[3] Cf. M. Dibelius, BuG II, p. 200, with reference to I Clem 5. The world of Paul was full of such itinerant missionaries with their 'gospel' of the supremacy of reason, and it is not difficult to image that Paul often came into contact with them; Acts 17:18 hardly presents an isolated instance of such a meeting. Cf. R. H. Pfeiffer, History of New Testament Times, pp. 142f.

[4] Cf. K. H. Rengstorf, TWNT I, pp. 398f. and 408f., also Pfeiffer. op.cit., p. 144.

Can Paul's apostolic self-consciousness be so easily paralleled with the self-consciousness of the wandering moral philosopher? The sage is called to preach the moral Agon, Paul is called into an Agon for the Gospel. His entire apostolic work bears the character of an Agon for the faith of the Gospel, that which he preaches being not morality but the λόγος τοῦ σταυροῦ (I Cor 1:18). When the Apostle defends his office under attack he points to the example of the athlete to illustrate the conditions of his work. But the front against which he fights is not the "Sendungsbewusstsein" of the moral athlete, but the opposition of those within the Church who have challenged the legitimacy of his calling. The πόνοι to which he frequently refers, are not the toils of the moralist, but the sufferings which, demanded by his calling, are at the same time the divine seal of his apostolicity. For they also serve the divine goal of his 'race', the extension of the Gospel and the glory of the Lord of the Gospel.

The favourite picture of Paul as a runner suggests another possible solution which must be briefly considered. Did he as an εὐαγγε-λιζόμενος and κηρύσσων picture himself as a messenger hastening to bring the news of victory—the victory of God over sin and death through the Christ—to the nations? The herald who bore good news of victory whether on the battlefield or at the games was treated with special honour and often crowned for his services. Thank-offerings (εὐαγγέλια) were offered to the gods and games of celebration organised.[1] But this solution to the problem is also unsatisfactory. Paul the εὐάγγελος is not only a messenger of victory. His 'race' is itself an intense striving for the victory of the Gospel. In the second place the metaphor of the runner suggests not the activity of the messenger but that of the athlete straining toward the goal. For the same reason it is highly improbable that a passage like Jer 23:21 from the LXX provided the impetus for the image of the runner in Paul's letters. Here again the τρέχων is the runner and not the athlete.[2]

---

[1] Cf. the examples collected by J. Schniewind, Euangelion, 2. Lieferung, Gütersloh 1927, pp. 137f., also in G. Friedrich, TWNT II, p. 719. The prototype of Paul as an εὐαγγελιζόμενος is, however, rather the OT and Jewish בְּכַשֵּׁר.

[2] It does, however, remain possible that the person, life and message of Jeremiah influenced the selfconsciousness and expression of Paul. The prophet's call, his inability to divorce his life from his God-sent mission, and his judgment on his sufferings as an essential part of his office, are all features of Paul's life and thinking. It is the last point which may also have influenced his thinking on the role of the Agon of suffering in his ministry, even if the

What prompted Paul again and again to grasp at the athletic image to illustrate the work of his own ministry and that of his coworkers? The most certain answer is also the most simple: *The image suggested itself not only as an illustration already popularised, but also as the most suitable since the conditions under which the athlete contested also applied, in a transferred sense, to the athlete of the Gospel.* In no other image, not even in that of the soldier, was there such a wealth of parallels.

The following, in summary, are the *features of the Agon for the Gospel*: self-renunciation and training in the endeavour to place everything in the service of the appointed task; within the contest itself the goal which dictates the earnestness of the struggle against opposition and error, the goal being the victory of the Gospel itself; the exertion and wholehearted endeavour and application of the will to the attainment of this goal; the wrestling against the natural opposition of men who refuse to submit to the claim of the Gospel or who falsify it, and consequently physical suffering in the process of this struggle; but also the heavenly prize and crown as the reward of faithfulness.

For Paul, the Apostle, the Agon of faith is identical with the Agon for the faith. For him they cannot be separated since the experience on the Damascus road was at the same time a call to faith and a call to Apostleship.

The *features of the Agon of faith* as it is demanded of every believer are the following: He also is required to practice self-renunciation that nothing may prove an obstacle to hinder the attainment of the goal. He who has entered the course and begun to run must persevere. The race is not won until the goal has been reached. The prime condition of his Agon is therefore, never to give up but to persevere in the faith even if this involves suffering.[1] The spiritual athlete strengthens and develops the gifts of the Spirit which are his and seeks to actualise these gifts in the Agon of faith. But as long as he lives in this existence he is like the athlete who stands between

---

image was not given to him from Jeremiah. For this point see K. H. Rengstorf, TWNT I, pp. 44of.

[1] This feature is also taken from the games. We read of falls in the horse races, of head injuries suffered in the boxing ring or in the pankration (Pindar Pyth. 5.65), of dislocated fingers (Pausanias 6.4.1f.), and even of the death of athletes as a result of over-exertion and exhaustion (cf. J. Burckhardt, Griechische Kulturgeschichte IV, p. 104).

starting post and goal. He who is still running in the course of faith knows that the prize awaits him, but can never claim it as won until the race is ended.

There are two important features in Paul which, even if not taken from the example of the athlete, nevertheless belong indispensibly to his concept of the Agon. Unlike the athlete who enrolls for the contest of his own free choice, Paul knows himself summoned as a δοῦλος of Christ. But it is just as a servant of Christ that he is called to match his will with the will of God. The second feature results from the first. As one who has been called into the contest for the faith of the Gospel the Apostle and his coworkers also know themselves to be responsible to the Judge on the last day. Nowhere does the picture of the ἀγωνοθέτης appear, but it is never far removed from Paul's picture of his Agon. The urgency of the contest is not only given with the situation in which he finds himself, but also by the knowledge of having to give account of his faithfulness to his commission.

If these are the features of the Agon in Paul, it is no longer difficult to see how he could have so gladly adopted the athletic image. He offers no Christianised version of the moral Agon of his pagan contemporaries. He does not even enter into a discussion with Hellenistic ethics in their own terms. The scope of the Agon has been completely changed, and because of this those offensive features contained in the traditional use of the image are avoided. Gone is the agonistic thinking connected with the image in the Greek mind. The Athlete of Christ strives not for his own supremacy and honour but for the honour and glory of Him Who has called him. A. Schlatter states the case perfectly: "Das Ehrprinzip in seiner agonistischen Ausbildung hört auf, der Antrieb zur Aktion zu sein. An die Stelle der Selbstbildung zur 'Tuchtigkeit' tritt die Dienstpflicht".[1] In the second place Paul replaces the Agon of virtue with the Agon of faith. In the place of the development of innate powers and strength to the peak of perfection appears the struggle to preserve and strengthen the gifts of the Spirit. The gift of faith puts an end to the old moral Agon and sets the believer on the new course of dependence on God. Self-perfection is replaced by

---

[1] A. Schlatter, "Paulus und das Griechentum", in: Das Paulus-Bild der neueren deutschen Forschung, ed. K. H. Rengstorf-U. Luck, Darmstadt 1964, p. 106; cf. also p. 111.

growth in faith and in the gifts of the Spirit. As these gifts are gifts shared within a community of believers the selfcentred moral Agon of the distribe is replaced by an ethic of love and service.[1]

The Agon motif in Paul's writings does not emphasise an ethic of exertion in the sense that salvation depends on the effort of the believer. But it does stress that the life of faith is not static. In this sense Karl Barth is correct when he says that the *gift* of righteousness provides at the same time the *goal* of righteousness.[2] Here the Agon of the evangelist and that of every believer is essentially the same. To strive for the extension of the Gospel and to strive to deepen its gifts in one's personal life are aspects of the one task given to man, to seek the goal of God Himself and His rule of righteousness.

This last point may be again seen by glancing back to the two central passages, I Cor 9:24-27 and Phil 3:12ff. In both cases Paul's self-apology is not a purpose in itself, but has a decided paraenetic goal. In the first instance his own Agon is ultimately only presented to illustrate the meaning of Christian freedom and self-control; in the second it is presented in order to refute the heretics and their claims to present perfection. In each case the Apostle's own Agon has paradigmatic character for the contest of all believers.

---

[1] Cf. Schlatter, op.cit., p. 110: "Den im griechischen 'Wettkampf' ausgeprägten Antrieb streicht Paulus ... Bei Paulus ist der Glaube der kraftschöpfende Akt, nicht trotzdem, sondern gerade weil er das Zentrum unseres Lebens aus uns selbst hinaus über uns hinauf verlegt". For Paul's rejection of the hellenistic 'Tugendethik', see pp. 107ff.

[2] Cf. p. 144 note 2.

C.

OUTLINES IN THE POST-PAULINE DEVELOPMENT

To complete the picture of the Agon tradition a few words are necessary in order to show Paul's relationship to the further Christian use of the image and its terminology. A detailed study is here not in place but certain broad lines of development must nevertheless be traced.

Within the NT only the Epistle to the *Hebrews* again uses the image extensively. Here, and in the isolated pale use of ἐπαγωνίζεσθαι in Jude 3, the Pauline emphasis—the struggle for the faith—is still retained. Hebr 10:32 (πολλὴν ἄθλησιν ὑπεμείνατε παθημάτων; cf. also θλίψεσιν θεατριζόμενοι in v.33) outlines the Agon as a contest of suffering in persecution. The task of the afflicted is summed up in the one word ὑπομονή, as can be seen from the more explicit metaphor of the foot-race in 12:1ff.: δι' ὑπομονῆς τρέχωμεν τὸν προκείμενον ἡμῖν ἀγῶνα. Christ who has already run the race has set the example of patient endurance despite the shame of the cross. Hebr 10:32ff. speaks of suffering, exposures, abuse and loss of property, but does not suggest that any of the faithful have as yet suffered death for the faith. This is probably how we should also understand Hebr 12:4: None have yet resisted to the point of shedding blood (ἀνταγωνίζεσθαι ... μέχρις αἵματος). Both passages are reminiscent of IV Macc, but it is also here unlikely that the author was dependent on this writing.[1] Nor have ἀγών or μάρτυς the technical meaning found in the later Martyr Acts. The second term has a double meaning in 12:1. The "witnesses" are those who (11:32-38) have already finished the course of faith, and who are now spectators of the Agon of the Christians. Amongst the earlier heroes of faith in the history of Israel are those who have overcome (καταγωνίζεσθαι 11:33) their enemies with the endurance of faith.[2]

Despite the Stoic colouring in the famous passage describing the toils and death of Peter and Paul in *I Clement* 5, the picture evolved

---

[1] IV Macc is usually placed in the first cent. A.D., but before the fall of Jerusalem. It is doubtful whether the Church could have so soon used the work (Mart Pol!) if it appeared later than the first cent.

[2] Hebr 11:35f. reflects rather the text of II Macc (cp. ἐτυμπανίσθησαν with τύμπανον in II Macc 6:19 and 28). In addition only II Macc contains the hope of resurrection.

is not so far removed from Paul's own concept of his apostolic Agon as M. Dibelius would have us believe. His argument for the Stoic influence in these verses can hardly be refuted,[1] as much as one can question the necessity of the conclusions which he draws as to the historicity of the account. It is, however, surprising that Dibelius fails to make a single reference to IV Macc in the course of his examination, since the theme of I Clem 5f. (ὑπομονή) which is illustrated by the examples of the Apostles and the Neronian martyrs is also a central theme illustrated by the Agones of the Jewish martyrs in IV Macc.

It is true that the deaths of the Apostles are not related with any stress on pain and agony as in IV Macc. But Dibelius is hardly right in emphasising the purely Stoic colour of the πόνοι in 5:4. Despite the parallels which he adduces (in any case the absense in I Clem 5 of certain important Stoic toils such as πενία, λοιδορία and ἀδοξία is striking), the theme of faithful endurance till death (ἕως θανάτου ἤθλησαν in 5:2; cf. IV Macc 6:30, 7:8, 13:1, 16:1, 17:7 and 10) gives the entire passage a tone which is far closer to IV Macc than to Stoic thought.[2] In addition vv.6ff. clearly connect the Apostle's πόνοι with his mission of proclamation; they are not to be paralleled with the moral toils of Hercules or of the sage.

For the present generation which finds itself in the same Agon of endurance (7:1) the lesson to be learnt from those who have already contested (cf. 6:2)[3] is again ὑπομονή. "Let us strive (ἀγωνίζεσθαι) to be found amongst the number of those who endure that we may share in the promised gifts" (35:4).

---

[1] M. Dibelius, "Rom und die Christen im ersten Jahrhundert", in: BuG II, pp. 192ff.; cf. supra in the Introduction. J. A. Fischer, Die apostolischen Väter, Darmstadt 1956, p. 31, also thinks that Clement follows diatribal thought and expression, and cites for support L. Sanders, L'Hellenisme de saint Clement de Rome et le Paulinisme, Löwen 1943, pp. 1-40.

[2] Cp. IV Macc 17:23—Antiochus proclaims the endurance of the martyrs to his soldiers εἰς ὑπόδειγμα—with I Clem 5:1 and 6:1 (ὑπόδειγμα) and 5:7 (ὑπομονῆς ... μέγιστος ὑπογραμμός). In both cases we have a loose counterpart to the examples of the famous moral athletes of Cynicism and Stoicism. —O. Perler, "Das vierte Makkabäerbich, Ignatius von Antiochien und die ältesten Märtyrerberichte", in: Riv. Arch. Crist. 25 (1949), pp. 65f. and 70ff., also sees influences from IV Macc—against A. Fridrichsen, "Propter Invidiam. Note sur I Clem V", in: Eranos 44 (1946), pp. 164f., who prefers to look to Hebr 11:32-40.

[3] Here it is even more clearly endurance in torture which is meant, as in IV Macc, although the image of the δρόμος is probably taken from II Tim 4:7 or Acts 20:24.

In less figurative language I Clem also speaks of an Agon as an intense struggle night and day "on behalf of the whole brotherhood that the number of the elect should be saved" (2:4—it is the intenseness of their prayers which is probably meant), and of running to the goal of peace (19:2; in 43:1 the σκοπός is the goal of truth).

Already less Pauline is the full use of the athletic image in *II Clement 7* where the Agon appears as the struggle to keep the seal of baptism pure and undefiled (6:9, 7:6). Even though the author shows traces of dependence on Paul,[1] the development of the image shows an almost Philonic love for detail. The sphere of the Agon has also been shifted to the struggle to "keep the flesh pure and observe the commandments of the Lord to obtain eternal life" (8:4). More in keeping with the image in the Pastorals is the contest for righteousness and training in godliness in 20:2f.

Barnabas 4:11 also speaks of striving (ἀγωνίζεσθαι) to keep the commandments of God, although the verb is very pale. The picture of the believers πάλη against Satan in *Shepherd of Hermas* Mand XII 5.2 and Sim VIII 3.6 may be taken from Eph 6:12, but the first passage (together with 4.7) bears striking linguistic parallels to Test Job 27 which also pictures a wrestling against Satan. The verse also clearly implies a reminiscence of Jam 4:7.

Paul's picture of the athlete of the Gospel is most perfectly preserved in the letters of *Ignatius* of Antioch, especially in his letter to Polycarp. The fellow-bishop is exhorted to "press on" in his δρόμος with the grace with which he has been endued, and to "bear the sicknesses of all as a perfect athlete. Where the toil is greatest, the gain is great" (1:2f.). He is to be "sober as God's athlete"[2] that he may gain the prize of immortality and eternal life (2:3), and, like Timothy, to endure suffering and yet win as becomes a great athlete (3:1). Here the Pauline scope of the Agon of the minister of the Gospel is clearly reflected. Perhaps it even lies behind the pale use of συντρέχειν; the faithful are to run in harmony with the will of their bishop (Eph 4:1),[3] as they are to run according to the will

---

[1] Verses 1f. parallel I Cor 9:24f., while v.4 appears to be an explication of νομίμως in I Tim 2:5.

[2] The verb νήφειν actually fits better into the military image (I Thess 5:6ff.), but the connection with the athletic image was probably suggested by II Tim 4:5.

[3] The word is colourless in Magn 7:2. Θεοδρόμος in Philad 2:2 suggests the picture of the runner in the stadium of faith, but the same word in Pol 7:2 means a messenger or courier of God (cf. θεοπρεσβεύτης in Smyrn 11:2).

of God (3:2). Those who hold office in the Church are called to "labour with one another, contend together, run together, suffer together..." (συγκοπιᾶτε ἀλλήλοις, συναθλεῖτε, συντρέχετε, συμπάσ-χετε—Pol 6:1). Here, in precise summary, are all the features and the terminology of Paul's own Agon for the faith of the Gospel!

The writings which after Ignatius best reflect the Agon of Paul himself are the *Apocryphal Acts of the Apostles*. Apart from the numerous citations from Paul and the Pastorals, or indirect references,[1] we find a further development of the picture of the Apostle as an athlete, striving, toiling, and suffering for Christ. Peter's struggles against Simon Magus and other preachers of Antichrist are called "certamina" for the true name of Christ (I 1,8f.).[2] The Apostle Philip carries on an Agon to fulfil the commission entrusted to him (ἀγῶνα ... ὅπως τελειώσω τὴν ἐμπιστευσθεῖσάν μοι οἰκονομίαν, II.2 23,16f.).[3] Andrew is addressed by Christ as καλὸς ἀγωνιστής μου and called to contend on behalf of humanity, to endure toils and persecution (II.1 117,20f.; cf. also 96,36). In the Acts of Thomas, Christ is himself addressed as the divine helper in the Agones of his servants, as the ἀληθὴς ἀθλητὴς ἡμῶν καὶ ἀήττητος (II.2 157,7ff.).

In more general applications of the image we read of the Agon of Perpetua for faith in Christ (I 218,11),[4] of the contest of meekness who alone overcomes all her enemies and receives the crown of victory (II.2 200,30f.), and of the contest for holiness, itself an "invincible athlete" (201,11ff.).

The *Martyrdom of Polycarp* provides not only the first literary Martyrdom of the early church. Here for the first time we may speak of a technical use of the athletic metaphor. By his death Poycarp gains the τῆς ἀφθαρσίας στέφανον καὶ βραβεῖον ἀναντίρρητον[5] (17:1; cf.

---

[1] Cf. the Indices in Bonn.-Lip.

[2] For the sake of brevity, references are to the volume, page, and line in the edition of Bonn.-Lip.—Cf. also I 60,16f.: "Petre, agonem magnum habebis contra Simonem inimicum Christi", and 62,23ff.: "Habebis autem agonem fidei ... et convertentur multo plures ... in nomine meo" (also 72,20).

[3] He who has been called to faith by the Apostle prays that it be granted to him to contend till death on his behalf (II.1 22,9f.). Note also "ὑπεραγω-νίζεσθαι for the truth" and ἀγωνίζεσθαι κατὰ 'Ιουδαίων (II.2 33,7), though in both cases it is not the Agon of the Apostle for the faith which is meant.

[4] The comprehensive metaphor of the runner and boxer in the Acts of John 67 (II.1 183,17ff.) is an illustration of the Christian ἄσκησις of faith.

[5] The phrase corresponds as closely to τὸ νῖκος ἀφθαρσία in IV Macc 17:12 as to the "crown of life" in Jam 1:12 and Rev 2:10.

19:2). His ashes are preserved that the faithful might celebrate the day of his martyrdom, "to commemorate those who have already contested (προαθλεῖν) and to prepare (εἰς ... ἄσκησιν) those who are still to suffer" (18:3). As in IV Macc the Agon is a contest against the godless ruler (τύραννος 2:4 and 17:1). The martyr wins the crown of immortality "having by endurance καταγωνισάμενος τὸν ἄδικον ἄρχοντα" (19:2; cf. IV Macc 1:11, 8:2, 16:14). Especially the second chapter shows distinct influence from IV Macc:[1] the wonder of the onlookers (2:2, 3:2; cf. IV Macc 17:16f.), the stress on the nobility of the martyrs in suffering (γενναῖος in 2:1f., 3:1, γενναιότης in 3:2; cf. IV Macc 6:10, 8:3, 16:16; also I Clem 5:1 and 6, 6:2), and their ὑπομονή while under torture (2:2ff., 3:1, 19:2; passim in IV Macc). Polycarp also prays that his death be accepted by God as an acceptable sacrifice (θυσία 14:1f.; also Ign Rom 4:2).[2]

The Martyrdom of Polycarp thus forms the bridge between the incipient martyr-terminology of IV Macc and the use of this terminology in an absolute sense in the later Christian martyr accounts. Only when the traditional character of the image is appreciated can its retention be fully understood, even though the contests of the martyrs were fought as gladiatorial spectacles in the arena and had nothing in common with the free Greek athletic games.[3]

---

[1] For the following cf. H. W. Surkau, Martyrien in jüdischer und frühchristlicher Zeit, Göttingen 1938, pp. 131f. and especially the verbal parallels between the two works pointed out by O. Perler, op.cit., pp. 49f. Dupont-Sommer, op.cit., p. 85, points to the following striking parallels: the fires are cold for the martyrs (Mart Pol 2:3, IV Macc 11:26), the tyrant respects the age of the sufferer (Mart Pol 9:2, IV Macc 5:6), the persecutors waver in their purpose (Mart Pol 11:2, IV Macc 6:23, 9:1); cp. also Mart Pol 11:2 with IV Macc 9:9.

[2] In IV Macc the martyr's death has an expiatory or propitiatory character. It is an ἀντίψυχον for the sin of the people (6:29, 17:22),a vicarious suffering of punishment (6:28); their blood acts as a καθάρσιον which purifies the nation (6:29; cf. 1:11, 17:21), a ἱλαστήριον or propitiatory sacrifice (17:22) which saves Israel and justifies her (17:10)—for the origins and further development of this idea cf. Strack-Bill. II, pp. 297f., W. D. Davies, Paul and Rabbinic Judaism, pp. 271ff., and R. H. Pfeiffer, op.cit., p. 220. Ignatius, about to die, also speaks of himself as an ἀντίψυχον for his readers (Pol 2:3, 6:1—both times in close proximity to Agon imagery—Eph 21:1, Smyrn 10:2). But Ignatius never conceives of his impending martyrdom in terms of an Agon, despite the frequent use of this image throughout his letters. Only in Eph 3:1 is there a hint at the picture of the athlete or gladiator; he speaks of himself being anointed, that is, prepared for the contest (ὑπολειφθῆναι) by the faith, endurance and longsuffering of his readers.

[3] Cf. F. Dölger, "Gladiatorenblut und Märtyrerblut—Eine Szene der

The traditional features of the *Agon of Martyrdom* in the Apocryphal Acts of the Apostles,[1] in the early Martyr Acts,[2] and especially
in the writings of Eusebius, are not difficult to trace. A few examples,
chiefly from the "Ecclesiastical History" and "Palestinian Martyrs"
of Eusebius, will suffice to show this. As in the diatribe, the contest
is again holy (H.E. VIII 2.3, 7.2, Mart. Pal. III); it is fought against
the tyrant as the instrument of Satan[3] (H.E. V 1.5f., 16,27,38,42,
IX 2, X 4.60, and Acta Ioannis 4, Bonn.-Lip. II.1, p. 153). The
'athletes' receive the customary epithet γενναῖος (H.E. V 1.17ff., 36,
Mart. Pal. IV 4, VIII 13, Origen, Exhort. ad Mart. 1); they carry
out a contest on behalf of and for εὐσέβεια and θεοσέβεια (H.E. VI
1.1, 4.3, VII 32.32 etc., Origen, Exhort. ad Mart. 5); their crown is
again the crown of immortality (ἀφθαρσίας στέφανος, H.E. V 1.36,
42); they again appear as a spectacle for the cosmos (H.E. V 1.40,
47, Passio S. Pauli VII —Bonn.-Lip. I, p. 30, Mart. Pal. I,IV,
IX, XI).[4]

Passio Perpetuae in kultur- und religionsgeschichtlicher Beleuchtung", in:
Bibliothek Warburg, Vorträge III, 1924, pp. 196ff.

[1] Cf. esp. Passio Andreae 7 and 15, Mart. Andreae Prius 16, Acta Ioannis
4, Acta Petri et Pauli 88, Acta Philippi 126 and 144ff. In the NT apocryphal
writings, see also the martyr-Agon in Or Sib II 45-47: "For Christ the lamb
will award (βραβεύειν) to them just prizes and crown those who have stood
the test, and he will give an immortal prize to the martyrs who have fought
the Agon even to death". In IV Ezra 2:42ff. the crowns awarded by the Son
of God to those who have confessed his name, are also the prize of martyrdom.

[2] For the best collections see O. von Gebhardt, Acta Martyrum Selecta,
Berlin 1902, and R. Knopf-G. Krüger, Ausgewählte Märtyrerakten, Tübingen
[3]1929. Note esp. the following passages: Passio Perpetuae 10; Test XL Mart. I
1 and 5, II; Passio S. Scilit. 15 and 17; Passio S. Mont. et Luc. 6f.; Mart.
Lugd. I 42; also Origen, Exhort. ad Mart. (MPG I, pp. 654ff.), and Augustine,
De Agone Christiano (MPL XL, pp. 289ff.). In Tertullian, ad Mart. 3, the
Father is the "agonothetes", the Spirit the "xystarches", and the Son the
"epistates" in the "bonus agon".

[3] Cf. H. Strathmann, TWNT IV, p. 513. In Herm Sim VIII 3.6, those
who are crowned after wrestling with the devil are the martyrs who have
"suffered for the law". Ignatius also speaks of suffering in martyrdom the
"cruel tortures of the devil" (Rom 5:3; cf. 7:1 and Magn 1:2). But the
classical example is offered by the Passio Perpetuae where the martyr-Agon
is pictured as a wrestling match with Satan as the opponent; cf. F. Dölger,
"Der Kampf mit dem Ägypter in der Perpetua Vision. Das Martyrium als
Kampf mit dem Teufel", in: AuC III, Münster/Westf. 1932, pp. 177ff.
Dölger refers to the same picture in Pseudo Augustine, De cataclysmo sermo
ad Catech. 2.2 (MPL XL 693), Cyprian Epistle 39.2, Prudentius Peristepha-
non XIV 112-118, Origen, Exhort. ad Mart. 36; also passim in Augustine,
De Christiano Agone.

[4] Particularly elaborate in Origen, Exhort. ad Mart. 18, with reference to
I Cor 4:9.

These features clearly reveal the influence of IV Macc,[1] but the Agon of martyrdom is still Pauline as long as the central stress lies on the endurance of faith, and not on ὑπομονή as a meritorious virtue. But since the growth of the cult of the martyrs from about the third century onwards there appears a false tendency towards a perfectionism which is decidedly un-Pauline. The martyr-athlete wins the prize not through the faith which he has preserved even in suffering, but through the merit of his Agon of fortitude and endurance.

The second major stream of development in the early church ends in the picture of the *Agon of Asceticism*. The trend appears as early as II Clem 7 where the struggle against the flesh to keep the seal of baptism pure and undefiled is portrayed in a style which is closer to that of the diatribe or Philo than to any passage in Paul's letters. The metaphor is also presented with hellenistic features by Clement of Alexandria in a large complex in Quis Dives Salv. In his struggles against wealth, the rich man is to submit to πόνοι and γυμνασία as an athlete. Though he is clothed with an "earthly covering" (the Greek body-soul dichotomy!) he is not debarred from the Saviour's prizes. The struggle is not to be won without dust and sweat but "let him come and subject himself to the γυμναστῇ μὲν τῷ λόγῳ, ἀγωνοθέτῃ δὲ τῷ Χριστῷ".[2]

It is unlikely that the use of the athletic metaphor to describe the struggles of the ascetic was taken directly from I Cor 9:24ff. But a passage such as Martyrium Matthaei 2 (Bonn.-Lip. II.1 219,3f.) has little in common with the Apostle's words on his 'enkrateia': The Christ-child says to the Apostle Matthew, "I am the strength of τῶν ἐγκρατευομένων ... ὁ στέφανος τῶν παρθένων ἐγώ ..." In the Christian additions to the Sibylline Oracles (II 48f.) the ascetic Agon is included after the picture of the Agon of Martyrdom: παρθενικοῖς δὲ δραμοῦσι καλῶς ἄφθαρτον ἄεθλον / δώσει τοῦ θέματος.[3]

---

[1] For the conscious use of the book—often with the result that the Jewish martyrs are almost drawn into the ranks of the Christian—by Gregory of Nazianzus, Chrysostom and Ambrose, Cf. J. Freudenthal, op. cit., pp. 29ff., R. B. Townshend, CAP II, p. 659, and O. Perler, op.cit., p. 47.

[2] The "logos" must be the Word rather than reason!

[3] Cf. also the grand picture of the ἀγὼν εἰσελαστικός in the preceding lines (II 34ff.). For the entire text see J. Geffcken, Oracula Sibyllina, Leipzig 1902, pp. 28ff., and the translation in E. Hennecke, Neutestamentliche Apokryphen, Tübingen ²1924, p. 417. In lines 56-148 there follows a long series of exhortations to justice, honestly, chastity, compassion, sobriety, moderation and

Instead of self-control and renunciation in the service of Paul's apostolic commission and in the service of the Christian Agon of faith, we now find the contest to keep the flesh pure through the self-negation of virginity and poverty. The growth of monastic ideals naturally furthered the picture of the ἀσκητικὸς ἀγών.[1] An excellent example for this, also showing the technical use of "aguna" (= ἀγών) in Syriac, can be found in the seventh treatise of Aphraates the Persian sage in "Concerning Penitents".[2] The candidate for baptism is called to the Agon of asceticism; baptism is itself called the "water of testing". "He who has completely purified his soul is fit for the Agon, because he no longer has anything behind him which he could remember or to which he could again lapse back."

Especially Gnosticism shows a return to the hellenistic Agon of asceticism, the struggle of the soul against its prison, the body and its passions. The Manichaean psalmist sings: "All hail o busy soul that has finished her fight (ἀγών) and subdued the ruling power, the body and its affections (πάθος). Receive the garland from the hand of the Judge".[3] The soul that has finished its Agon and ascended on high has been released from the grievous bonds of the flesh. "I have not mingled with the intercourse of the flesh, for it is a thing that perishes. Thy good fight (ἀγών) I have set myself to ... I strip myself of the body of destruction." "I was victorious in the first struggle (ἄθλον), yet another fight (ἀγών) arose for me ... Since I was bound in the flesh I forgot my divinity."[4] Here, as in Pistis Sophia 249,[5] the Agon has again become the struggle of the mystic

---

contentment, with the conclusion: "Οὗτος ἀγών, ταῦτ᾽ ἐστὶν ἀέθλια, ταῦτα βραβεῖα, this is the door to life and the entrance to immortality / which God in heaven has set as the prize / of victory for just men; but those who receive / the crowns with glory shall pass through it".

[1] Cf. Theodorus Studita (8.-9. cent.), Encomium in Theophanem, in: Analecta Bollandiana 31 (1912), 22.9.

[2] Text in Patrologia Syriaca I, Ed. J. Parisot, Paris 1894, cols. 341-350; German translation in: Liturgische Texte I (LKIT 5), new edition by A. Adam, Berlin ³1960. The loan-word "'aguna" ceases to suggest the athletic metaphor in this technical use, as can be seen from the repeated references to the armour necessary for the struggle.

[3] Cf. A Manichaean Psalm-Book, Ed. C. R. A. Allberry, Stuttgart 1938, p. 57.27ff.

[4] Op.cit., pp. 65.13ff., 86.31ff., 117.17ff.; cf. also pp. 145.9ff., 148.23ff., 149.18ff.

[5] Cf. Koptisch-gnostische Schriften I, Ed. C. Schmidt, Leipzig 1905, p. 160: "Und nach all diesen Leiden durch euch selbst habt ihr gewetteifert (ἀγωνίζεσθαι) und gekämpft, in dem ihr der ganzen Welt und der in ihr befindlichen Materie (ὕλη) entsagt (ἀποτάσσεσθαι) habt, und habt nicht nach-

to escape the body and to preserve the divine spark implanted in his soul.[1]

The Church Fathers have been given little attention in the main body of this study, since their exegesis of Paul is often more misleading than helpful. A decided hellenisation of the Christian Agon of faith can be detected especially in the writings of Chrysostom and Gregory of Nazianzus.[2] Both show a return to the Stoic features of the Agon against the passions in the pursuit of virtue. This is a development which can only be expected as soon as Pauline ethics, based on the justification of the sinner by grace, and the gift of the Spirit, are fused with the hellenistic "Tugendeithk".

Both the Agon of martyrdom and the Agon of asceticism begin —and certainly continue to contain—a genuine Pauline aspect, but both tend towards a false development. At the end one can say that the circle has been closed—the Christian Agon bears features which closely parallel the Agon of Hellenism. The unique position of Paul within the Agon tradition has been surrendered!

---

gelassen zu suchen, bis das ihr alle Mysterien (μυστήρια) des Lichtreiches fändet, welche euch ... zu reinigem Lichte ... gemacht haben ..." Cf. also pp. 350, 356f.

[1] Cf. supra ch.II 3 on the Mystery Religions.

[2] J. Geffcken (Kynika und Verwandtes, Heidelberg 1900) points out that both Fathers share the Cynic-Stoic aversion for athletics and likewise replace the rejected agonistics with an ethical Agon (cf. pp. 18ff., where he quotes Poem. mor. X 735 from Gregory, 37, 89, and esp. 102ff.). It is surprising that O. A. Sawhill (The Use of Athletic Metaphors in the Biblical Homilies of St. John Chrysostom, Dissertation Princeton 1928) has not recognised the traditional character of the imagery in Chrysostom, although he does observe the reference to Plato's picture of the reinsman and the horses in Phaedrus 247 in several passages (op.cit., p. 26). A glance at the passages which Sawhill has collected shows that the Christian Agon appears almost exclusively as an ἀγὼν ὑπὲρ ἀρετῆς. The typically Greek antagonism against the body as opposed to the higher principle in man, the soul, and the picture of the Agon as the asceticism of virgins, monks and priests, is far removed from anything in the letters of Paul.

BIBLIOGRAPHY

I. COMMENTARIES

Apocrypha and Pseudepigrapha

Bensly R. L.-James M. R., The Fourth Book of Ezra. The Latin Version edited from the MSS with an Introduction, in: Texts and Studies III 2. Cambridge 1895.

Charles R. H., The Greek Versions of the Testaments of the Twelve Patriarchs. Oxford 1908; reprint Darmstadt 1960.

Dupont-Sommer A., Le Quatrieme Livre des Machabees. Paris 1939.

Fichtner J., Die Weisheit Salomos (HAT 2. Reihe 6). Tübingen 1938.

Freudenthal J., Die Flavius Josephus beigelegte Schrift über die Herrschaft der Vernunft. Breslau 1869.

Fritzsche O. F.-Grimm C. L. W., Kurzgefasstes exegetisches Handbuch zu den Apokryphen des Alten Testaments. Leipzig 1851-1860.

Goodrick A. T. S., The Book of Wisdom with Introduction and Notes. London 1913.

Hadas M., The Third and Fourth Books of the Maccabees (Dropsie College Edition of the Jewish Apocryphal Literature). New York 1953.

James M. R., Apocrypha Anecdota II, in: Texts and Studies V 1. Cambridge 1897.

Reider J., The Book of Wisdom (Dropsie College Edition of the Jewish Apocryphal Literature). New York 1957.

Riessler P., Altjüdisches Schrifttum ausserhalb der Bibel. Augsburg 1928.

Smend R., Die Weisheit des Jesus Sirach erklart. Berlin 1906.

Zöckler O., Die Apokryphen nebst einem Anhang über die Pseudepigraphen-literatur (Strack and Zöckler's Kurzgefasster Kommentar, AT, Abteilung IX). München 1891.

New Testament

Abbott T. K., Ephesians and Colossians (ICC). Edinburgh[4] 1922.

Althaus P., Der Brief an die Römer (NTD 6). Göttingen [9]1961.

Bachmann Ph., Erster Korintherbrief (KNT VII). Leipzig [3]1921.

——,Zweiter Korintherbrief (KNT VIII). Leipzig [4]1922.

Barth K., Der Römerbrief, neunter Abdruck der neuen Bearbeitung. Zürich 1954.

——,Erklärung des Philipperbriefes. Zürich [6]1947.

Beare F. W., A Commentary to the Epistle to the Philippians. London 1957.

Bengel J. A., Gnomon Novi Testamenti. Tübingen 1773.

Bornemann W., Die Thessalonicherbriefe (KEK X). Göttingen [5&6]1894.

Bousset W., Die Paulinischen Briefe (SNT II). Göttingen [3]1917.

Bring R., Commentary on Galatians (ET). Philadelphia 1961.

Burton E. de W., Galatians (ICC). Edinburgh 1921.

Dibelius M., An die Thessalonicher I und II. An die Philipper (HNT 11). Tübingen [3]1937.

——,Der Brief des Jakobus (KEK XV). Göttingen [10]1959.

Dibelius M.-Greeven H., An die Kolosser. An die Epheser. An Philemon
    (HNT 12). Tübingen ³1952.
Dibelius M.-Conzelmann H., Die Pastoralbriefe (HNT 13). Tübingen ³1955.
Duncan G. S., The Epistle of Paul to the Galatians (MNTC). London 1955.
Ewald P., Epheser, Philemon, Kolosserbrief (KNT X). Leipzig ²1910.
Ewald P.-Wohlenberg G., Philipperbrief (KNT XI). Leipzig ³1927.
Frame J. E., Thessalonians (ICC). Edinburgh 1953.
Heinrici G., Erster Korintherbrief (KEK V). Göttingen ⁷1888.
Hendriksen W., Exposition of I and II Thessalonians. Grand Rapids 1955.
——,Commentary on I and II Timothy and Titus. London 1959.
Hering J., The First Epistle of St. Paul to the Corinthians (ET). London 1962.
Jeremias J., Die Briefe an Timotheus und Titus (NTD 9). Göttingen ⁸1963
    (including H. Strathmann: Der Brief an die Hebräer).
Klostermann E., Das Lukasevangelium (HNT 5). Tübingen ²1929.
Lietzmann H., An die Römer (HNT 8). Tübingen ⁴1933.
——,An die Galater (HNT 10). Tübingen ³1932.
Lietzmann H.-Kümmel W. G., An die Korinther I und II (HNT 9). Tübingen
    ⁴1949.
Lightfoot J. B., St. Paul's Epistle to the Galatians. London ¹⁰1890.
——,St. Paul's Epistle to the Philippians. London 1879.
Lock W., The Pastoral Epistles (ICC). Edinburgh 1924.
Lohmeyer E., Die Briefe an die Philipper, Kolosser und an Philemon (KEK
    IX). Göttingen ¹²1961.
Meyer H. A. W., Der Brief an die Epheser (KEK VIII). Göttingen ⁶1886.
Michael J. H., The Epistle of Paul to the Philippians (MNTC). London 1928.
Michaelis W., Der Brief des Paulus an die Philipper (ThHK 11). Berlin 1935.
Michel O., Der Brief an die Römer (KEK IV). Göttingen ¹²1963.
——,Der Brief an die Hebräer (KEK VIII). Göttingen ¹¹1960.
Oepke A., Der Brief des Paulus an die Galater (ThHK 9). Berlin ²1957.
Plummer A., II Corinthians (ICC). Edinburgh 1915.
Rengstorf K. H., Das Evangelium nach Lukas (NTD 3). Göttingen ⁹1962.
Robertson A.-Plummer A., I Corinthians (ICC). Edinburgh ²1914.
Sanday W.-Headlam A. C., Romans (ICC). Edinburgh ⁵1902.
Schlatter A., Erläuterungen zum Neuen Testament II. Stuttgart 1909.
——,Gottes Gerechtigkeit. Ein Kommentar zum Römerbrief. Stuttgart ³1959.
——,Paulus der Bote Jesu. Eine Deutung seiner Briefe an die Korinther.
    Stuttgart ³1962.
——,Die Kirche der Griechen im Urteil des Paulus. Eine Auslegung seiner
    Briefe an Timotheus und Titus. Stuttgart ²1958.
Schlier H., Der Brief an die Galater (KEK VII). Göttingen ¹²1962.
——,Der Brief an die Epheser. Düsseldorf ³1962.
Schmidt H. W., Der Brief des Paulus an die Römer (ThHK 6). Berlin 1962.
Schmiedel P. W., I Korintherbrief (HC II). Freiburg 1892.
Sieffert F., Galaterbrief (KEK VII). Göttingen ⁹1899.
Strack H. L.-Billerbeck P., Kommentar zum Neuen Testament aus Talmud
    und Midrasch, Bd. III. München ²1954. (Strack-Bill.)
Vincent M. R., Philippians and Philemon (ICC). Edinburgh ⁵1955.
Weiss B., Das Neue Testament, Bd. II, Die Paulinischen Briefe und der
    Hebräerbrief. Leipzig 1902.
——,Der Brief an die Römer (KEK IV). Göttingen ⁹1899.
——,Die Briefe Paulus an Timotheus und Titus (KEK XI). Göttingen ⁷1902.
Weiss J., Der Erster Korintherbrief (KEK V). Göttingen ¹⁰1925.
Wendland H. D., Die Briefe an Die Korinther (NTD 7). Göttingen ⁸1962.

Wettstein J. J., Novum Testamentum Graecum. Amsterdam 1752; reprint
    Graz/Austria 1962.
Windisch H.-Preisker H., Die katholischen Briefe (HNT 15). Tübingen ³1951.
Windisch H., Der Zweite Korintherbrief (KEK VI). Göttingen ⁹1924.
Wohlenberg G., Die Pastoralbriefe (KNT XIII). Leipzig ³1923.
——,Der Erste und Zweite Thessalonicherbrief (KNT XII). Leipzig ²1909.
Zahn Th., Galaterbrief (KNT IX). Leipzig ³1922.
——,Römerbrief (KNT VI). Leipzig ³1925.

II. REFERENCE WORKS AND LITERATURE

Almqvist H., Plutarch und das Neue Testament. Ein Beitrag zum Corpus
    Hellenisticum Novi Testamenti. Uppsala 1946.
Bacher W., Die Agada der Tannaiten. Strassburg ²1903.
Barrett C. K., The New Testament Background: Selected Documents.
    London 1958.
Baus K., Der Kranz in Antike und Christentum. Bonn 1940.
Beardslee W. A., Human Achievement and Divine Vocation in the Message
    of Paul (Studies in Biblical Theology No. 21). London 1961.
Bentzen A., Introduction to the Old Testament I-II. Copenhagen 1958.
Bergmann J., "Die stoische Philosophie und die jüdische Frömmigkeit", in:
    Judaica, Festschrift zu Hermann Cohens siebsigstem Geburtstag. Berlin
    1912.
——,Jüdische Apologetik im neutestamentlichen Zeitalter. Berlin 1908.
Bonhöffer A., Die Ethik des Stoikers Epiktet. Stuttgart 1894.
——,Epiktet und das Neue Testament. Giessen 1911.
——,"Epiktet und das Neue Testament". ZNW 13 (1912), pp. 281ff.
Bornkamm G., "Der köstlichere Weg. 1 Kor. 13", in: Jahrb. der Theol. Schule
    Bethel 8 (Friedrich von Bodelschwingh zum 60. Geburtstag), 1937, pp.
    132ff.; reprint in: Das Ende des Gesetzes, Paulusstudien, Gesammelte
    Aufsätze I. München 1961, pp. 93ff.
——,"Der Lohngedanke im Neuen Testament", in: Evang. Theol. 1946, pp.
    143ff.; reprint in: Studien zu Antike und Urchristentum, Gesammelte
    Aufsätze II. München 1959.
Bousset W.-Gressmann H., Die Religion des Judentums im späthellenisti-
    schen Zeitalter (HNT 21). Tübingen ³1926.
Braun H., "Die Indifferenz gegenüber der Welt bei Paulus und bei Epiktet",
    in: Gesammelte Studien zum Neuen Testament und seiner Umwelt.
    Tübingen 1962, pp. 159-167.
Brun L., "Engel und Blutschweiss, Lk. 22.43-44", ZNW 32 (1933), pp. 265ff.
Bultmann R., "Das religiöse Moment in der ethischen Unterweisung des
    Epiktet und das Neue Testament", ZNW 13 (1912), pp. 97ff, and 177ff.
——,Das Urchristentum im Rahmen der antiken Religionen, Zürich 1947
    (ET: Primitive Christianity in its Primitive Setting, transl. by R. H.
    Fuller. London 1956).
——,Der Stil der Paulinischen Predigt und die kynisch-stoische Diatribe
    (FRLANT). Göttingen 1910.
——,"Ignatius und Paulus", in: Studia Paulina in Honorem Johannis de
    Zwaan Septuagenarii. Haarlem 1953.
——,Theologie des NT. Tübingen ⁴1961; ET: Theology of the NT, transl. by
    K. Grobel. Vol. I London 1952.
Burckhardt J., Griechische Kulturgeschichte IV. Berlin/Stuttgart 1889ff.

Cumont F., Die Mysterien des Mithra. Leipzig/Berlin ³1923.

Curtius E., "Der Wettkampf", in: Göttinger Festreden. Berlin 1864, pp. 1-22.

——,"Paulus in Athen", SAB, 1893.

Davies W. D., Paul and Rabbinic Judaism. London ²1955.

Deissmann A., Licht vom Osten. Tübingen ⁴1923 (ET: Light from the Ancient East, transl. by L. R. M. Strachan. London ²1911).

——,Paulus—Eine Kultur—und religionsgeschichtliche Skizze. Tübingen ²1925 (ET: Paul—A Study in Social and Religious History, transl. by W. E. Wilson. New York 1957).

Deubner L., "Die Bedeutung des Kranzes im klassischen Altertum", in: Archiv für Religionswissenschaft 30 (1933), pp. 71-104.

Dibelius M., Die Formgeschichte des Evangeliums, herausg. von G. Bornkamm. Tübingen ⁴1961.

——,"Ἐπίγνωσις ἀληθείας", Neutest. Studien G. Heinrici zum 70. Geburtstag. Leipzig 1914; reprint in: BuG II, pp. 1-13.

——,"Paulus und die Mystik". München 1941; reprint in: BuG II, pp. 134ff.

——,"Rom und die Christen im ersten Jahrhundert", Sitzungsbericht der Heidelberger Akademie der Wissenschaft Phil.-hist. Kl. 2/1941-1942; reprint in: BuG II, pp. 177ff.

Dibelius M.-Kümmel W. G., Paulus (Sammlung Göschen 1130). Berlin ²1956 (ET: Paul, transl. by F. Clarke. London/New York/Toronto 1953).

Dölger F., "Gladiatorenblut und Märtyrerblut—Eine Szene der Passio Perpetuae in kultur- und religionsgeschichtlicher Beleuchtung", Bibliothek Warburg, Vorträge III, 1924.

——,"Der Kampf mit dem Aegypter in der Perpetua-Vision. Das Martyrium als Kampf mit dem Teufel", in: AuC III, Münster/Westf. 1932, pp. 177ff.

Edmonds H., "Geistlicher Kriegsdienst. Der Topos der militia spiritualis in der antiken Philosophie", in: Heilige Überlieferung, Festgabe J. Herwegen, 1938, pp. 21-50.

Ehelolf H., "Wettlauf und szenisches Spiel im hethitischen Ritual", in: SAB, 1925, pp. 267ff.

Ehrhardt A., "An Unknown Orphic Writing in the Demosthenes Scholia and St. Paul", ZNW 56 (1957), pp. 101-110.

Eidem E., Pauli bildvärld I, Athletae et Milites Christi. Lund 1913. (Eidem) Beiträge zur Religionswissenschaft der religionsw. Gesellschaft zu Stockholm 1 (1913/14), pp. 212ff.

Eissfeld O., Einleitung in das Alte Testament. Tübingen ³1964.

Ellis E. E., Paul's Use of the Old Testament. Edinburgh 1957.

Farrar F. W., The Life and Work of St. Paul. London 1896.

Gardiner E. N., Athletics of the Ancient World. London 1930.

——,Greek Athletic Sports and Festivals. London 1910.

Geffcken J., Kynika und Verwandtes. Heidelberg 1909.

Gelzer T., Der epirrhematische Agon bei Aristophanes. Untersuchungen zur Struktur der attischen alten Tragödie — Zetema 23, München 1966

Grobel K., "Σῶμα as 'Self, Person' in the Septuagint", in: Neutestamentliche Studien für Rudolf Bultmann. Berlin ²1957, pp. 52ff.

Harder G., Paulus und das Gebet. Gütersloh 1936.

Harnack A. von, Die Mission und Ausbreitung des Christentums. Leipzig ⁴1924 (ET: The Mission and Expansion of Christianity, transl. by J. Moffatt. New York 1961).

——,"κόπος (κοπιᾶν, οἱ κοπιῶντες) im frühchristlichen Sprachgebrauch", ZNW 27 (1928), pp. 1ff.

——,Militia Christi. Die christliche Religion und der Soldatenstand in den ersten drei Jahrhunderten. Tübingen 1905.

Hatch E., The Influence of Greek Ideas on Christianity, reissued with a foreword by F. C. Grant. New York 1957.

Heinze R., "Anacharsis", in: Philologus, Zeitschrift für das klassische Altertum 50(1891), pp. 458ff.

Hijmans B. L., ᾽ΑΣΚΗΣΙΣ —Notes on Epictetus' educational system. Assen 1959.

Hirschfeld G., "Νίκη τοῦ δεῖνος", Philologus 50(1891).

Höistad R., Cynic Hero and Cynic King. Uppsala 1948.

Howson J. S., The Metaphors of St. Paul. London ³1883.

Juncker A., Die Ethik des Apostels Paulus I-II. Halle 1904-1919.

Jüthner J., "Das Alter der Olympischen Spiele", in: Geistige Arbeit 4 (1937), No. 11 3/5.

Jüthner J., "Herkunft und natürliche Grundlagen der griechischen Nationalspiele", in: Die Antike 15 (1939), pp. 231-261.

Käsemann E., "Das Formular einer neutestamentlichen Ordinationsparänese", in: Neutestamentliche Studien für Rudolf Bultmann. Berlin ²1957, pp. 261ff.; reprint in: Exegetische Versuche und Besinnungen I. Göttingen 1960, pp. 101ff.

Kerényi K., Die Griechisch-Orientalische Romanliteratur in religionsgeschichtlicher Beleuchtung. Tübingen 1927.

Krause J. H., Gymnastik und Agonistik der Hellenen. Leipzig 1841.

Krauss S., Talmudische Archäologie I-III. Leipzig 1910ff.

Kroll J., Die Lehren des Hermes Trismegistos. Münster/Westf. 1914.

Lightfoot J. B., Notes on the Epistles of St. Paul. London 1904.

Marrou H.-J., Geschichte der Erziehung im klassischen Altertum (German transl. of Histoire de l'education dans l'antiquité). München 1957.

McNeile A. H., An Introduction to the Study of the New Testament. Oxford ²1953.

Meyers Konversationslexicon I. Leipzig/Wien 1907.

Milligan M., "Lexical Notes from the Papyri", in: ExT VII Vol. 6, 1908.

Moore G. F., Judaism in the First Centuries of the Christian Era. The Age of the Tannaim I-III. Harvard 1927 and 1930.

Nägeli T., Der Wortschatz des Apostels Paulus. Göttingen 1905.

Norden E., Die antike Kunstprosa vom VI Jahrhundert vor Christus bis in die Zeit der Renaissance I. Leipzig ⁴1923.

——,"In Varronis Saturas Menippeas Observationes Selectae", in: Fleckeisen's Jahrbücher für klassische Philologie, Supplement XVIII, Leipzig 1891, pp. 298ff.

Perler O., "Das vierte Makkabäerbuch, Ignatius von Antiochien und die ältesten Märtyrerberichte", in: Riv. Arch. Crist. 25, 1949.

Pfeiffer R. H., History of New Testament Times with an Introduction to the Apocrypha. London 1949.

Pohlenz M., Die Stoa. Geschichte einer geistigen Bewegung. Göttingen 1948.

——,"Paulus und die Stoa", ZNW 42 (1949), pp. 69ff.

Ramsay W. M., Pauline and Other Studies. London 1906.

——,St. Paul the Traveller and the Roman Citizen. London 1895.

Reallexikon für Antike und Christentum I. Stuttgart 1950.

Reitzenstein R., Die hellenistischen Mysterienreligionen nach ihren Grundgedanken und Wirkungen. Stuttgart ³1927; reprint Darmstadt 1956.

Rengstorf K. H., Apostolat und Predigtamt. Ein Beitrag zur neutestamentlichen Grundlegung einer Lehre vom Amt der Kirche. Stuttgart/Köln ²1954.

——,Die Auferstehung Jesu. Form, Art und Sinn der urchristlichen Oster-
botschaft. Witten/Ruhr ⁴1960.
Richardson A., An Introduction to the Theology of the New Testament.
London 1958.
Schlatter A., Die Theologie des Neuen Testaments II. Stuttgart 1910.
——,Die Theologie der Apostel. Stuttgart 1922.
——,Der Märtyrer in den Anfängen der Kirche (BFChTh 19. Jahrgang, Heft
3). Gütersloh 1915.
——,"Paulus und das Griechentum", in: Die X christliche Studentenkonfe-
renz. Aarau and Bern 1906, pp. 9-22; reprint in: Das Paulus-Bild in der
neueren deutschen Forschung, Ed. K. H. Rengstorf, U. Luck. Darm-
stadt 1964, pp. 98ff.
——,Wie sprach Josephus von Gott (BFChTh 14 Jahrgang, Heft 1). Güters-
loh 1910.
Sawhill O. A., The Use of Athletic Metaphors in the Biblical Homilies of St.
John Chrysostom. Dissertation Princeton 1928.
Schmid L., Der Ἀγών bei Paulus. Type-written Dissertation, Tübingen 1921.
(Schmid)
Schneider C., Einführung in die neutestamentliche Zeitgeschichte. Leipzig
1934.
Schniewind J., Euangelion, 2. Lieferung. Gütersloh 1927.
Schrage W., Die konkreten Einzelgebote in der paulinischen Paränese. Ein
Beitrag zur neutestamentlichen Ethik. Gütersloh 1961.
Schürer E., Geschichte des jüdischen Volkes im Zeitalter Jesu Christi I-III.
Leipzig ³&⁴1901ff. (Schürer)
Schweitzer A., Die Mystik des Apostels Paulus. Tübingen ²1954 (ET: The
Mysticism of Paul the Apostle, transl. by W. Montgomery. London
²1953).
Schwyzer E., Griechische Grammatik II. München 1950.
Sevenster J., Paul and Seneca. Leiden/Brill 1961.
Soden H. von, "ΜΥΣΤΗΡΙΟΝ und sacramentum in den ersten zwei Jahr-
hunderten der Kirche", ZNW 12 (1911), pp. 188ff.
Spicq C., "Gymnastique et morale d'apres I Tim 4:7-8", in: RB 54 (1947).
——,"L'Image Sportive de II Cor 4:7-9", in: Eph Th Lov 1937, pp. 209-229.
Stauffer E., Theologie des Neuen Testaments. Tübingen 1941 (ET: Theology
of the New Testament, transl. by J. Marsh. London 1955).
Stengel P., Die griechischen Kultur-Altertümer, in: Handbuch der klassischen
Altertumswissenschaft, herausg. von I. Müller, München 1920.
Straub W., Die Bildersprache des Apostels Paulus. Tübingen 1937.
Streeter B. H., The Four Gospels. A Study of Origins. London 1927.
Surkau H. W., Martyrien in jüdischer und frühchristlicher Zeit. Göttingen
1938.
Torrey C. C., The Apocryphal Literature. Yale 1945.
Treitel L., Gesamte Theologie und Philosophie Philo's von Alexandria. Berlin
1923.
Völker W., "Fortschritt und Vollendung bei Philo von Alexandrien", in:
Texte und Untersuchungen 49, 1 (1938).
Vollmer H., Die alttestamentlichen Citate bei Paulus. Freiburg 1896.
Weiss J., "Beiträge zur paulinischen Rhetorik", in: Theologische Studien.
Festschrift für B. Weiss. Göttingen 1897.
——,Das Urchristentum, ergänzt von R. Knopf. Göttingen 1917 (ET:
Primitive Christianity, Ed. F. C. Grant. New York 1959).
Wendland P., Die hellenistisch-römische Kultur in ihrer Beziehung zu Juden-

tum und Christentum. Die urchristlichen Literaturformen (HNT I 2/3). Tübingen ²&³1912.

——,"Philo und die kynisch-stoische Diatribe", in: Beiträge zur Geschichte der griechischen Philosophie und Religion. Berlin 1895.

Windisch H., Die Frömmigkeit Philos und ihre Bedeutung für das Christentum. Leipzig 1909.

Wolfson H. A., Philo I-II. Cambridge/Mass. ²1948.

INDEX OF AUTHORS

INDEX OF REFERENCES

I. OLD TESTAMENT

(most references are to the LXX)

II. NEW TESTAMENT

III. APOCRYPHIA AND PSEUDEPIGRAPHA

IV. CLASSICAL AND HELLENISTIC AUTHORS

VII. CHURCH FATHERS